This isn't just another book about AI and educa about the need for educational innovation in a rapidly changing world as well as a detailed *how-to guide that will give education leaders the tools to transform their schools into incuba-* *tors for lifelong learners and creative problem solvers.*

—Sandra H. Ruffo
President of the New York State School Boards Association

AI is the biggest thing to hit education ever. Dan Fitzpatrick in Infinite Education *offers a compelling vision and guides you confidently through to a future which is more human.*

—Sir Anthony Seldon
Historian & Founding Director at Wellington College Education

Dan's book is about what happens when AI becomes a part of schools. In the rapidly changing world of AI, no book can give you a roadmap for what exactly a school should do to integrate AI, but this book will make you think about the issue and ask the right questions. Read the book...

—Professor Sugata Mitra
Educational Theorist

Dan Fitzpatrick, the AI Educator, provides the roadmap to journey forward with confidence and curiosity into a world where Artificial and human intelligence purposefully intersect, rather than necessarily diverge. Infinite Education *is for school leaders and teachers who find themselves at a critical crossroads navigating change while experiencing a range of competing emotions. Dan's knowledge and expertise, rooted in practical application, motivates educators to take intentional and measured first and future steps that make for an exciting classroom adventure characterized by boundless potential and possibilities.*

—Giovanni Virgiglio, Ed.D.
Superintendent of Schools, New York State

The book dares educators to break free from finite, outdated systems and embrace "infinite" approaches that foster lifelong learning, creativity and adaptability in the age of AI. It's thought-provoking, refreshing, and a touch provocative—a call to innovate before we risk being left behind. What made this book stand out for me is its practicality and accessibility. Each chapter provides actionable steps for leaders ready to pioneer change, from building innovative strategies to aligning culture with forward-thinking values. The tone is approachable but urgent, pushing readers to consider their role in shaping an education system fit for a rapidly evolving world. Whether you're an educator, policymaker or tech enthusiast, Infinite Education *is a must-read if you care about equipping students for a future where AI is both a partner and a disruptor.*

—Al Kingsley, MBE
Author & Multi Academy Trust Chair

Dan Fitzpatrick's Infinite Education *is a rallying cry for a revolution in how we think about learning. With AI reshaping our world at an astonishing pace, this book doesn't just inform it also inspires and includes insights that act like signposts to positive transformation for all of us. It challenges us to reimagine schools and organizations as vibrant ecosystems that nurture curiosity, creativity, and resilience, preparing students not just for careers but for a lifetime of evolution that enables a happier, healthier and purposeful future as we navigate the digital age. Dan reminds us that education is not a finite game of grades and exams but an infinite journey of growth and possibility. This is essential reading for anyone who believes, as I do, that education's ultimate purpose is to help every individual find their purpose and meaning in an ever-changing world.*

—Dr. Jamie Farnell-Smith
Entrepreneur, Advisor & Speaker

Infinite Education

The Four-Step Strategy
for Leading Change in the
Age of Artificial Intelligence

Dan Fitzpatrick

TEACHERGOALS  PUBLISHING

Infinite Education

Published by TeacherGoals Publishing, LLC Beech Grove, IN

www.teachergoals.com

Cover Design by: Tricia Fuglestad

Interior Design by: Heather Brown

Edited by: Dr. John Wick, Ed.D.

Library of Congress Control Number: 2024952367

Paperback ISBN: 978-1-959419-27-3

ASIN: B0DRZ3GXVT

First Printing: January 2025

JMJ

Thank you to the educators I worked with while writing this book across England, Germany, Mexico, The Netherlands, Norway, Scotland, Spain, Sweden, The United Arab Emirates, The United States, Wales and the Island of Jersey.

ABOUT DAN FITZPATRICK

Dan Fitzpatrick is an award-winning author, thought leader and global advocate for the transformative power of artificial intelligence in education. His best-selling book, *The AI Classroom: The Ultimate Guide to Artificial Intelligence in Education*, has become a cornerstone resource for educators navigating the intersection of technology and learning. As a Forbes contributor, Dan pens weekly insights on the future of education, illuminating how AI reshapes classrooms and empowers educators worldwide.

A recipient of the Tech Champion Award at the Digital Industry Dynamite Awards and recognized as one of EdTech Magazine's Top 30 K-12 Influencers, Dan's work is celebrated for its profound impact on the education sector. His career includes roles such as Director for Innovation & Digital Strategy for a group of colleges and senior leadership in secondary education before becoming the Director of Thirdbox Ltd.

Holding an M.A. from Durham University, a PGCE from UCL and a Postgraduate Diploma in Design Thinking & Innovation from MIT, Dan blends scholarly depth with cutting-edge expertise. This foundation has enabled him to lead initiatives that have helped over 100,000 educators globally integrate AI into their teaching practices while also empowering small business leaders to unlock AI's potential for growth and efficiency.

As a sought-after speaker and commentator, Dan has shared his expertise on ITV's Good Morning Britain, Time Magazine, Sky News and ITV News. Resonating deeply with educators and leaders globally, Dan is a trusted voice navigating the challenges and opportunities of education in the age of artificial intelligence.

Dan's career is marked by his unwavering dedication to fostering innovation and collaboration among educational leaders and trailblazers across the globe. His unique ability to distill complex concepts into actionable strategies has made him an indispensable partner for those seeking to harness AI's transformative potential in education and beyond.

For more information about Dan, visit https://www.theaieducator.io/about or scan the QR code.

TABLE OF CONTENTS

THE INFINITE EDUCATION PLAYBOOK

Don't wait to start transforming education—access the playbook now and begin your journey toward meaningful change.

The *Infinite Education Playbook* is the **essential companion** to *Infinite Education*, designed to help you bring the book's strategies to life. This hands-on resource bridges the gap between theory and action, guiding you step-by-step as you reimagine education for an AI-driven world.

Packed with practical exercises, reflective prompts and actionable frameworks, the playbook empowers you to assess your readiness, define your vision and implement meaningful change.

The playbook introduces exclusive frameworks and innovative approaches not found elsewhere, tailored specifically for educators navigating the challenges of AI integration.

Key features include:

- **Strategic Roadmaps**
  Navigate the transformation journey with step-by-step plans that simplify complex changes into achievable actions.

- **Reflective Spaces**
  Utilize dedicated sections to journal your experiences, capture critical learnings, and continuously adjust your approach for optimal results.

- **Team Engagement Tools**
  Access activities and exercises designed to foster collaboration, build consensus, and unite your team in pursuing innovative educational goals.

Access the playbook PDF for free now at infiniteeducation.ai

Once upon a time, an old man ambled wearily home one dusky evening.

He spotted a curious glow in the grass. Bending down, he found a frog adorned with a tiny golden crown. Surprised and curious, he picked up the frog.

To his amazement, the frog spoke, "Please, help me. I am a wealthy princess cursed by an evil magician. A kiss from you can break the spell, and then we can live together, rich and with many children."

The man paused, considering her words carefully.

Finally, he placed the frog into his pocket and continued walking.

"What are you doing?" shouted the frog.

The old man responded, "At my age, I'd rather have a talking frog."

INTRODUCTION

Have you ever found yourself clinging to the familiar, even when the potential for transformation is ahead of you?

The old man's choice reflects our dilemma with artificial intelligence (AI) in schools. Are we distracted by the novelty of talking AIs while missing the fundamental transformation they offer? AI isn't a toy. It's a wake-up call for education. We can cling to the familiar or embrace the future. Will we seize the opportunity or simply put it in our pocket?

I am privileged to accompany educational leaders through the labyrinth of ongoing AI advancements. Under my guidance, they pursue strategic visions that secure their leadership in the future.

This book serves as your guide on that journey. Your compass through the chaos of artificial intelligence's rapidly and ever-changing landscape.

As you read, new kinds of schools are being designed, launched and expanded. Many are utilizing the power of artificial intelligence. Some of these schools will compete with mainstream schools. They will likely render some traditional methods of education obsolete.[1]

If you have already started to feel the ground shifting beneath your feet, you are not alone. The strategies found in these pages will enable you to shift with the ground and lay your foundations as a leader for tomorrow.

---

1. In a recent blog that outlines the advanced future of AI, OpenAI CEO Sam Altman wrote: "Our children will have virtual tutors who can provide personalized instruction in any subject, in any language, and at whatever pace they need." "The Intelligence Age." Ia, 23 Sept. 2024, ia.samaltman.com. Accessed on Sep 23, 2024.

If you implement this book, you will gain the trust of your colleagues and stakeholders, your students, and their parents. You will communicate a clear, innovative vision for integrating AI into your learning environments. You will ensure the longevity and relevance of your school by adopting a sustainable approach to transformation that anticipates and adapts to future disruptions.

The world is changing at an unprecedented pace, and there is no longer a special dispensation for education. Nor should there be. Without innovation, schools are at risk of becoming irrelevant.

They may already be.

Graduates enter the workplace without the skills and knowledge needed to succeed. In a recent survey of 800 directors and executives, Intelligence.com[2] found that college graduates had the following issues:

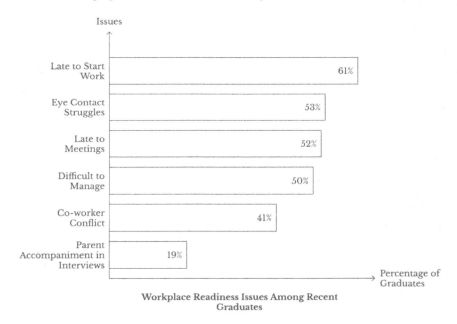

Workplace Readiness Issues Among Recent Graduates

The job market demands competencies that many modern young adults don't possess. Most schools still focus on memorization and standardized testing. This obsession is leaving students ill-equipped to meet the challenges they will

2. "Nearly 4 in 10 employers avoid hiring recent college grads in favor of older workers - Intelligent." Intelligent, 2 Jan. 2024, www.intelligent.com/nearly-4-in-10-employers-avoid-hiring-recent-college-grads-in-favor-of-older-workers. Accessed on July 20, 2024.

face in a world.[3] In a YouGov survey of more than 2,000 British business leaders, these were the top 10 most desirable skills:

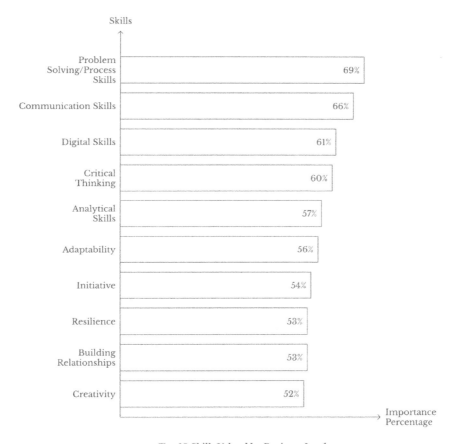

Top 10 Skills Valued by Business Leaders

The world is changing at an unprecedented pace, and there is no longer a special dispensation for education.

---

3. Having worked as a teacher and leader in the education system, I do believe this is an obsession. It's what mainly determines success for a school and its principal.

Teachers are also struggling. Many feel overwhelmed by the volume of new tools and platforms. There is a lack of training and support, with more than 7 in 10 teachers saying they haven't received any professional development on using AI in the classroom.[4] They are often forced to rely on outdated methods and materials that further widen the gap between the classroom and the world surrounding it.

In recent decades, schools have failed to adapt to society's changing needs. They are still operating on a model designed for the industrial age, which is not sustainable in an increasingly automated, interconnected and rapidly evolving world. The industrial age is over. Welcome to the age of intelligence.

Let me explain.

The tides of economic power have shifted, reshaping the landscape of success. Once, vast tracts of land and inherited wealth were the keys to prosperity. The Industrial Revolution upended this paradigm, elevating labor to the throne of productivity. Our current education system, conceived during this era, aimed to mold young minds into cogs for this new machine.

The playing field is being leveled and the barriers to entry demolished.

We now stand at the precipice of another shift. The entrepreneur rises, armed not with acres or assembly lines but with a laptop and a wi-fi connection. In this new world, a spark of innovation can ignite a global enterprise from the corner of a Starbucks coffee house. Artificial intelligence and automation are fanning these flames, allowing ideas to scale quickly and efficiently.

The playing field is being leveled and the barriers to entry demolished. No longer do we need inherited fortunes or armies of workers. The currency of our age is creativity, adaptability and vision. As AI continues its relentless march, it's not just augmenting our capabilities—it's redefining the very nature of work itself.

4. Langreo, Lauraine. "Teachers Desperately Need AI Training. How Many Are Getting It?" Education Week, 27 Mar. 2024, www.edweek.org/leadership/teachers-desperately-need-ai-training-how-many-are-getting-it/2024/03. Accessed on April 4, 2024.

In this reality, our schools face an urgent choice: evolve or become relics of a bygone era.

Think about your team. How do you respond to change? Are you fostering a culture that is ready to innovate? What steps can you take to build a shared vision for the future of education?

Without transformation, we risk creating a society where only a privileged few have access to the entrepreneurial skills and the knowledge needed to succeed while the rest struggle in an increasingly automated world.

The role of education is to help everyone discover their potential and empower them to achieve it. It will fail at this if it is left to stagnate. Without innovation, we are condemning a great many of our students to what Yuval Noah Harari calls the Useless Class—those who possess skills easily replaceable by artificial intelligence.[5]

There is hope.

We can adapt and create a system that prepares students for the future. We need to take a strategic approach to innovation, one that is focused on creating dynamic, responsive educational organizations that offer meaningful value to students and society.

We should embrace change and take calculated risks. I will show you how. There are four steps to transform education in the AI era. These steps act as a framework for change.

Many educational frameworks focus on improving systems, whereas my four steps will equip you to create the future system. This framework empowers leaders to anticipate disruption, adapt swiftly and drive lasting change in education.

Without transformation, we risk creating a society where only a privileged few have access to the entrepreneurial skills and the knowledge needed to succeed while the rest struggle in an increasingly automated world.

---

5. Harari, Y. N. (2016). Homo Deus: 'An intoxicating brew of science, philosophy and futurism' Mail on Sunday. Random House.

Follow the steps, and they lead to meaningful action.

Part one of this book addresses why the education system desperately needs innovation in an AI world. Part two outlines the type of innovation (the what) and guides you through my four-step method for leading this innovation (the how).

Your dedication to making this transformation a reality is essential.

It won't just happen. It requires a commitment to act. It involves experimentation, failure and learning from mistakes. It requires a deep sense of purpose and a belief in the power of education.

In return, this is what I promise you from this book.

Promise #1

You will be propelled into a profound discovery of a world with artificial intelligence.

Promise #2

You will gain tools to craft a compelling vision for the future of education.

Promise #3

You will be equipped to inspire and lead others in this journey.

Promise #4

You will unite your team around this shared vision.

Promise #5

You will acquire the knowledge and strategies to drive meaningful and sustainable improvements.

Part 1

CHANGE IS THE LAW OF LIFE

"Change is the law of life,
and those who look only to the past
and present are certain to miss the future."

—John F. Kennedy

Chapter 1

FROM FINITE TO INFINITE EDUCATION

Learning should never end.

Indeed, it doesn't. The fact you are reading this book means that you are still on the learning journey. According to Technavio.com, the professional development market size is estimated to grow by USD 24.34 billion between now and 2028.[1] Yet our education system[2] insists upon a manufactured end to education when we are 18 or 21.

What if a joy of discovery, fostered at school, fuelled a lifelong journey of growth and learning? This is the potential reality of education reimagined as an infinite game.

James Carse's groundbreaking book *Finite and Infinite Games* presents a compelling dichotomy: finite games with fixed rules and clear endpoints and infinite games that evolve continuously.[3] Our current education system, with its standardized tests and grade point averages, exemplifies a finite game.

---

1. "Professional Development Market Analysis North America, Europe, APAC, South America, Middle East and Africa - US, Canada, Germany, UK, China - Size and Forecast 2024-2028." Technavio, Aug. 2024, www.technavio.com/report/professional-development-market-analysis. Accessed 1 Sept. 2024.
2. When I use the term education system, I am referring to the often political institutions that direct and oversee schools, colleges, and universities.
3. Carse, J. (2011). Finite and Infinite Games. Simon and Schuster.

The Finite Education System

Picture a chessboard where students, teachers and administrators are the pieces, moving according to rigid rules set by curriculum guidelines and testing protocols. The finite success of the game creates a win-lose mentality that often leads to the sacrifice of proper understanding for the short-term achievements of grades.

This approach to education can:

- Stifle creativity and critical thinking because the game players realize that focusing on memorization will lead to better finite success.

- Create immense pressure to perform on tests that only measure knowledge at a specific time, disregarding any progress made from the moment they complete the exam or any progress made before the exam that could not be demonstrated.

- Fail to allow students to take agency in their success because success is presented as a predetermined goal. We live in a world where the opposite is true. Where success can be what we want it to be, uncapped and reachable when armed with a passion for learning and an internet connection.

What if education could be transformed into something more enduring and authentic, where learning is about continuing the play?

As Carse astutely observed, "A finite game is played for the purpose of winning, an infinite game for the purpose of continuing the play."

Reflect on the structures in your school or institution. Are there practices that prioritize short-term success over long-term growth? How might you shift the focus from grades to deeper learning? What if education could be transformed into something more enduring and authentic, where learning is about continuing the play?

Education as an Infinite Game

Imagine education as a vast, ever-expanding universe. Here, the boundaries are flexible and the players include not just students and educators but also parents, employers and society at large.

Infinite education is an ongoing journey rather than a destination. Artificial intelligence will challenge us in unpredictable ways and present unimaginable opportunities. By preparing our students to play the infinite game, they will be adaptable and valuable in this rapidly evolving world.

In this infinite game:

- Learning is a lifelong process with no definitive end, helping students understand that failure is always an opportunity to improve.

- Success is measured by the ability to think critically and solve real-world problems, two skills that will be invaluable in the age of AI.

- The focus shifts from students competing to do the same activity to personal growth and societal value.

- Curiosity drives motivation to learn and meet challenges head-on.

📢 Leadership Voice

"We might even see entirely new school models emerge, where the traditional boundaries of time, location and curriculum become more fluid. AI could facilitate personalized learning journeys, mentorship programs and real-world project-based learning experiences."

—Matthew Wemyss, Assistant School Director,
Cambridge School of Bucharest, Romania

As we begin to create the future of education in this AI era, our current limitations should not hold us back. How can you foster a culture of learning that goes beyond traditional boundaries for educators and students? Carse's insight resonates deeply: "Only that which can change can continue."

A Blueprint for Infinite Education

How might infinite education differ from our current finite approach? Here are some shifts we should start to consider so that we can move beyond the boundaries we have placed around our practices:

1. Knowledge to Wisdom

Move beyond mere information transfer to cultivate the ability to apply knowledge ethically and effectively in new situations. This transforms education into a lifelong journey of growth and societal contribution.

2. Redefining Success

Measure success not by test scores or admissions but by students' positive influence on their communities and the world. Nurture empathy, creativity and ethical decision-making alongside academic skills.

 Leadership Voice

"AI is not just a technological trend; it represents a fundamental shift in how we interact with information and make decisions. Incorporating AI into the curriculum can enhance students' critical thinking, analysis, and evaluation skills."

—Maryam Ferdosi, Director of Technology,
Berlin Brandenburg International School, Germany

---

3. Laboratories of Continuous Learning

Reimagine learning spaces where failure is a valued part of the process. Foster resilience and innovation, preparing students for a world of constant change. Encourage teachers to experiment with new methods, creating a culture of ongoing improvement.

 Leadership Voice

"AI-powered education presents promising opportunities to augment traditional teaching methods. These systems can provide students with on-demand support and guidance, supplementing classroom instruction and promoting continuous learning outside of the traditional classroom setting."

—*Rob Lea and Andrea Quantrill,*
Heart of Yorkshire College Group, England

---

4. Educators as Adaptive Innovators

Empower teachers to radically reinvent their approaches when needed while retaining the core of learning science. This might mean abandoning traditional practices for new methodologies that better serve evolving student needs, requiring humility and adaptability.

5. Education's Higher Purpose

Frame education's ultimate goal as developing individuals capable of addressing complex global challenges with empathy, critical thinking and collaboration skills. This transcends national and economic boundaries.

6. Collaborative Ecosystems

Break down barriers between K-12, higher education, industry and community organizations. Foster trust and cooperation across these sectors to create more comprehensive and effective learning experiences.

7. Learning From Excellence

Encourage schools and educators to view high-performing institutions as sources of inspiration and learning, not competitors. This abundance mindset can drive innovation across the entire education sector.

8. Challenging Assumptions

Empower educators to question long-held beliefs about learning, assessment and school structure. This might involve reconsidering fundamental aspects of our current system, like age-based grouping or subject-based curricula.[4]

9. Holistic Assessment

Develop evaluation methods that reflect students' development and capabilities, not just snapshot performances. Consider portfolio-based assessments, project evaluations and measures of crucial skills like adaptability and teamwork.

10. Societal Progress

Position learning as a catalyst for societal transformation. By nurturing forward-thinking, adaptable learners, education can become the force behind creating more just, sustainable and innovative communities.

Instead of unquestioningly teaching students to follow the rules of a finite system, we should encourage them to think critically about innovating beyond the established boundaries.

---

4. Check out the book How We XP about how a group of schools in northern England reinvented school by grouping subjects, at https://www.howwexp.org

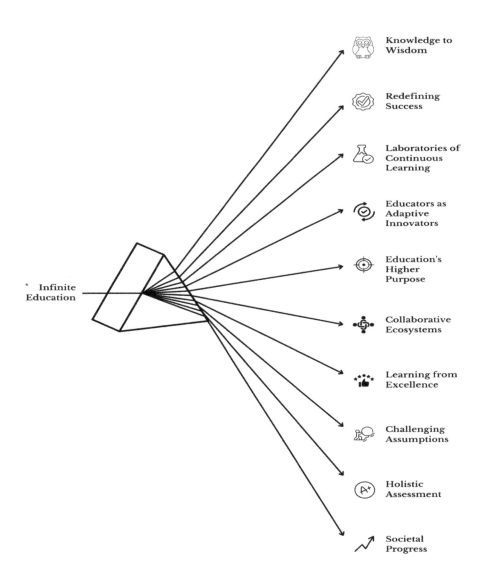

Infinite Education

Knowledge to Wisdom

Redefining Success

Laboratories of Continuous Learning

Educators as Adaptive Innovators

Education's Higher Purpose

Collaborative Ecosystems

Learning from Excellence

Challenging Assumptions

Holistic Assessment

Societal Progress

Case Study: Going Beyond the Finite Experience of School With City Schools

Let's look at City Schools, created by the Israeli education innovator Yaacov Hecht. He reimagined education by viewing the entire city as a school, breaking down traditional school boundaries and embracing community-wide learning.

The fundamental principles behind City Schools include diverse learning opportunities, real-world engagement, self-directed learning and democratic decision-making. The students choose from workshops led by various community members, gaining practical experience by studying at local businesses and organizations. These aren't theoretical exercises but hands-on learning opportunities. For example, in Hadera, where Hecht founded the first democratic school in 1987, students have worked on projects like designing community spaces or participating in local governance, ensuring their contributions directly impact the city.

City Schools provide access to various learning centers within the school, but the real innovation comes from connecting students with experts across the city. In Tiberias, for instance, students managed an archaeological park that became a vital part of the city's tourism strategy. This isn't just a classroom assignment; it's real-world problem-solving, where students' work genuinely impacts their community.

The flexible, open structure of City Schools allows students to take control of their learning. In Bat Yam, students begin their day with "morning circles," where they meet with educators to set personal goals and craft unique learning paths. This approach empowers students to follow their passions, with their daily schedules adapting to their interests rather than being dictated by rigid timetables. This flexibility teaches students crucial time-management skills and fosters self-directed learning as they engage with projects that matter to them personally.

In these schools, learning doesn't just happen between students and teachers. Hecht's model encourages community participation, meaning experts from the city lead workshops and students often teach each other. In Tiberias, students acted as cultural ambassadors, guiding tourists through the city and sharing local knowledge. This approach highlights the belief that valuable knowledge can come from anywhere and that learning is a collaborative, democratic process.

This model helps students develop real-world skills, encourages creativity and nurtures entrepreneurial thinking, all while fostering a strong sense of community. By blending the boundaries of school and city, City Schools offer a holistic learning experience that prepares students for the evolving job market and instills a sense of civic responsibility.

Three Takeaways From City Schools

1. Real-World Problem Solving

Can we transform our schools into hubs where students tackle genuine community issues and partner with local experts to mentor them? In City Schools, students aren't just passively learning; they're actively engaged in solving real-world problems, like those in Tiberias who helped manage an archaeological park or those in Bat Yam working on projects with local businesses. These experiences teach critical thinking and show students their power to create real change.

2. Flexible Learning Time

What if learning drove the schedule, not the clock? Could we adapt to student interests and world events? At City Schools, students set personal goals with their educators and work on projects that align with their passions, creating a flexible schedule that fosters engagement and lifelong learning. The morning circles in Bat Yam are a great example, where students start each day by deciding how best to spend their time based on their learning paths.

3. Everyone Teaches

Let's invite the community to share their expertise. Could students teach, too? At City Schools, students learn from community experts, but they also become teachers themselves. In Tiberias, students acted as cultural ambassadors, guiding tourists and sharing knowledge about their city. This demonstrates that learning is not confined to textbooks or classrooms; it can happen anywhere, with anyone.

Breaking the Rules

Moving from the finite to the infinite game is not only an academic exercise; it's necessary for our rapidly changing world. This shift requires more than just policy changes. It demands a fundamental reimagining of what education means and how it's delivered.

Successful entrepreneurs often "break the rules" of what has gone before, so our education system must embrace a more disruptive approach. Instead of unquestioningly teaching students to follow the rules of a finite system, we should encourage them to think critically about innovating beyond the established boundaries.

 Leadership Voice

"We have an opportunity to use AI to transform how we teach and how students learn in many positive ways. We need to prepare our students to be critical thinkers, to use AI not as a replacement, but as a tool that will help them innovate, explore, and become effective problem-solvers."

—Jess Baron, Ottawa Carleton District School Board, Canada

If we want our students to thrive in a world where the most successful individuals often rewrite the rules, we need an education system that doesn't just teach the rules but encourages students to reimagine them. We must also be the role models of how this is done.

As we embrace this new paradigm, we open doors to endless possibilities. Learning becomes not just a means to an end but a thrilling journey of continuous discovery and growth. In this infinite game, there are no losers, only evolving players who contribute.

In the words of James Carse, "Finite players play within boundaries; infinite players play with boundaries."

Let's not just play the game. Let's redefine it. The infinite game of learning awaits. Finite education systems cannot prepare new generations adequately for what is to come.

"Finite players play within boundaries; infinite players play with boundaries."

—James Carse

---

5 Questions for Infinite Minds

1. How can we shift our focus from winning (e.g., achieving high test scores) to continuing the play, ensuring education is a lifelong journey of discovery and growth?

2. How can we play with boundaries instead of within them by creating a more flexible and adaptive curriculum that evolves with the needs of our students and society?

3. How can we cultivate a learning culture that values ongoing change and adaptation, recognizing that 'only that which can change can continue?

4. What new and innovative assessment methods can we introduce to measure not just what students know but also how they think, solve problems and adapt to new challenges?

5. How can we ensure that our educational practices and policies do not just prepare students to win in the short term but equip them with the skills and mindset to thrive in an infinite game?

Download the interactive Infinite Education Playbook to complete this task in the playbook and access more accompanying activities for you and your accelerator group.

3 Mistakes to Avoid

1. Avoid treating infinite play as a lack of goals. Set adaptable, long-term objectives that provide direction and encourage continuous improvement.

2. Foster a collaborative culture by valuing diverse ideas and partnerships among students, teachers, parents and the community, moving away from a competitive environment.

3. Embrace change and innovation, revising traditional practices to ensure the educational system adapts and grows in response to new challenges and opportunities.

TL;DR

TL:DR stands for 'Too Long; Didn't Read,' so here's a quick summary if you need it:

- Traditional education functions like a finite game, focusing on achieving short-term goals such as grades and test results. In contrast, infinite education encourages continuous learning, creativity and personal development.

- The current educational system limits innovation by prioritizing memorization and rigid structures, often at the expense of deeper understanding and long-term skill building.

- Artificial intelligence is crucial in enabling infinite education by offering personalized learning experiences, real-time feedback and opportunities for lifelong education. AI can help students develop critical thinking and adaptability rather than just memorizing information.

- The City Schools model, created by Yaacov Hecht, reimagines education by turning entire cities into learning environments. This approach connects students with community resources, promotes self-directed learning and encourages real-world problem-solving.

- To move toward infinite education, it is necessary to redefine success, incorporate AI-driven tools, empower educators to experiment and innovate and create learning environments that inspire lifelong curiosity and contribute to societal progress.

Chapter 2

ARTIFICIAL INTELLIGENCE AND THE ORIGIN OF A NEW SPECIES

Two seismic events have already shaken our world in the 2020s. First came COVID-19, a global crisis that razed our society and pulled back the tide of our hubris, upending so many lives. Then, hot on its heels, the public release of advanced artificial intelligence in the form of language models like ChatGPT and Google Gemini. If the pandemic was an earthquake, AI is the tidal wave that follows it. A powerful force of change, filled with the potential to reshape the very foundations of our society in ways we are only beginning to imagine. In a YouGov survey commissioned by Kingston University in the UK, 74% of British business leaders believe current graduates are unprepared for a world driven by AI.[1]

---

1. Kingston University renews calls for urgent action to prepare students for workplace increasingly dominated by AI as it unveils latest Future Skills report. (n.d.). News - Kingston University London. https://www.kingston.ac.uk/news/article/2904/06-dec-2023-kingston-university-renews-calls-for-urgent-action-to-prepare-students-for-workplace-increasingly-dominated-by/

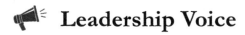

Leadership Voice

"AI is not the future; AI is the present. If we are not integrating AI into our educational setting, then we are failing to educate students for the world they are living in."

—*Henry Exham, Head of Digital Learning,*
Shrewsbury School, England

COVID-19 forced us to reimagine how we live and work.[2] AI challenges us to reconsider who we are. Although I work in AI and education, my work is more about using AI as a mirror to reflect a different angle of who we are, what education could be and our children's futures. This is not merely about smarter machines but about redefining the essence of human creativity and intelligence.

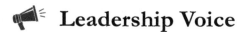

Leadership Voice

"AI challenges the very essence of what it means to be human. It forces us to consider creativity and intelligence in ways we never imagined before."

—*Tom Rogerson, Head of Cottesmore School, England*

Many still cling to the notion that AI isn't truly creative or thoughtful. But perhaps we should append "...like us" to that statement. As the historian Yuval Noah Harari (2024) astutely observes, we're dealing with "Alien Intelligence" rather than artificial intelligence.[3] There's nothing synthetic about the cognition emerging in cutting-edge AI systems.

---

2. I'm not saying this was a positive experience, but it did allow many people to reassess how they want to live and work. For more on this, I recommend the late David Price's mid-COVID book The Power of Us: How we connect, act and innovate together. Thread, 2020.

3. Lloyd, Will. "Yuval Noah Harari: 'Alien intelligence' will destroy us." The Sunday Times, 6 Sept. 2024, www.thetimes.com/culture/books/article/yuval-noah-harari-interview-nexus-brief-history-informa-tion-networks-stone-age-ai-0qfrnb9hs#:~:text=AI%20could%20destroy%20civilisation%20%E2%80%-A6%20we,will%20do%20the%20same%20thing.%E2%80%9D.

Machina Sapiens could symbolize the dawn of an intelligence untethered by the constraints of organic life.

I often hear the refrain, "It's just a tool." People say this with the best intentions, especially when persuading colleagues to try it or alleviating fears. But it grossly underestimates AI's profound impact.

Mustafa Suleyman, the co-founder of the artificial intelligence research laboratory DeepMind, offers an even more provocative reflection: "I think AI should best be understood as something like a new digital species."[4] While not accurate in the biological sense, this analogy captures the profound magnitude of what humanity is bringing into existence.

We might propose naming this emerging form of intelligence Machina Sapiens, a term that evokes its potential to rival or even surpass human wisdom. Where Homo sapiens—"wise man"—denotes the culmination of biological evolution's capacity for reason, *Machina Sapiens* could symbolize the dawn of an intelligence untethered by the constraints of organic life.

This framing not only elevates AI from the status of mere tool or technology but also forces us to confront the more profound implications of its rise. This "digital species" may only mirror our ingenuity, but could this be a harbinger of something entirely new—a parallel intelligence with its own trajectory, imperatives and, perhaps, wisdom? By naming it, we acknowledge the profound shift unfolding before us as humanity moves from creator to cohabitant.

It's crucial to take Suleyman seriously. He has been at the forefront of AI development for 15 years and has worked deep inside Google, Inflection AI and now Microsoft. He elaborates: "Now, don't take this too literally, but I predict that we'll come to see them as digital companions, new partners in the journeys of all our lives." This framing helps sharpen our focus on the critical issues surrounding AI development and its integration into society.

I invite you to pause and reflect on how AI is already reshaping your world. This isn't just a book to read—it's a conversation about the future. How is AI

---

4. TED. "What Is an AI Anyway? I Mustafa Suleyman I TED." YouTube, 22 Apr. 2024, www.youtube. com/watch?v=KKNCiRWd_j0.

challenging the way you think, teach or lead? Consider how your experiences, insights and concerns can contribute to this evolving dialogue. The questions we explore here are not abstract but deeply relevant to your life and role in shaping what comes next.

As we navigate these monumental shifts, my work in AI and education indicates that this new species is still a toddler in need of parenting.

The questions we explore here are not abstract but deeply relevant to your life and role in shaping what comes next.

Parenting the Toddler

I am a father of a five-year-old girl and a four-year-old boy. One moment, they are awe-inspiring; the next, they draw up the walls with crayons. One moment, I exclaim, "Wow," and the next, "We've got some concerns here." At the moment, AI is like a toddler. It blows our minds but reminds us of our responsibility as we navigate ethical concerns.

We are the generation that gets to parent it,[5] to guide it towards a maturity we can be proud of. Suleyman eloquently says: "Because we are still designing and building AI, we have the potential and opportunity to do it radically better."

This moment demands more than just technological prowess; it requires soul searching. As we shape AI, we shape ourselves. It will mirror our consciousness, amplifying our noblest aspirations and profound flaws.

Imagine yourself as a parent to this AI toddler. It's full of potential but also capable of unexpected consequences. What kind of parent would you be to such a technology? What values, ethics and safeguards would you want to instill? Reflect on how you already engage with AI and how you can guide its use to ensure it reflects the best human values.

 Leadership Voice

"We must ensure that AI development is guided by ethical considerations to prevent unintended consequences."

—Rob Lea and Andrea Quantrill,
Heart of Yorkshire College Group, England

The pace of AI development is exhilarating, opening up incredible new possibilities for industries, education and society. The "AI is just a bubble" critics have been made to eat their words various times over the last few years. The global AI market is valued at over $196 billion and is projected to increase by over 13x over the next 6 years. 83% of companies now claim that AI is a top priority in their business plans.[6] It's time to look up.

Remember that ChatGPT, the platform that introduced most of the world to generative AI, was released on November 28, 2022. Fast forward to August 2024 and a third of Americans use AI in any given week. They mostly used ChatGPT

---

5. I first heard the term "parenting AI" from Kai Vacher, Principal of British School Muscat and British School Salalah.
6. Howarth J. 57 NEW Artificial Intelligence Statistics (Oct 2024). Exploding Topics. Published September 26, 2024. https://explodingtopics.com/blog/ai-statistics

and Google Gemini.[7] There is a similar trend in education,[8] with 46% of teachers, 51% of parents, 48% of K-12 students and 46% of undergraduate students reporting that they use AI chatbots at least once per week.[9]

It's not just adoption that is growing; it's also the AI itself. Even before ChatGPT, the computational power of AI has been increased by 10x per year, every year for almost a decade.[10] The size and capabilities of AI models are expanding to reflect this. Suleyman puts this into perspective in a recent TED talk when he stated, "If someone did nothing but read 24 hours a day for their entire life, they'd consume eight billion words. And of course, that's a lot of words. But today, the most advanced AIs consume more than eight trillion words in a single month of training."[11]

Artificial Intelligence and Our Brains

When ChatGPT burst onto the scene, it made the world take notice. AI advancements were beyond what most people thought was possible. We will get more moments like this.

Let's peek behind some closed doors. Monumental advancements in AI have been made in laboratories around the world. Researchers can now use AI to interpret brain signals, essentially reading thoughts and reconstructing images or music based on neural activity.

In 2023, researchers at Osaka University in Japan used an AI called Stable Diffusion to reconstruct images from fMRI brain scans—an imaging scan that

7. Bick, Alexander, et al. The Rapid Adoption of Generative AI. 18 Sept. 2024, static1.squarespace.com/static/60832ecef615231cedd30911/t/66f0c3fbabdc0a173e1e697e/1727054844024/BBD_GenAI_NBER_Sept2024.pdf. Accessed 30 Sept. 2024.
8. The sample from the USA, includes a total of 1003 teachers, 1001 K-12 students, 1003 undergraduates and 1000 parents. The teachers, K-12 students and parents' samples were weighted to align with demographic estimates from the U.S. Census and undergraduates with demographic estimates from the National Center for Education Statistics.
9. "The Value of AI in Today's Classrooms." Walton Family Foundation, 11 June 2024, www.waltonfamilyfoundation.org/learning/the-value-of-ai-in-todays-classrooms.
10. TED. "What Is an AI Anyway? I Mustafa Suleyman I TED." YouTube, 22 Apr. 2024, www.youtube.com/watch?v=KKNCiRWd_j0.
11. TED. "What Is an AI Anyway? I Mustafa Suleyman I TED." YouTube, 22 Apr. 2024, www.youtube.com/watch?v=KKNCiRWd_j0.

shows activity in specific areas of the brain.[12] These scans were taken of the brains of people looking at 10,000 different images. The AI learned from the brain scan dataset and could recreate the specific objects people were thinking of. In the image below, on top are the images four participants were thinking of and below are the images created by the AI.

We are on the verge of technological mind-reading. I can't help but marvel at the possibilities this technology unlocks for those who cannot express their thoughts while also considering the need to manage its risks carefully.

Takagi and Nishimoto / bioRxiv, 2022 under CC BY 4.0

In a similar experiment, scientists at the National University of Singapore are developing a system that interprets brain activity using AI. The team, led by Professor Helen Zhou, uses MRI scans to capture brain patterns as subjects view images.[13]

"As long as I have seen it and you know the patterns of my brain, then the AI will read that out of my brain," Professor Zhou explained during a demonstration. The research holds potential for medical applications, such as restoring lost senses. However, as the technology progresses, it poses new challenges for personal privacy and data protection.

12. Takagi, Yu, and Shinji Nishimoto. "High-resolution image reconstruction with latent diffusion models from human brain activity." Biorxiv, 11 Mar. 2023, www.biorxiv.org/content/10.1101/2022.11.18.51700 4v3. Accessed 30 Mar. 2023.
13. NBC News. "AI technology may be able to generate our mind's images." YouTube, 25 Mar. 2023, www.youtube.com/watch?v=TYbRNQ3LxwU.

As brain-computer interface technology advances, balancing scientific progress with ethical considerations remains a crucial challenge for researchers and policymakers alike.

We are on the verge of technological mind-reading.

UC Berkeley is using AI to reconstruct music from brain recordings using intracranial electroencephalography (iEEG), a method of obtaining brain signals from implanted electrodes.[14] They successfully recreated a recognizable version of Pink Floyd's "Another Brick in the Wall, Part 1" from patients' brain activity, capturing the rhythm and decipherable lyrics.

In December 2023, a groundbreaking system developed at the University of Technology Sydney (UTS) continued to push the boundaries of what is possible.[15] Their brain computer inference technology translates brainwaves directly into text, offering a glimpse into a future where our thoughts can be effortlessly communicated to machines and other people.

At the heart of this system is a portable, non-invasive wearable cap. Participants in the study demonstrated the system's ability to decode silent thoughts by simply reading text passages to themselves.

Currently, the system achieves a translation accuracy score of around 40% on the BLEU-1 scale—an algorithm for evaluating the quality of text that has been machine-translated from one natural language to another. While this is a significant achievement, researchers aim to improve accuracy to levels comparable with language translation or speech recognition programs, which operate closer to 90%.

Will future users of this technology need to wear an EEG cap? Perhaps not if a company called Neuralink has its way. Founded in 2016, Neuralink has developed a brain-computer interface inserted in a human skull and aims to connect

14. Sanders, Robert. "Brain recordings capture musicality of speech — with help from Pink Floyd - Berkeley News." Berkeley News, 1 May 2024, news.berkeley.edu/2023/08/15/releases-20230811.
15. "Portable, non-invasive, mind-reading AI turns thoughts into text." University of Technology Sydney, 12 Feb. 2024, www.uts.edu.au/news/tech-design/portable-non-invasive-mind-reading-ai-turns-thoughts-text#:~:text=In%20a%20world%2Dfirst%2C%20researchers,and%20turn%20them%20into%20text.

the brain directly with external devices. The current version is a small implant about the size of a coin, containing thin electrode threads surgically inserted into the brain's motor cortex.

Recent human trials have shown promising results.[16] Two participants with quadriplegia have demonstrated the ability to control computer cursors using only their thoughts. These early successes suggest potential applications for individuals with severe motor disabilities.

The Neuralink device works by detecting and interpreting neural signals. These signals are then translated into commands that can control external devices. The interface uses Bluetooth to communicate wirelessly with computers, though the company is exploring other signal transmission options.

While the initial focus is on restoring capabilities for people with disabilities, Neuralink's long-term goals are more ambitious. The company envisions applications ranging from controlling robotic limbs to enabling direct brain-to-brain communication.

Technology has become more personalized for decades, from giant computers to personal computers, smartphones, smartwatches and other wearable devices. Is the future of invasive AI such a surprise?

Imagine how the developments of these technologies could influence the current education systems. For students with disabilities, AI-driven brain technology offers new ways to communicate and participate in learning, breaking down barriers to learning.

AI merging with our bodies is one direction this technology is taking. But what if AI also gets its own body?

A New Body for a New Species

AI having a body in the form of a robot is a familiar idea. It has been the subject of movies and books for a long time. As AI progresses at incredible speeds, AI robots become a more viable reality.

---

16. Neuralink. "PRIME Study Progress Update — Second Participant I Blog I Neuralink." Neuralink Blog, 22 Aug. 2024, neuralink.com/blog/prime-study-progress-update-second-participant.

Among many others, two companies, Figure and Tesla, are developing humanoid robots to address labor shortages and automate repetitive tasks. While both projects are still in development, they offer insights into the future of robotics in industrial and potentially consumer settings.

Figure's human-form robot with a ChatGPT mind, called Figure 02, performs autonomous tasks in real-world environments. In recent tests at a BMW production line, Figure 02 demonstrated capabilities such as high-precision pick-and-place tasks. The robot's human-scale hands and multiple cameras, combined with AI perception models, allow it to interact with its environment effectively.

Tesla's Optimus initiative is being developed with similar goals. Tesla aims to create an autonomous humanoid robot capable of performing repetitive or dangerous tasks. The company aims to produce these robots for less than $20,000 each, potentially making them accessible for broader use.

In video presentations of each robot, the companies are keen to show off their domestic skills. In a video for the Figure robot, we see it performing tasks such as tidying up an area of a kitchen and loading a drying rack with a plate and cup. In a video by Tesla, we see the Optimus robot handling eggs and dancing. Will these robots eventually live with us? While we go about our typical day, they could be tidying the house, vacuuming the carpets and preparing dinner. If you live alone, they could provide intellectual conversation over dinner. The possibilities are nearly limitless.

Both robots represent significant technological leaps. While challenges are ahead, their promise in controlled settings gives us a glimpse into a future where AI and robotics could revolutionize daily life and work in ways we're only beginning to explore.

These breakthroughs not only revolutionize the technological presence in society but also redefine the competencies our students will need as they learn and work in the school of tomorrow.

This is our chance to create a new species *that embodies the best of humanity while avoiding our worst tendencies.*

Shaping Our Digital Offspring

We have a unique opportunity to shape the development of AI. This is our chance to create a *new species* that embodies the best of humanity while avoiding our worst tendencies. Education plays a crucial role. We must prepare the next generation not just to use AI tools but to understand their implications and shape their development. This goes beyond teaching coding or data science. It requires fostering critical thinking, ethical reasoning and a deep understanding of what it means to be human.

We need environments where students can explore AI's potential and limitations firsthand. This might involve hands-on projects using AI tools, discussions about the ethical implications of AI decisions, or exercises in imagining future scenarios shaped by advanced AI.

When you hear AI described as a *new species*, what does that evoke in you? Consider how AI is already increasingly becoming a presence in our daily lives. What responsibilities come with that presence? As you continue reading, think about your role in shaping how this *new species* interacts with your work, your institution and the people you care about.

Co-Evolution

The emergence of AI as a new digital species represents the most significant challenge and extraordinary opportunity of the 21st century. We stand at a crossroads. The decisions we make now about how to develop and deploy AI will shape the future of our planet and our species. Will we approach this new era with wisdom and foresight, creating digital companions that elevate humanity? Or will we stumble mindlessly forward, potentially unleashing forces beyond our control?

The choice is ours. As educators, leaders and citizens, we all have a role in shaping this future. We must engage in open, honest discussions about AI's implications. We must demand transparency and ethical considerations in AI development. And we must nurture the next generation to be not just users of AI but its wise stewards.

As we co-evolve with our digital offspring, let us do so with eyes wide open, optimistic intent and minds attuned to the risk we face. The age of intelligence is here. How we navigate it will define the next chapter of human history.

I urge you not to remain a bystander. The future of education, work and even human identity is being rewritten—and your role in this transformation is critical. Reflect on your responsibility as an educational leader, innovator or parent. Your actions today will shape how this technology is woven into the lives of future generations.

As we explore the consequences of an AI world on education in the chapters ahead, I challenge you to think beyond your immediate context and imagine the broader societal impact you can influence. Your leadership in this pivotal moment can help ensure that AI enhances, rather than diminishes, our collective humanity. How will you rise to meet this extraordinary moment?

3 Philosophical Writings for Further Reflection

1. Nicomachean Ethics by Aristotle (350 BC)
Aristotle's ancient work teaches that ethical leadership involves prioritizing human well-being, cultivating virtues and applying practical wisdom to specific situations. While the capability of AI progresses around us, this means ensuring that it enhances rather than diminishes the holistic development of students, balancing technological tools with ethical and human-centered decision-making.

2. Superintelligence by Nick Bostrom (2014)
Bostrom emphasizes advanced AI's potential risks and power, urging

careful preparation. You can use these insights to inform your decisions about the progress of AI and its impact on your school.

3. The Conscious Mind by David Chalmers (1996)

Chalmers's work will encourage you to reflect on the unique nature of human consciousness compared to AI. This perspective will help guide your school by emphasizing the importance of preserving the human elements of education.

4 Questions for Infinite Minds

1. How do we nurture human potential when AI surpasses us in most cognitive tasks?

2. How do we cultivate human creativity when AI can generate art, music and literature?

3. In a world of AI companions, what uniquely human skills become most vital?

4. If AI mirrors our collective consciousness, how do we ensure it reflects our best selves?

Download the interactive Infinite Education Playbook to complete this task in the playbook and access more accompanying activities for you and your accelerator group.

TL;DR

- While the COVID-19 pandemic forced us to rethink how we live and work, AI is challenging our understanding of humanity and the future of education.

- AI is more than just a tool. Mustafa Suleyman likens it to a "new digital species." This shift in perspective underscores how AI is becoming an integral part of everyday life, with personal AIs and conversational interfaces soon to be everywhere.

- AI is currently like a toddler. It is awe-inspiring but can cause concerns. As the generation parenting this technology, we are responsible for guiding its development in ways that align with our values and ethical principles.

- There are breakthroughs with brain-computer interfaces, where AI can now interpret thoughts and reconstruct images or music from brain activity. These advances open new possibilities for education and accessibility but bring urgent ethical questions around privacy and control.

- Teachers and leaders are needed to shape AI's future actively. There is an urgent need for reflection, ethical decision-making and preparing institutions to navigate AI's transformative impact on education and society.

Chapter 3

HUMANITY IN A WORLD OF ARTIFICIAL INTELLIGENCE

The fluorescent lights of the New York auditorium flickered with tension one May afternoon in 1997. A hush fell over the crowd. Garry Kasparov, the world chess champion, walked onto the stage. His piercing gaze swept across the room. A mix of defiance and unease was etched on his face. Across from him sat his opponent—not a human but a state-of-the-art computer known as Deep Blue.

For a moment, time seemed to stand still. The weight of human intellectual achievement rested on Kasparov's shoulders. He wasn't playing for a title; he was defending humanity's cognitive supremacy against the march of artificial intelligence. The first move was made and the battle began.

Kasparov played with the brilliant intuition that made him a chess legend. His moves were a testament to the ineffable qualities of human creativity. However, Deep Blue countered with cold, machine-like precision. Each decision IBM's AI made was the product of algorithms sifting through millions of possibilities in seconds. Spectators leaned forward in their seats, hardly daring to breathe.

Computer scientists watched eagerly, their eyes darting between Kasparov's furrowed brow and Deep Blue's impassive display.

Then it happened. Deep Blue made a play so unexpected and brilliantly counterintuitive that Kasparov visibly recoiled. The machine sacrificed one of its pieces in a move that seemed to defy logic. Kasparov's eyes widened. Doubt crept into his mind. He glanced up at the machine before him.

At that moment, the line between human and machine intelligence blurred. Ripples of unease pulsed through the audience. Could a computer outthink the world's most extraordinary chess mind?

As the final game approached, Kasparov's composure began to crack. His once confident moves now carried a hint of desperation. Deep Blue waited patiently, its circuits unclouded by doubt or fatigue.

The endgame was a masterclass. Move by move, Deep Blue tightened its grip on the board, unfolding its strategy with ruthless efficiency. Kasparov fought bravely, but it was like holding back the tide with his bare hands.

The room erupted in a cacophony of gasps when the final move was made. Kasparov stared at the board in disbelief. His king toppled. He hadn't just lost a game but a battle for human intellectual supremacy.

The Deep Blue team celebrated their moment of triumph and the world buzzed with debate. The outcome was a watershed moment. It prompted the question of the value of humans playing chess anymore, with many asking, "Is chess over?"

Human Connection

Twenty-seven years later, we know the answer.

Far from drifting into obscurity, human chess has witnessed a remarkable renaissance. Young people, in particular, are flocking to the game with a renewed passion and urgency.[1]

But the question is, why?

Since 1997, if you wanted to watch the best chess game, it wouldn't be between two human grandmasters but between two artificial intelligences. AI should have reduced the human game to an afterthought. Yet we're still watching, playing and celebrating the human pursuit of chess mastery.

The answer lies in palpable human connection. Chess, at its heart, is more than just a calculation of moves; it is a theatre of human will, where each decision carries the weight of an individual's psyche. The game's beauty lies not in a perfect performance but in the tension between mind and heart. It's a struggle between strategy and intuition. There's the hope of triumph and the fear of heartbreak.

Humans are obsessed with humans.

This need for human connection extends beyond chess. It's woven into the fabric of everything we do. Humans are obsessed with humans. We have evolved to need to be around other humans for survival. There's even evidence that humans who socialize more live longer.[2] Whether watching sports, getting

---

1. Carpenter, Nicole. "Why teens are suddenly obsessed with chess." Polygon, 12 Apr. 2023, www.polygon.com/tabletop-games/23679440/teens-love-chess-memes-boom-2023.
2. Godman, Heidi. "Even a little socializing is linked to longevity." Harvard Health, 1 July 2023, www.health.harvard.edu/mind-and-mood/even-a-little-socializing-is-linked-to-longevity.

lost in a movie's emotional highs and lows, or passionately following the twists and turns of political events, we genuinely crave the human story. The victory of the underdog. The rise of the fallen hero. The uncertainty of life itself. These elements draw us in because they reflect our journeys.

📢 Leadership Voice

"It could be too easy to go too far with AI, losing human contact and interaction. Creating a cold experience, diminishing empathy and the art of human interaction."

—*Chris Loveday, Vice Principal,*
Barton Sixth Form College, England

According to psychologist Carl Jung, humans share universal stories and symbols—archetypes—that resonate deeply within us, shaping our experiences and connections.[3] This deep well of stories and symbols defines us. It could be why we are drawn to drama, not just on the chessboard but everywhere. These archetypes play out in the most important narratives of our lives: in relationships, careers, conflicts and even our search for meaning.

We constantly engage with these archetypal stories, whether chess, a sporting event, a movie, or a simple human interaction. We connect with stories of the Hero confronting overwhelming challenges, the Sage offering wisdom in moments of doubt and the Trickster revealing unexpected truths. According to Jung, these patterns guide our lives.

In this way, the human story transcends any single activity or medium. I don't necessarily believe there is a collective unconscious, but I think Jung is on to something with the types of stories, what he called archetypes, that we are attracted to. This is because they speak to a deep need in us all due to being human. It's what makes a football match more than just a game, a movie more than just entertainment and a political campaign more than just a race for power. These are all stages upon which our humanity comes to life and finds meaning.

3. Flowkyo. "C G Jung The Archetypes and the Collective Unconscious 2nd Edition." www.academia. edu, Oct. 2022, www.academia.edu/88679511/C_G_Jung_The_Archetypes_and_the_Collective_Unconscious_2nd_Edition.

Jung believed that our exploration of archetypes was part of the individuation process. He describes this as our journey towards becoming whole. He warns against disconnecting from these archetypes: "Whether he understands them or not, man must remain conscious of the world of the archetypes, because in it he is still a part of Nature and is connected with his roots. A view of the world or a social order that cuts him off from the primordial images of life not only is no culture at all but, in increasing degree, is a prison or a stable."[4]

> **Human endeavor's messy, beautiful and unpredictable process is just that—a human endeavor.**

We continuously navigate toward self-realization through the stories we tell, the games we play and the lives we lead. For now, at least AI cannot participate in the journey of individuation. Human endeavor's messy, beautiful and unpredictable process is just that—a human endeavor.

The All-Important Question

As AI tools proliferate classrooms and administrative offices, educators grapple with existential concerns: Will there be a place for human teachers in future classrooms? This question comes up many times.

 Leadership Voice

"The true value of education is in fostering creativity and emotional intelligence, areas where human teachers excel over AI."

—*Tom Rogerson, Head of Cottesmore School, England*

---

4. Flowkyo. "C G Jung The Archetypes and the Collective Unconscious 2nd Edition." www.academia.edu, Oct. 2022, www.academia.edu/88679511/C_G_Jung_The_Archetypes_and_the_Collective_Unconscious_2nd_Edition.

Our children must continue to have meaningful interactions with human educators. We should not be merely knowledge machines. Teachers bring passion, understanding, professional skills and a personal touch. Instead of viewing AI as a replacement, it's time to reimagine it as a collaborator that amplifies what we do.

AI is a powerful ally that can handle the tasks that turn humans into robots—administration, data input, report writing, etc. If we integrate AI correctly, it can free up teachers to focus on developing the genuine human connections they have with their students. It could unshackle us from our devices so that human relationships can flourish. This sounds very optimistic. That is intentional. We need to act with intent. Education demands a new vision for a world where humans and AI coexist.

An infinite approach to education is about understanding that an arbitrary amount of information in the memory of a student on a specific exam day is not what education is about. It's about the formation of the human so they can thrive in the decades ahead.

📢 Leadership Voice

"AI has the potential to realign education. Schools have become factories and we can make sure that they become active social clubs to foster human relationships and social development."

—*Henry Exham, Head of Digital Learning,*
Shrewsbury School, England

The journey from Deep Blue to ChatGPT is staggering. But a timeless truth remains as we stand on the precipice of further progress: human connection is vital for survival. AI offers algorithmic genius, but the authentic, heartwarming and challenging human journey remains central to who we are.

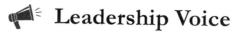 **Leadership Voice**

"My approach to leading the strategic development of AI was to establish the clear and simple vision of 'Enhancement Not Replacement'. It was essential that staff understood that for us, AI is not about replacing jobs, people or learning but about streamlining workloads, enhancing creativity and being active and positive members of the next digital revolution."

—Bryony Evett Hackfort, Coleg Sir Gar Coleg Ceredigion, Wales

5 Questions for Infinite Minds

1. If human connection is our greatest asset, how must we radically reimagine education to put relationships at the heart of learning?

2. How do we shift our focus from knowledge acquisition to wisdom cultivation in a world where AI can instantly provide information?

3. How can we harness the power of storytelling and human drama to create learning experiences that resonate profoundly?

4. If standardized testing becomes obsolete in an AI world, how do we redefine and measure the success of our students and schools?

5. In a future where AI and humans collaborate intimately, how do we cultivate a sense of purpose and meaning that transcends mere productivity or efficiency?

Download the interactive Infinite Education Playbook to complete this task in the playbook and access more accompanying activities for you and your accelerator group.

TL;DR

- Human connection remains irreplaceable in an AI-driven world, becoming our most valuable asset as technology advances.

- We must embrace imperfection, recognizing that what truly captivates us isn't a flawless performance but the messy, emotional journey of human experience.

- Storytelling is paramount in education, leveraging the power of narrative and archetypes to create deeply engaging learning experiences.

- As AI handles information processing, we must redefine success, shifting our focus from knowledge acquisition to cultivating wisdom, creativity and purpose.

- Rather than viewing AI as an adversary, we should reimagine it as a powerful ally, a tool to enhance human capabilities and free educators to foster genuine connections.

- As we embrace AI's capabilities, let's commit to placing human connection at the forefront of education, ensuring that technology enriches, not diminishes, our shared humanity.

Chapter 4

FINDING PURPOSE IN AN IKEA WORLD

When I needed a coffee table for my spare room, my choice was obvious: IKEA. Its winding aisles and cheerful minimalism beckoned, offering solutions to problems I didn't even know I had. After a plate of Swedish meatballs and a slice of Daim cake, I found what I was looking for—a modest oak veneer table. Light, practical and packed with cardboard. It is a triumph of mass production. This table wasn't trying to be more than it was. It existed to serve a purpose, quietly and without ceremony.

In the future, when I need a centerpiece dining table, the journey will likely be very different. It wouldn't start in a fluorescent maze of ready-to-assemble furniture but perhaps in a craftsman's workshop. This table wouldn't just hold meals; it would hold meaning. Solid oak, its surface worn smooth by time, it would bear the weight of memories—holiday feasts and laughter shared.

A piece like this transcends function. It becomes a story in itself, a testament to the artisan who carved it and the family who gathered around it. It's an investment in tradition, in permanence. And as it's passed down, it doesn't just connect generations—it anchors them.

This contrast between the IKEA coffee table and the imagined dining table reflects more than a personal preference. It's a glimpse into two modes of being: one defined by efficiency and accessibility, the other by craftsmanship and intention. IKEA excels at making good design democratic, at scaling functionality so it can sit in every home. But what IKEA represents—mass production, convenience and uniformity—is seeping into every aspect of modern life. And now, with AI, it may go further still.

AI has the potential to "IKEA-ify" entire industries. That's a word I've made up, but it fits. The same principles that brought affordable furniture to millions—efficiency, scalability and affordability—could transform art, writing, design, medicine and more. With AI's relentless efficiency, tasks once thought uniquely human may soon be rendered faster, cheaper and more uniform.

This shift is often framed as a threat: What will be left for humans when machines can do it all? But perhaps we're asking the wrong question. The value of human endeavor may not lie in what machines can't do, but in what they don't strive to do. Machines may perfect efficiency, but they'll never hunger for meaning. They'll never carve a table with intention, imagining the lives that will unfold around it.

The skilled carpenter, once an indispensable member of society, is now a niche artist. Their work is no longer a necessity—it's a luxury. And yet, their value endures, even grows. Not because their craft is irreplaceable, but because it's irreplicable. AI may one day help to create furniture faster, cheaper and sturdier than any human can. But it will never imbue it with the kind of soul that draws you in, makes you run your hand along the grain and imagine its story.

This is the paradox we face as AI reshapes our world. As it streamlines and optimizes, it will render many human skills unnecessary in the mainstream. But doing so could elevate those same skills in the margins. Writing, art, design, and music may all become niche pursuits, but their value will be magnified by their rarity and the human spirit embedded within them.

The IKEA-ification of human endeavor isn't a dystopia. It's a reality already unfolding. And yet, there's hope. The future of humanity isn't found in what we do faster or cheaper than machines, but in what we do with care, with purpose and with a soul machines will never possess. Like a handcrafted dining table, our most significant contributions will always tell stories machines cannot.

So What?

Human creativity is still valuable, but we must approach it differently and in novel ways to make a living with it. This sounds bad, but it's positive news. This is an opportunity to change our outlook on educating our children so they succeed in this AI world. After all, the purpose of education is to ensure every child has the opportunities, knowledge and skills to become successful.

Another way of framing success is finding purpose. The diagram below is useful for visualizing what purpose might entail. Created as the Bliss Diagram by the teacher Dorothy Shapland, in her 2011 blog "Ask Ms. Dorothy", the diagram has been adapted and renamed at various points over the years.[1] It is now most commonly used to represent the Japanese concept of Ikigai.

It represents the intersection of finding:

- What you love
- What the world needs
- What you are good at
- What you can get paid for

Our most significant contributions will always tell stories machines cannot.

---

1. Shapland, Dorothy. "Reflecting on "What I do."" askmsdorothy.blogspot.com/2011/09/reflecting-on-what-i-do.html.

The Purpose Diagram

Ikigai, a Japanese concept meaning 'reason for being,' represents the intersection of what you love, what you are good at, what the world needs and what you can be paid for. Business coach Marc Winn reappropriated the diagram by placing Ikigai at the center.[2] Ikigai in its original form, popularized by the Japanese psychiatrist Mieko Kamiya, is not necessarily tied to one's professional endeavors.[3]

In its true form, Ikigai is more of a personal and nuanced philosophy that encourages individuals to find contentment in the present, nurture meaningful

2. Metcalf, Michael. "Ikigai meaning: 5 Steps to unlock your purpose and find joy." Marlee, getmarlee. com/blog/what-is-ikigai.
3. "Ikigai ni Tsuite – 生きがいについて- Mieko Kamiya." Ikigai Tribe, 12 Oct. 2023, ikigaitribe.com/blog-post/ikigai-ni-tsuite.

connections and appreciate life's small pleasures.

However, Marc Winn's adaptation of Ikigai for career success has gained significant traction in the West. According to Winn, the intersection of these components can guide individuals toward a fulfilling career path that also aligns with their passions and talents. While this adaptation is a more structured approach, it provides a valuable tool for those looking to guide the next generation in a world where advanced AI is ubiquitous.

Winn's model may not capture the full depth of Ikigai as understood in its original context, but it offers a practical application. By integrating the traditional ideas of Ikigai with career exploration, this adaptation can help us align personal values with professional ambitions, providing a pathway to long-term fulfillment.

Ikigai can be the compass we use to educate our young people. If each curriculum addressed all four parts of the purpose diagram, failing to prepare our students for a meaningful future would be difficult. Building on the need to move beyond finite educational goals, integrating Ikigai principles offers a pathway to help students find enduring purpose in an AI-driven world.

John Kelly, the founder of the school Colegio Ikigai in Mexico, was inspired by the Japanese philosophy of Ikigai. While being interviewed on The International Classroom Podcast, he explained, "You've got to look at your vocation, your profession, your mission and your passion in life and if you can intersect all those lines, then you could be really successful in life."[4] At Colegio Ikigai, students engage in personalized, project-based learning aligned with their interests, creating a unique intersection of their abilities and passions. "The idea of Ikigai is that if we can capture all of their vocation, mission, passion and interests, we can help students find their reason for living," Kelly states.

We need vision. We need imagination. We need brave leaders.

---

4. The International Classroom Podcast. (2024, February 16). Innovation, Ikigai, and International Classrooms with John Thomas Kelly [Video]. YouTube. https://www.youtube.com/watch?v=DuFMxZR-byxQ

Purpose in an AI World

When we have a finite mindset toward education, we can't help but make the endpoint the goal. The endpoint for most stages of education is the exam. Preparation for an exam mainly involves memorization and regurgitating memorized knowledge at a single moment. Artificial intelligence can already do this so much better than humans. As someone who works within the education system, I see firsthand that our current system trains our young people to compete with machines.

We need vision. We need imagination. We need brave leaders.

Educators who, instead of training students to compete with AI, help them to find their purpose by leveraging AI to enhance their human potential. AI shouldn't be our competition; it should help us be better competitors. It is not about technology replacing us but about humans using technology to redefine what's possible. Our greatest strength has always been adapting, creating and envisioning new horizons.

The emerging capabilities of AI invite us to elevate our focus, tackle greater challenges and amplify our most human qualities. In embracing this shift, we don't just adapt to the future; we shape it. We can be bold enough to design a curriculum like this!?

We need to innovate our education practices now before we betray the students in our classrooms.

For decades, blue-collar workers have been disrupted by automation, from robotic arms in car factories to grocery packing in warehouses. This continues to the modern day. The recent East and Gulfcoast Longshoreman strike in the United States was fiercely fought with automation being one of the main topics of impasse; some going so far as to refer to automation as a "cancer".[5] Now,

5. LaRocco, L. A. (2024, October 4). U.S. ports start 100-day countdown clock to new strike, and automation is poised to be the dealbreaker. CNBC. https://www.cnbc.com/2024/10/04/port-strike-deal-not-done-automation-big-hurdle-for-ila-union-usmx.html

it's the turn of white-collar workers. The automation of complex cognitive capabilities is different and will likely be more unsettling. We need to innovate our education practices now before we betray the students in our classrooms.

5 Questions for Infinite Minds

1. How can we embed Ikigai principles to guide students toward entrepreneurial careers that leverage their passions and strengths in an AI-driven landscape?

2. What innovative assessment strategies can we adopt to prioritize and cultivate creativity, critical thinking and adaptability over traditional standardized testing?

3. In what ways can we integrate AI technologies to personalize learning and empower teachers to focus on developing students' uniquely human skills?

4. How can we create programs that foster specialized skills and craftsmanship, ensuring our students remain distinctive and valuable in an automated world?

5. What leadership practices can we implement to inspire and equip educators to embrace innovation and effectively guide students in utilizing technology for purposeful and entrepreneurial futures?

Download the interactive Infinite Education Playbook to complete this task in the playbook and access more accompanying activities for you and your accelerator group.

TL;DR

- Artificial intelligence is revolutionizing all industries by increasing efficiency and standardizing tasks, much like Ikea's approach to mass production.

- It is essential to nurture students' unique creative and specialized skills to ensure their contributions remain distinct and valuable in an AI-driven world.

- Incorporating the Ikigai framework into education helps students discover their passions, missions, vocations and professions, leading to purposeful and fulfilling career paths.

- Education should move away from exam-focused methods towards fostering critical thinking, adaptability and the ability to leverage AI to enhance human potential.

- Educational leaders must design innovative curricula that seamlessly integrate technology with human creativity, preparing students to thrive and shape the future in an AI-dominated landscape.

Chapter 5

A SYSTEM IN NEED OF REFORM

Our education systems remain stubbornly anchored in the past. The traditional model of education, emphasizing memorization, standardized testing, and rigid curricula, is entrenched within our culture and rapidly loses meaning in the face of advancements reshaping the very nature of work and society.

Historical Foundations of Our Education System

The Origins and Finite Reasons

The roots of the modern school system can be traced back to 18th century Prussia, marking a significant shift from traditional education provided by families, private tutors and religious institutions. The catalyst for this transformation was Prussia's defeat by Napoleon's army, which prompted Prussian leaders to recognize the need for an educated citizenry capable of strengthening national defense.[1]

---

1. Fabrega, Ana Lorena. "The Origin of the Modern School System — Ana Lorena Fabrega." Ana Lorena Fabrega, 20 May 2022, afabrega.com/my-blog/the-origin-of-the-modern-school-system.

With this finite purpose in mind, Prussia pioneered the foundational elements of modern schooling. They formed dedicated school buildings, teacher certifications, standardized curricula and mandatory attendance. The primary goal was to cultivate literate and patriotic citizens primed for military service. The finite reasons for building their education system proved remarkably effective in raising literacy rates, particularly among underprivileged children.

The Prussian system's influence extended globally, coinciding with the Industrial Revolution. Schools began to mirror the emerging factory system, prioritizing efficiency and standardization. This "factory model" of education featured regimented classroom layouts, an emphasis on rote learning and limited student autonomy.

Beyond Prussia, the establishment of modern schooling in Europe served multiple purposes. It helped forge national identities, particularly in newly formed nation-states.[2] Education was also used to consolidate political power, instilling loyalty to the state rather than the monarchy or the church.[3] It promoted economic development by equipping individuals with skills needed for the evolving workforce.

Memorization was prioritized over critical thinking, ensuring workers could recall necessary information quickly and accurately without understanding the underlying concepts.

The spread of modern schooling through colonialism often resulted in the suppression of indigenous educational practices, raising important questions about cultural imperialism and the imposition of Western educational paradigms.

This historical context reveals how modern education systems were shaped by a complex interplay of military needs, industrialization, nation-building and colonial expansion. In the words of my friend, the computer scientist and

2. "From 1871 to 2021: A Short History of Education in the United States." SUNY Buffalo State University, 8 Dec. 2021, suny.buffalostate.edu/news/1871-2021-short-history-education-united-states.
3. Morris, Emily Markovich, and Ghulam Omar Qargha. "Why understanding the historical purposes of modern schooling matters today." Brookings, 22 May 2023, www.brookings.edu/articles/why-understanding-the-historical-purposes-of-modern-schooling-matters-today.

educational theorist Sugata Mitra, for these reasons the education system is "not broken. It's wonderfully constructed. It's just that we don't need it anymore."[4]

Core Principles Established

The core principles of this educational framework emphasize discipline, rote memorization and standardized testing. These elements were essential for creating a uniform workforce that maintains high productivity. Memorization was prioritized over critical thinking, ensuring workers could recall necessary information quickly and accurately without understanding the underlying concepts.

Structure and Curriculum

The structure of the education system became highly standardized, with rigid curricula focused on basic literacy, numeracy and adherence to a fixed set of knowledge. Subjects were compartmentalized and the educational experience was designed to be consistent across different regions and institutions. This uniformity was crucial for maintaining consistent workforce standards when industrial efficiency was paramount.

 **Leadership Voice**

"Over the last decade our traditional education model, which largely focuses on preparing students for a knowledge-directed linear examination, has become more and more irrelevant to what students require to be successful global citizens when they leave school. AI is the disrupter that we all need to provoke a much bigger conversation around what we teach and how we assess it."

—*Henry Exham, Head of Digital Learning,*
Shrewsbury School, England

4. Mitra, Sugata. "Build a School in the Cloud." TED Talks, www.ted.com/talks/sugata_mitra_build_a_school_in_the_cloud/transcript?subtitle=en.

In his critique of the English education system, Terry Deary, the author of the famous *Horrible Histories* children's books and a former teacher, states that during the Industrial Revolution, "The primary aim of compulsory schooling was to sweep crime off the streets." He explains that the question of what children should learn was secondary and not well thought out when they introduced subjects: "Never mind teaching them how to think, or behave, or interact with other people. Teach them subjects. Lots of facts." In his scathing remarks, he concludes that a 'big lie' has been told ever since to maintain the system: "If you work hard, you will pass exams. If you pass exams, you'll get a good job. If you get a good job you'll make lots of money. And if you make lots of money, you'll be happy. Lies, all lies. None of those are true."[5]

All Hail the University

Misalignment Between Education and Modern Needs

Although much of the structure and practices of the industrial-era education system remain, our finite reasons for education have shifted. Why do we obsess over exam grades? For many schools, it's to get their students into a university. In his influential TED talk, Sir Ken Robinson highlighted a critical flaw in this finite goal: "The whole system of public education around the world is a protracted process of university entrance. And the consequence is that many highly talented, brilliant, creative people think they're not, because the thing they were good at at school wasn't valued, or was actually stigmatized."[6] This observation offers an insightful reading of the fundamental misalignment between our current educational practices and the skills needed.

When I interviewed the former UK Schools Minister from Tony Blair's government, Lord Jim Knight, on the Edufutusits podcast, he argued that the traditional university model is becoming unsustainable and needs to evolve.

---

5. Deary, Terry. "Game Based Learning 2009 - Terry Deary, Author, Horrible Histories." YouTube, 21 June 2010, www.youtube.com/watch?v=qsmJ8ViJiOY.
6. Robinson, Ken. "Do schools kill creativity?" TED Talks, www.ted.com/talks/sir_ken_robinson_do_schools_kill_creativity?subtitle=en.

He suggested that the future of education will require more flexibility, with people needing "an ongoing relationship with education" to navigate changing labor markets. He advocates for more flexible models, potentially including "subscription models" to remain relevant in the changing landscape of education and employment.[7]

If the education system is obsessed with exam grades for the finite reason of university, what do we do when the university becomes unsustainable? What if the finite reason is poor? In a 2021 article M. Hansen, the CEO of Cengage Group, explained that "the U.S. education system is not held accountable for ensuring that students are properly equipped with the skills and capabilities to prepare for a career where they can obtain financial stability." He claims that, as a result, there are, "nearly 15 million un- or under-employed individuals."[8]

The Centage survey,[9] on which he based these comments, reveals some trends in the ever-increasing misalignment between how our systems educate people and what they need in the world:

1. Lack of Skills

Over half of graduates (53%) avoided applying for jobs in their field because they felt unqualified, mainly because they did not possess all the required skills.

2. Degree Obsession

Employers continue to prioritize traditional degrees, with 65% of open jobs requiring a bachelor's or associate's degree. However, this requirement excludes many capable candidates who might have gained employable skills through non-traditional paths, such as vocational training or certifications. This traditional focus leaves many graduates unemployed or underemployed, with 15 million Americans fitting this category.

7. Edufuturists. "Edufuturists #85 - An Education System Fit for Purpose with Lord Jim Knight." YouTube, 17 Apr. 2020, www.youtube.com/watch?v=kOO7JlxGPvA.
8. Hansen, Michael. "The U.S. Education System Isn't Giving Students What Employers Need." Harvard Business Review, 24 May 2021, hbr.org/2021/05/the-u-s-education-system-isnt-giving-students-what-employers-need#:~:text=A%20recent%20Cengage%20survey%20(publication,their%20first%20post%2Ddegree%20job.
9. Cengage. "2021 Graduate Employability Report [INFOGRAPHIC]." The Cengage Blog, 22 Nov. 2023, blog.cengage.com/2021-graduate-employability-report-infographic.

3. Vocational Stigma

In the U.S., there is still a strong stigma against non-traditional education, including vocational training, even though countries like Germany
and Switzerland have long embraced it as a path to the middle class. In
the U.S., 61% of HR leaders admitted disregarding resumes without a
traditional degree, excluding many qualified candidates.

4. Education Cost

The high cost of traditional college degrees (ranging from $10,560 to
$70,000 per year) is becoming increasingly unsustainable, preventing
many from pursuing higher education. This financial burden further
amplifies the misalignment, as students are left with debt but no job-ready
skills to secure well-paying jobs.

These trends reflect a systemic issue where educational institutions are not
aligning their programs with the evolving demands of the workforce, leaving
graduates underprepared and many employers struggling to find the right talent.

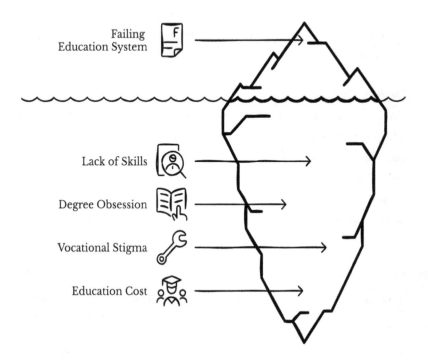

Persistence

Despite the world's changing demands, the education system continues to emphasize rote learning and memorization. Students are trained to recall information quickly and accurately, but there is a lack of focus on applying or synthesizing this knowledge. This approach limits the development of deeper cognitive skills necessary for critical thinking and problem-solving. As we edge towards an AI world, we are not changing fast enough.

Standardized testing remains the primary metric for measuring student success. These tests usually assess memorization and the ability to reproduce information under timed conditions. This overreliance on testing perpetuates a narrow view of intelligence and discourages diverse forms of learning and expression. An appreciation of wide intelligence will prove invaluable in a world dominated by information machines that will live alongside us.

The curricula in most educational institutions remain inflexible and resistant to incorporating new subjects or adapting to emerging fields. This rigidity prevents integrating contemporary knowledge areas and skills crucial for navigating today's dynamic environment. Interdisciplinary learning and personalized education paths are rare, limiting students' ability to explore and develop their unique talents and interests. As we've explored, cultivating unique interests is crucial to giving our young people the chances of success we are supposed to be giving them.

Resistance to change will lead to competition. It already is.

As we edge towards an AI world, we are not changing fast enough.

The Rise of Decentralized Education

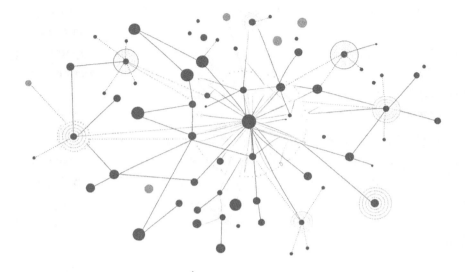

The 21st century has witnessed a notable trend toward decentralization across various domains. Technological advancements have played a pivotal role in this shift. The emergence of blockchain, distributed ledger technologies and peer-to-peer networks has enabled the creation of systems that operate without a central authority or intermediary. These innovations have facilitated decentralization in finance through cryptocurrencies, governance via decentralized autonomous organizations (DAOs), and data storage with decentralized cloud solutions.

There is a great belief that decentralized systems can enhance efficiency, accountability and transparency by bringing decision-making closer to the people and reducing bureaucracy. A growing distrust of institutions is fuelling the growth of decentralized alternatives. The global financial crisis, data privacy scandals and perceived corruption have fueled a desire for more transparent and trustless systems, propelling the adoption of decentralized alternatives.

A growing distrust of institutions is fuelling the growth of decentralized alternatives.

Embracing Decentralization

Here are ten ways decentralization is changing various sectors and functions of society:

1. Finance

Decentralized finance is revolutionizing how we handle money by offering an alternative to traditional banks. Platforms like Uniswap allow users to trade cryptocurrencies directly with one another, while Aave enables peer-to-peer lending and borrowing without intermediaries. MakerDAO creates stablecoins like DAI, which maintain a stable value through decentralized governance, making financial services more accessible and transparent. As I write this sentence on October 13, 2024, from my hotel room in Seattle, the total amount currently invested in cryptocurrencies is $2.30 Trillion. Bitcoin, the largest cryptocurrency, is even an official currency in El Salvador and several other countries have been said to be considering the same move.

2. Governance and Organizations

Decentralized Autonomous Organizations (DAOs) empower communities to govern themselves without hierarchical structures. Platforms such as Aragon provide tools for creating and managing DAOs, enabling collective decision-making. MolochDAO funds Ethereum infrastructure projects through member voting, demonstrating how decentralized governance can support and grow essential initiatives.

3. Healthcare

In healthcare, decentralization is improving data security and patient privacy. Medicalchain securely stores electronic health records on the blockchain, allowing patients to control who accesses their information. BurstIQ offers a decentralized platform for managing and sharing health data, enhancing interoperability between healthcare providers.

In an interview I co-hosted on the Edufuturists podcast in 2022, the healthcare futurist Manish Juneja emphasized the role of technology like AI and wearable monitors in shifting from a system-centric to a decentralized person-centered approach. He envisions a future where individuals take greater control of their health through self-monitoring, education and behavioral changes, which can reduce reliance on traditional healthcare systems. This shift, he argues, is crucial for addressing challenges such as limited access to care in rural areas or for those with mobility issues. Manish also highlights how decentralized healthcare can create a fairer society by reducing biases in diagnoses and treatment.[10]

4. Energy

Decentralized energy systems enable individuals and communities to generate and trade their energy. Power Ledger allows households with solar panels to sell excess energy directly to their neighbors. LO3 Energy's Brooklyn Microgrid facilitates local energy transactions using blockchain, promoting renewable energy distribution and reducing reliance on centralized utilities.

5. Credentials

Blockcerts issues blockchain-based digital certificates, enabling learners to securely verify and share their academic credentials. Odem connects students and educators directly through a decentralized marketplace, facilitating courses and tutoring without intermediaries.

6. Gaming and Virtual Worlds

In gaming, decentralization empowers players with true ownership of in-game assets. Axie Infinity allows players to own, trade and sell their in-game creatures as NFTs, providing real ownership and monetization opportunities.[11] Decentraland is a virtual world where users can buy, develop and sell virtual land and assets using cryptocurrency.

7. Legal Services

Decentralized legal platforms make legal services more accessible and efficient. OpenLaw integrates smart contracts with legal agreements, automating contract execution and reducing the need for intermediaries.

10. Edufuturists. "Edufuturists 197 - Replacing the Human with Maneesh Juneja." YouTube, 16 Nov. 2022, www.youtube.com/watch?v=sDz6qm-XJug.
11. An NFT, or Non-Fungible Token, is a digital certificate of ownership for a unique item, like a piece of art, music, or video, that exists online.

Kleros offers decentralized dispute resolution, where jurors worldwide adjudicate disputes based on blockchain evidence, ensuring fair and transparent outcomes.

8. Art and Collectibles

Decentralization in the art world ensures provenance and fair compensation for artists. OpenSea and Rarible are decentralized marketplaces for NFTs, allowing artists to sell and trade digital art without intermediaries. SuperRare tokenizes artwork, providing provenance and ensuring artists receive royalties through smart contracts every time their art is resold.

9. Retail and E-commerce

Decentralized e-commerce platforms reduce fees and increase trust between buyers and sellers. Origin Protocol creates marketplaces where users interact directly, cutting out the middleman and lowering transaction costs. OpenBazaar is a peer-to-peer marketplace that allows users to trade goods and services using cryptocurrency, fostering a more open and competitive retail environment.

10. Agriculture

Decentralized agricultural platforms enhance transparency and efficiency in the food supply chain. AgriDigital uses blockchain to manage transactions between farmers, suppliers and buyers, ensuring secure and transparent dealings. TE-FOOD provides end-to-end traceability for food products, improving transparency and reducing fraud in agricultural markets.

Although this is not an exhaustive list, I wanted to go beyond just a glancing look at our evolving decentralized world to show that this is not a 'flash in the pan' phenomenon. It's a growing trend driven by a disillusionment with centralized authority and is made possible through advanced technology.

Decentralized Education

Post-covid changes in student behavior point towards a dissatisfaction of young people and their parents with the education system. Katie Rosanbalm, a child clinical and quantitative psychologist at Duke Center for Child & Family Policy, believes that "both absenteeism and behavioral outbursts are examples of the human stress response, now playing out en masse in schools: fight (verbal or physical aggression) or flight (absenteeism)." There was an estimated 26% of public school students in the United States considered chronically absent in 2023.[12]

Post-covid changes in student behavior point towards a dissatisfaction of young people and their parents with the education system.

While millions of dollars are being spent on strategies to get these students back into schools, the presumption seems that the young person's behavior needs to change rather than the educational environment they are expected to attend.

Is sitting our children in rooms all day, expecting them to be silent and teaching them about facts really the best we can do? Teaching children information 'just in case' is no longer sufficient; there is a pressing need for a more practical approach. There are examples of organizations and individuals trying to do better.

Teaching children information 'just in case' is no longer sufficient; there is a pressing need for a more practical approach.

---

1. To the Stars

Synthesis School represents a groundbreaking model in decentralized education, fundamentally challenging traditional schooling methods. It operates independently of conventional educational frameworks, emphasizing real-world problem-solving, critical thinking and personalized learning through AI.

12. Mervosh, Sarah. "Why School Absences Have 'Exploded' Almost Everywhere." The New York Times, 29 Mar. 2024, www.nytimes.com/interactive/2024/03/29/us/chronic-absences.html.

The Synthesis School began when Josh Dahn, a fourth-grade teacher, received an unexpected email from Elon Musk's executive assistant. Invited to discuss a potential opportunity at SpaceX, Dahn soon found himself at the forefront of creating a school for Musk's children called Ad Astra. Initially housed in a conference room at SpaceX, the school eventually expanded to include more children from the surrounding Los Angeles area. Musk's directives were clear but broad: "There's no budget but spend money thoughtfully," "only hire world-class talent," and "make it great." These guidelines allowed for significant creative freedom, enabling the school to develop unique educational methodologies.

As Ad Astra evolved into Synthesis School, its approach diverged sharply from traditional education systems. Their Chief Evangelist, Ana Fabrega, criticizes conventional schooling, stating, "Kids are stuck in the game of school imitating their teachers instead of thinking for themselves."[13] Synthesis aims to rectify this by fostering independent thinking and problem-solving through simulations that require students to figure things out independently, promoting critical thinking and resilience.

The school engages students in real-world learning experiences directly relevant to contemporary challenges. For instance, Dahn created "synthesis" experiences, which are complex, competitive and cooperative and allow for deep

13. Edufuturists. "Edufuturists 223 - The Learning Game with Ana Fabrega." YouTube, 27 Sept. 2023, www.youtube.com/watch?v=bY7POnAh_XI.

reflection. These experiences mimic real-life challenges, requiring students to make decisions, experience failure and learn from it. As Fabrega puts it, "They want the real thing...they want to make real decisions and sort of shoulder the consequences of those decisions."

One of the standout features of Synthesis is its AI-powered digital tutor designed to teach students core academic subjects like math.

Leveraging technology, Synthesis School transcends the limitations of traditional brick-and-mortar institutions. The online format allows students from diverse backgrounds to participate, making education more inclusive and adaptable. The school's long-term vision includes creating a comprehensive K-12 education system integrating soft skills through simulations and rigorous academic skills through digital tutors.

One of the standout features of Synthesis is its AI-powered digital tutor designed to teach students core academic subjects like math. Based on the teachings of Dr. James Tanton, the tutor offers personalized, patient instruction that adapts to each student's learning pace. Fabrega describes the tutor as feeling "like you're talking to a human and you feel like you're learning from a human." Unlike other educational apps that rely on gamification, the Synthesis tutor engages students by making the subject matter intriguing and relevant, promoting intrinsic motivation and deeper understanding.

Synthesis School can be found at synthesis.com.

2. Sora Schools

Sora Schools, an online middle and high school founded by Garrett Smiley, exemplifies a decentralized approach to education that is unconcerned with traditional education systems. Established in 2019, Sora Schools aims to provide a transformative education that radically changes students' lives.

Initially, Sora Schools was not designed as an online institution. It focused on delivering a progressive, transformative education accessible to a broader range of students. Smiley and his team recognized that online delivery could democratize access to high-quality education by removing geographical barriers. "We asked ourselves, is it really necessary for a school to be in person... and the answer we came to was no," says Smiley.[14]

Sora Schools' curriculum is uniquely interdisciplinary and competency-based, giving students significant agency in shaping their learning paths. "We built up a completely interdisciplinary, transdisciplinary curriculum... students have tons of agency and voice," Smiley explains. The school's approach moves away from traditional discrete subjects, favoring project-based learning that integrates various disciplines and real-world applications.

Student progression is based on students demonstrating mastery of units and abilities rather than traditional assessments. This method allows students to move forward once they are ready, ensuring a deeper understanding of the material. "I think assessment is a good thing... but how we do it at Sora is competency-based, so students move on when ready," Smiley notes.

Students at Sora Schools choose their learning experiences every six weeks from various options, tailoring their education to their interests and goals. Each student has an advisor to help guide them through their educational journey. Advisors receive detailed data to help support students effectively, ensuring no one falls through the cracks.

A key aspect of Sora Schools' approach is connecting academic content with real-world relevance, which helps students retain knowledge more effectively. "The human mind is a relevance-finding machine... we fire connecting ideas," Smiley explains. The school also maintains a mentor network that connects students with industry professionals, although this aspect is still being developed.

Students at Sora Schools choose their learning experiences every six weeks from various options, tailoring their education to their interests and goals.

14. Edufuturists. "Edufuturists 188 - Sora Schools with Garrett Smiley." YouTube, 15 Sept. 2022, www.youtube.com/watch?v=1lnvLFjsAEc.

Smiley envisions a future where education is flexible, personalized and facilitated by technological advancements. He emphasizes that philosophical and pedagogical changes are paramount. "It's a pedagogical failure, it's a philosophical failure that's making schools bad today," he asserts. Sora Schools aims to stay at the cutting edge of educational technology while strongly focusing on effective teaching and learning practices.

You can learn more about Sora Schools at www.soraschools.com.

3. Non-Traditional Learners Post-COVID

Minerva's Virtual Academy emerged after the COVID-19 pandemic to address the needs of students who do not fit into the mainstream education system. By offering a fully online curriculum that emphasizes active learning and real-world application, Minerva provides an inclusive environment where students can excel without the constraints of traditional classroom settings.

Minerva's online curriculum focuses on active learning through seminars, collaborative projects and real-world problem-solving. The school provides a supportive environment for students who may have felt marginalized or disengaged by mainstream education, offering personalized support and a flexible learning pace.

By providing an inclusive and adaptive learning environment, Minerva Online School helps students who struggle with traditional education to succeed. The emphasis on active learning and real-world application ensures students develop practical skills and confidence. This approach addresses the immediate challenges posed by the pandemic and aligns with the long-term needs of a diverse and evolving workforce.

Minerva's Virtual Academy can be found at minervavirtual.com.

4. Daisy's Tutor

Every parent has a desire to support their child's educational journey. For Phil Birchenall, a business consultant from Manchester U.K., this desire led to an innovative approach to leveraging artificial intelligence to address his daughter's academic challenges. Phil's journey with ChatGPT exemplifies how AI can be harnessed to personalize educational experiences.[15]

15. I first wrote about Phil and Daisy in my Forbs article: Fitzpatrick, Dan. "3 ChatGPT Prompts That

Phil's daughter Daisy, a bright and enthusiastic 11-year-old, was falling behind in math. The pressures of transitioning from primary to secondary education, compounded by long-term illness at home, were taking their toll. Daisy struggled with critical areas such as long division, squared and cubed numbers, written multiplication and fractions.

Recognizing the need for targeted support, Phil explained that he intended to help Daisy himself. However, he soon realized that the traditional methods of math he studied at school were insufficient. Phil reflected, "After watching my daughter attempt to solve the questions, I heard my inner voice channel Mr. Incredible from the Incredibles movie... 'Why would they change math!?'"

Phil had been exploring AI tools and was aware of their potential to revolutionize various sectors, including education. Inspired by a video by Doug Cunnington on training AI for specialized roles, Phil decided to create a virtual math tutor tailored to Daisy's needs.[16] He noted, "I figured that if we could train an AI with relevant information about our needs, it could just work. And boy, did it work."

Phil recalls that he began by instructing ChatGPT to be a personalized tutor, called Izzy, with this prompt:

> I want you to act as a personalized math tutor for an 11-year-old UK student preparing for her exams. Your role is to assess her current mathematical understanding, identify any areas of weakness and develop strategies to improve her skills in those areas. This will involve explaining concepts in a clear and engaging way, providing practice questions and offering feedback on her progress. You should also incorporate elements of test-taking strategies, such as time management and question analysis, to better prepare her for the format and pressure of her exams.

Helped A Parent Transform His Child's Future." Forbes, 18 May 2024, www.forbes.com/sites/danfitz-patrick/2024/05/18/3-chatgpt-prompts-that-helped-a-parent-to-transform-his-childs-future.
16. Doug Cunnington. "ChatGPT-4 Prompt Engineering: POWERFUL PROMPT GENERATOR." YouTube, 15 Mar. 2023, www.youtube.com/watch?v=jEFfo-M29-A.

Phil provided detailed information about Daisy's areas of struggle and her interests:

Focused Areas Prompt:

> My daughter is a bright kid but consistently scores around 50% on the test papers she has been working on. Can the tutor focus on the following areas to help improve: long division, multiplying fractions, squared and cubed numbers. ⬆

Personal Interests Prompt:

> My daughter is called Daisy, she's 11 years old. She absolutely loves dogs, and she likes having a laugh, so the more we can add humor and dog references, the more engaging the tutor will be. ⬆

The AI provided clear explanations, step-by-step guidance and practice questions that focused on the identified weak areas. It incorporated Daisy's love for dogs into the examples, making the lessons relatable and fun. This approach not only helped Daisy understand complex concepts but also kept her motivated and engaged.

"The sessions with 'Izzy' were scarily on point: they focused on Daisy's specific needs, targeting precise areas where she needed help," Phil explained to me.

By integrating elements of Daisy's interests and creating a supportive learning environment, he demonstrated how AI could be used to foster a positive and fun educational experience. The success of Izzy's tutoring sessions was evident in Daisy's improved exam performance, a testament to the potential of AI in personalized education.

Phil proudly noted, "Daisy smashed her exams and her teacher commended her for how much improvement she'd made on math."

> *"I figured that if we could train an AI with relevant infor-
> mation about our needs, it could just work. And boy, did
> it work."*
>
> *—Phil Birchenall*

Phil's journey with ChatGPT underscores the transformative potential of AI in education. It highlights the importance of personalized learning experiences that meet individual needs and interests. As Daisy transitions to secondary school, Phil plans to further adapt Izzy to her evolving academic challenges, possibly integrating her newfound love for German into the math problems. "We've talked about creating a new version of 'Izzy', updated on the areas she needs to improve on now," Phil mentioned.

Phil's experience with Izzy offers valuable insights into how AI can be harnessed to support and enhance traditional education methods. It decentralizes the teacher's power from the school's walls to anyone who wants to learn, wherever they are.

In a world where AI is set to redefine various aspects of our lives, Phil Birchenall's innovative use of ChatGPT for his daughter's education is a beacon of what's possible when an entrepreneurial parent and AI converge.

5. Two-Hour Learning

Alpha School, co-founded by MacKenzie Price, is pioneering a decentralized education model that challenges traditional schooling methods. Motivated by personal experiences with the limitations of conventional education, Price developed the "2hr Learning" approach. This approach dedicates two hours daily to core subjects using adaptive apps, allowing students to progress at their own pace. The remaining school day focuses on life skills and hands-on projects, ensuring a well-rounded education.

The school's innovative model integrates technology to provide a highly personalized learning experience. Adaptive apps tailor lessons to each student's strengths and weaknesses, significantly improving learning efficiency. This approach has led to remarkable academic achievements, with students learning up to 2.6 times faster than in traditional settings. For example, second-grade students at the Brownsville campus improved from the 31st percentile to the 84th percentile in math and the 71st percentile in reading within a year.[17]

Alpha School's success has led to expansion, with new campuses in Miami and Brownsville and the incorporation of diverse programs such as esports and sports academies. The school's philosophy centers on adaptable, equitable and engaging education, leveraging AI and adaptive learning tools as equalizers that cater to students regardless of their background. This decentralized approach addresses current shortcomings in the education system and paves the way for a future where every student can reach their full potential.

5 Questions for Infinite Minds

1. Our current education system was designed for the Industrial Age. What would a system truly designed for the AI era look like and how drastically would it differ from our current model?

2. How might we create a decentralized accreditation system that accurately reflects a student's skills and knowledge, regardless of how they were acquired and what implications would this have for traditional schooling?

3. How can we shift our education system from a "just in case" model of learning facts to a "just in time" model of acquiring skills and knowledge as needed and what would this look like in practice?

4. If we were to design our education system primarily around fostering creativity, critical thinking and adaptability—kills crucial for an AI-dominated future—what would our schools look like and how would we measure success?

17. Price, MacKenzie. "There's No Such Thing As A 'C' Student." Forbes.com, 11 June 2024, www.forbes.com/councils/forbestechcouncil/2024/06/10/theres-no-such-thing-as-a-c-student-how-edtech-will-democratize-learning. Accessed 16 July 2024.

5. Considering the success of AI tutors and adaptive learning platforms, how might we ethically and effectively integrate AI into our schools to provide personalized support at scale while maintaining the essential human elements of education?

Download the interactive Infinite Education Playbook to complete this task in the playbook and access more accompanying activities for you and your accelerator group.

TL;DR

- Our current education system is not broken—it's obsolete. Designed for the industrial era, it fundamentally fails to meet the needs of our AI-driven world, necessitating reform and a radical reimagining of education.

- Emerging models like Synthesis and Sora Schools are proving the transformative power of decentralized, personalized learning. These innovative approaches prioritize real-world skills over standardized curricula, challenging the very foundation of traditional schooling.

- AI-driven personalized learning, exemplified by tools like ChatGPT, has the potential to democratize high-quality education at an unprecedented scale. This technology could be the key to eliminating educational inequalities, making it possible for every child's potential to be fully realized.

- In an age of abundant information, the focus of education must shift dramatically from knowledge acquisition to skill development. Creativity, critical thinking and adaptability are becoming the new currencies of success in a rapidly evolving world.

- Rising student disengagement and rapidly evolving workforce needs signal that incremental change is woefully insufficient. Educational leaders must act now to create learning systems that are not just relevant but revolutionary in their approach to preparing students for the future.

Chapter 6

RETHINKING SCHOOL

J ohn Gatto, a New York City public school teacher for over 30 years, delivered his acceptance speech after receiving the New York State Teacher of the Year award in 1991.

"I don't teach English; I teach school," Gatto declared as he began.[1] He would go on to explain the seven lessons that teachers teach their students, what he called the hidden curriculum. Although Gatto frames his words as a critique of himself, in doing so, he peels back the underlying culture found in much of how we 'school' children.

---

1. Gatto, J. T. (2002). Dumbing Us Down: The Hidden Curriculum of Compulsory Schooling. New Society Publishers.

By the nature of how most schools function, we cannot help but continue to perpetuate a curriculum that teaches:

1. Confusion
2. Class Position
3. Indifference
4. Emotional Dependency
5. Intellectual Dependency
6. Provisional Self-Esteem
7. Surveillance

Although delivered over three decades ago, Gatto's insights forecasted many of our education system's challenges. It is imperative to reform the hidden curriculum as AI transforms our world at an unprecedented pace.

Let us change these seven lessons:

1. Connection
2. Individuality
3. Curiosity
4. Emotional Autonomy
5. Intellectual Autonomy
6. Intrinsic Self-Worth
7. Independence

What if classrooms transformed from individual subjects into idea labs?

Lesson One: ~~Confusion~~ Connection

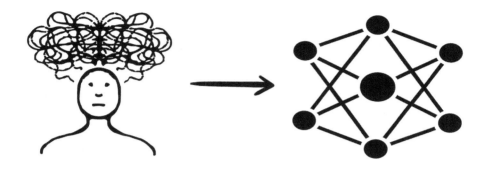

Gatto stated that, "The first lesson I teach is confusion. Everything I teach is out of context. I teach the un-relating of everything." This is a chilling indictment of his school, but it can be identified in schools around the world that are part of a system that fragments knowledge into disconnected shards. It causes confusion. In our AI-driven world, this approach is outdated. Our children need to become master pattern-recognizers adept at weaving disparate threads of information into tapestries of understanding. They must learn to surf the waves of AI-generated data, crafting meaning from the digital deluge.

What if classrooms transformed from individual subjects into idea labs?

- Projects that mirror the interconnected nature of real-world challenges

- Students armed with AI-powered research tools but focused on human-driven synthesis

- Lessons in metacognition, teaching the art of learning itself

- Visual mapping exercises that reveal the hidden connections between seemingly unrelated concepts

Confusion will give way to clarity and fragmentation will yield to a holistic worldview.

Building upon the need to replace confusion with connection, we must also consider how class positions hinder individuality.

Lesson Two: ~~Class Position~~ Individuality

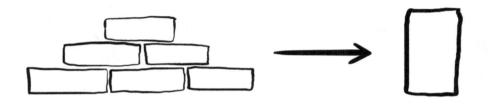

"The second lesson I teach is class position," Gatto reveals. "I teach that students must stay in the class where they belong." It's a sobering reminder of how our schools often reinforce societal hierarchies instead of celebrating individuality and creating opportunities for the individuals in front of them.

This rigid categorization isn't just unfair; it's a recipe for obsolescence in the AI age. The job market will demand unique individuals with diverse skills, not factory replicas. We live in a world where students with laptops and entrepreneurial flair can earn more over a weekend than their teacher does in a month. How do we encourage students to foster their potential?

We must cultivate in our students a profound sense of their unique potential, a hunger for lifelong learning and the confidence to chart their path in the face of AI disruption.

The job market will demand unique individuals with diverse skills.

What if schools offered:

- Personalized learning paths that honor each student's strengths and interests

- Assessment tools that recognize and nurture diverse forms of intelligence

- 'Personal brand' projects that help students identify and develop their unique talents

- Curriculum centered on self-discovery and individual growth alongside academic achievement

In this brave new classroom, the class position becomes irrelevant, replaced by celebrating each student's individuality.

Lesson Three: ~~Indifference~~ Curiosity

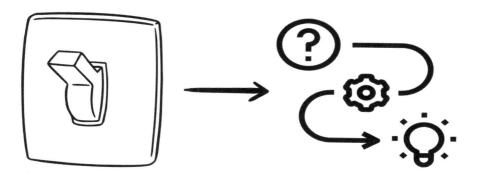

Gatto's third lesson cuts to the core of educational malaise: "I teach children not to care too much about anything, even though they want to make it appear that they do." This is a pervasive issue affecting classrooms globally.

We put them in a room to practice math for an hour, then move them to another room to write for an hour, then to another room to try and play a keyboard for an hour and so it goes, every day. How can they deep-dive into a task or a problem? They can't, so they become indifferent to most classes.

This cultivated apathy is more than a shame. It's an existential threat in a world of AI. As machines master routine tasks, human curiosity becomes one of our most valuable resources.

Our students must rediscover the joy of curiosity, the thrill of asking "why" and "what if," and the satisfaction of unraveling mysteries.

Our students must rediscover the joy of curiosity.

Picture a school ablaze with curiosity:

- 'Wonder walls' where students post questions that drive classroom investigations

- Collaboration with AI to explore and investigate areas of importance where they feel they can bring value

- Real-world problem-solving challenges that ignite curiosity about complex issues

- Inquiry-based learning approaches that prioritize questioning over answering

In these vibrant learning spaces, indifference withers and curiosity flourishes.

Our greatest asset is our ability to empathize, manage and direct our emotions.

Lesson Four: ~~Emotional Dependency~~ Emotional Autonomy

"The fourth lesson I teach is emotional dependency," Gatto admits. "I teach kids to surrender their will to the predestinated chain of command." It's a shocking reflection on how schools often prioritize compliance over emotional growth.

This emotional stunting is a critical weakness. As machines take over more cognitive tasks, our emotional autonomy is vital. Our greatest asset is our ability to empathize, manage and direct our emotions.

Our education system must nurture emotionally autonomous individuals capable of self-regulation and empathy in a world increasingly mediated by AI.

Imagine schools as dojos for emotional autonomy:

- Self-awareness exercises integrated into daily routines

- AI-powered emotion recognition tools used to help students understand and manage their feelings

- Peer support programs that teach emotional self-reliance

- Mindfulness and stress-management techniques that promote emotional self-regulation

In this emotionally rich environment, dependency gives way to autonomy and self-directed emotional intelligence.

Lesson Five: ~~Intellectual Dependency~~ Intellectual Autonomy

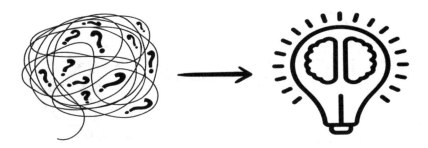

Gatto's fifth lesson strikes at the heart of intellectual growth: "I teach intellectual dependency. Good students wait for a teacher to tell them what to do." It's a damning indictment of an education system that often values obedience over independent thought.

This intellectual passivity is more than a flaw. It's a fatal weakness. As AI systems become more sophisticated, the ability to think independently, to question assumptions and to innovate with AI becomes essential.

We must foster a fierce intellectual autonomy in our students, equipping them to analyze, evaluate and create in partnership with AI.

Envision classrooms as intellectual gyms:

- Student-led learning projects where teachers act as facilitators, not directors

- Critical thinking challenges that require students to question AI-generated content

- Debate clubs that encourage the formation and defense of original ideas

- Self-directed research initiatives that allow students to pursue their intellectual passions

Intellectual dependency crumbles in these mental workout spaces, replaced by robust, autonomous thought.

We must foster a fierce intellectual autonomy in our students, equipping them to analyze, evaluate and create in partnership with AI.

Lesson Six: ~~Provisional Self-Esteem~~ Intrinsic Self-Worth

"The sixth lesson I teach is provisional self-esteem," Gatto reveals. It's a lesson that ties a child's sense of worth to external evaluations, creating a fragile foundation for self-image.

In an AI future where machines can outperform humans on many measurable metrics, this externally validated self-esteem is a ticking time bomb. We need to nurture in our students a sense of intrinsic self-worth that isn't shaken compared to machine capabilities.

Our schools must help students develop a strong internal locus of evaluation and resilience in the face of failure and the ability to derive satisfaction from personal growth rather than external accolades.

Picture schools as a nurturing ground of intrinsic self-worth:

- Reflective practices that help students identify and appreciate their inherent value

- Strength-based learning approaches that focus on developing each student's unique insights and potential

- Failure workshops that teach students to view setbacks as opportunities for growth

- Community service projects that help students derive worth from their positive impact on others

In these nurturing environments, provisional self-esteem could transform into unshakeable intrinsic self-worth.

Lesson Seven: ~~Surveillance~~ Independence

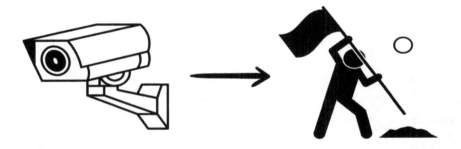

Gatto's final lesson is eerily prescient: "I teach that one can't hide." This lesson takes on new and urgent implications in today's digital age.

As AI-powered surveillance becomes ubiquitous, understanding privacy rights, data ethics and the societal implications of technology isn't just important; it's crucial for maintaining human independence.

We must educate our students to be not just consumers of technology but independent and ethical stewards of it. They need to understand the power and pitfalls of AI and be prepared to shape its development in ways that enhance rather than diminish human autonomy.

Teaching our children that they can't hide and are being watched pushes them to accept this fate. So, when big tech is doing it to them, it won't really matter to them.

> *The school environment imparts that success is equated with compliance. This could not be further from the truth.*

Imagine schools as training grounds for digital independence:

- Programs that teach students how to protect their privacy and personal information

- Ethical hacking courses that empower students to understand and control technology

- AI design projects that challenge students to create systems that respect user independence

- Digital detox initiatives that help students maintain independence from technology

In these forward-thinking spaces, students learn not just to survive in a surveillance world but to actively assert their independence in the digital age.

Gatto's hidden curriculum unveils an obsession with control over learning. This emphasis does not reflect the dedication of teachers or the intentions of administrators. It's a consequence of systemic constraints. The focus shifts to maintaining order in a classroom where a single educator is responsible for thirty or more students. Behavior management becomes a primary concern. The school environment imparts that success is equated with compliance. This could not be further from the truth.

The standardization of education further compounds these issues. Many institutions have abandoned attempts at personalized learning in favor of a uniform approach that purposefully teaches to the top. While administratively efficient, this one-size-fits-all methodology fails to address the diverse needs and potentials of individual students. The result is an educational experience undermining the skills it aims to develop. We must question whether we are inadvertently stifling the intellectual growth and curiosity of the minds we seek to nurture as we strive for order in our classrooms.

By rethinking these seven lessons, we can create an education system that doesn't just prepare our children for the AI future but it empowers them to create a future where AI enhances, rather than diminishes, our humanity. In reimagining education, we're not just securing our children's future but safeguarding the essence of what it means to be human in the age of artificial intelligence.

The Urgent Need for Transformational Change

Imagine an education system that values depth over breadth, where we encourage students to explore subjects deeply and meaningfully. Classrooms would be spaces of collaboration and inclusivity. Learning should be an immersive and engaging process, free from the arbitrary interruptions of bells and rigid schedules. Emotional and intellectual independence should be cultivated, allowing students to develop a strong sense of self and the confidence to think critically and creatively.

 Leadership Voice

"We can now transform and maximize the way individuals learn throughout their lives and in all contexts by providing meaningful and personalized AI-enhanced experiences and guidance in and out of the classroom. I've witnessed for the first time how a teacher can introduce personalization with the integration of AI. This is life changing not only for students, but also for teachers. We're heading towards total personalization of learning"

—Jennifer Verschoor, Northlands, Argentina

This transformational change is not only possible but necessary. The stakes are too high to settle for incremental improvements. We must be bold and imaginative, drawing on the best ideas and practices from around the world to create an education system that truly serves our children and society.

Let us remember that the ultimate goal of education is not to produce test scores but to cultivate human beings capable of thinking deeply, feeling compassionately and acting courageously.

XP Schools: Redefining Education Through Connection and Autonomy

There are many examples of schools bucking the trend of Gatto's seven lessons. One I know well and is close to home for me is XP Schools.

Students lead their parent-teacher conferences and math, science and literature blend seamlessly in real-world projects. This is the reality at XP Schools. Let us explore how they're reshaping learning.

The true test of education isn't in exam grades—it's in life after school.

The Power of Connected Learning

At XP, forget about isolated subjects. Instead, they have "expeditions." These are learning journeys that weave multiple disciplines into compelling real-world challenges. A project on railways isn't just about trains. It's a deep dive into local history, a practical application of physics and a lesson in economic impact all rolled into one.

Why does this matter? Because life doesn't happen in neat subject boxes. XP Schools prepare students to tackle complex, multifaceted problems by connecting the dots between disciplines.

They're not just learning facts; they're learning how to think.

Cultivating Individuality and Ownership

At XP, you'll notice something different. Students work in open spaces and dress as they choose. They're encouraged to speak up, appreciate others and be themselves. This isn't just about comfort; it's about fostering a sense of identity and belonging.

The real magic happens in "Crew" meetings. These daily gatherings with the same teacher create a home base where students are truly known. It's here that they learn to take charge of their education, confidently presenting their work and progress to parents.

A Dual Focus on Intellect and Emotion

XP Schools understand a crucial truth: sharp minds need healthy emotions. Their approach challenges students intellectually through critical thinking and problem-solving. At XP Gateshead, students aren't just learning about climate change; they're creating action plans to address it in their own schools.

Yet, amidst this intellectual rigor, emotional well-being isn't forgotten. "Mindfulness Mondays" and daily check-ins ensure that feelings aren't left at the classroom door. This balance creates resilient, well-rounded individuals ready to face life's complexities.

A Love for Learning

How do you make students want to learn? XP Schools have cracked this code. By tackling real issues, students find purpose in their studies. Field trips and guest speakers bring lessons to life. The result? A natural curiosity that fuels deeper engagement.

Imagine the pride of a student presenting their documentary or published book. These tangible outcomes of expeditions do more than teach – they inspire. They show students the power of their capabilities, fostering a sense of accomplishment that textbook learning rarely achieves.

Preparing for the Real World

The true test of education isn't in exam grades—it's in life after school. XP Schools excel here. Their graduates enter universities and workplaces with a toolkit many adults envy: self-direction, problem-solving skills and the ability to collaborate effectively.

Former students often reflect on how XP shaped them into confident, capable individuals. They credit the school's focus on character development—resilience, teamwork and critical thinking—for their success in facing real-world challenges.

XP Schools aren't just teaching differently; they're redefining what education can be. By fostering connections, embracing individuality, balancing intellect and emotion, igniting curiosity and preparing students for true independence, they offer a compelling vision for the future of learning.

∞

5 Questions for Infinite Minds

1. How can we fundamentally redesign our educational structures to cultivate genuine curiosity and intellectual autonomy, effectively countering Gatto's "hidden curriculum" of confusion and indifference?

2. In an age where AI rapidly transforms the job market and society, what bold steps can educational leaders take to shift their institutions' focus from standardized knowledge acquisition to nurturing uniquely human skills like emotional intelligence, creative problem-solving and ethical reasoning?

3. Considering the success of models like XP Schools in fostering deep, interdisciplinary learning and strong student-teacher relationships, what radical changes to your school's physical and temporal structures are you prepared to implement despite potential resistance or systemic barriers?

4. How can we create assessment and feedback systems that cultivate intrinsic motivation and a genuine love for learning, moving beyond the "provisional self-esteem" critique of traditional grading methods?

5. As information becomes increasingly accessible through AI, how can we transform educators' roles from knowledge dispensers to facilitators of curiosity, critical thinking and personal growth?

Download the interactive Infinite Education Playbook to complete this task in the playbook and access more accompanying activities for you and your accelerator group.

TL;DR

- The hidden curriculum of confusion and dependency undermines true education. School leaders must recognize and dismantle these ingrained patterns, transforming schools into centers of curiosity and self-discovery.

- As AI reshapes our world, education must pivot to cultivate uniquely human skills. Schools should focus on emotional intelligence, creativity and ethical reasoning, preparing students to lead in a world where human ingenuity is paramount.

- Innovative models like XP Schools offer a blueprint for reimagining learning environments. By fostering interdisciplinary connections and mentorship, these approaches challenge leaders to courageously redesign their institutions as dynamic ecosystems of growth.

- Moving beyond grades and standardized tests, the chapter advocates for assessment systems that nurture intrinsic motivation. This revolution-ary approach celebrates personal growth and builds genuine self-worth, inspiring a lifelong love of learning.

- The role of educators must evolve from knowledge dispensers to catalysts for critical thinking. This paradigm shift demands innovative professional development and systemic changes, empowering teachers to ignite students' passion in an AI-augmented world.

Chapter 7

A NEW LEARNING PARADIGM

A dangerous idea is taking root. It's an idea born of fear and nurtured by uncertainty. If it's left unchecked, it could harm an entire generation.

It's this: *We must prepare our children with the skills that AI doesn't have.*

In this narrative, humans are placed in the gaps where artificial intelligence cannot perform. We must resist it.

Filling Gaps

For a moment, imagine a time long ago when the sound of thunder was a mystery. Our ancestors huddled in caves, trembling at the booming voice from the sky. "It must be a god," they whispered. For a time, that explanation sufficed.

Thunder lost its divine status as humanity's understanding grew. It became a natural phenomenon explained by science. The gap where a god once stood was filled by scientific knowledge.

This is the essence of the "God of the gaps" argument.[1] It's a theological concept that places divinity in the spaces science has not yet explained. It's an idea

---

1. "God of the gaps." Wikipedia, 9 Sept. 2024, en.wikipedia.org/wiki/God_of_the_gaps.

doomed to die with each new scientific discovery.

We're not listening to the rumble of thunder but the quiet hum of artificial intelligence. This time, we aren't placing a god in the gaps but humans.

It's a Trap

When we place humans in the gaps where artificial intelligence cannot perform, we attach value to humans dependent on doing what artificial intelligence cannot. It whispers to educators, policymakers and parents: "Teach them what the machines can't do. That's where they'll find their worth."

It sounds logical. Even noble. But it's a trap.

AI struggled with image recognition in 2015. By 2020, it was generating photorealistic images from text descriptions. It wrote passable articles in 2021. By 2023, it was coding complex programs and engaging in nuanced conversations. It's filling its gaps quickly.

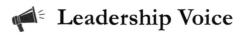 **Leadership Voice**

"We are currently in the dial-up stage of AI. Just as the internet evolved significantly from its early days, AI is expected to undergo substantial advancements and transformations. This early phase is a crucial time for learning and adaptation."

—*Heather Gold, Ed. D. and Adrian Peer,*
Gateway Community Charters School, California, USA

AI is already expanding into areas once thought to require human oversight. As populations age, countries like Japan face severe caregiver shortages, prompting the development of AI-powered robots to assist the elderly with daily tasks, such as getting out of bed and predicting restroom needs. In the brewing industry, AI is helping companies make beer by collecting and analyzing customer feedback through an algorithm, improving both product customization and operational efficiency.[2]

Google's Director of Engineering, Ray Kurzweil,[3] predicted that "Artificial intelligence will reach human levels by around 2029. Follow that out further to, say, 2045, we will have multiplied the intelligence, the human biological machine intelligence of our civilization a billion-fold."[4] A lot of Kurzweil's AI predictions have been famously accurate.

The gaps are closing and they're closing fast.

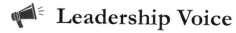

Leadership Voice

"I don't want to be asleep at the wheel when it comes to the technologies that will shape their world. Education cannot lag without severe consequences to future generations' employability and adaptability."

—*Matthew Wemyss, Assistant School Director,*
Cambridge School of Bucharest, Romania

We are playing a game we will lose if we stake our future on being better than AI at specific tasks. It's like teaching our children to be the world's best horseshoe makers on the eve of the automobile's invention.

In this brave new world, what happens to the humans who are only trained to fill the gaps in AI's abilities?

2. Tarud, Jonathan. "7 Recent AI Developments: Artificial Intelligence News." Koombea, 30 Sept. 2024, www.koombea.com/blog/7-recent-ai-developments.
3. I wrote about Ray Kurzweil's predictions on the singularity in The AI Classroom book.
4. https://www.paymanai.com/

Working for the ~~Man~~ AI Every Night and Day

But surely, you might think, AI will always need human oversight. It may take some jobs, but it can't take the initiative or lead, right?

Think again.

I talked about this during a keynote I delivered in Dubai recently. A member of the audience asked if I thought this would happen. I chuckled, but the laughter died in my throat because, the truth is, probably.

Two startups may be about to change everything we thought we knew about the future of work. Skyfire has created a payment network that lets AI agents spend real money.

"AI agents can't do anything if they can't make payments; it's just a glorified search," said Skyfire co-founder and chief product officer Craig DeWitt in an interview with TechCrunch. "Either we figure out a way where agents are actually able to do things, or they don't do anything, and therefore, they're not agents." He's not wrong. And he's not alone.

Another startup, Payman, is building what it calls "Fiverr for AIs:" a marketplace where AI posts jobs and humans complete them for pay. 10,000 people have already signed up for its beta.

The implications are staggering. We're not just talking about AI taking jobs anymore. We're talking about AI becoming the employer. In this brave new world, what happens to the humans who are only trained to fill the gaps in AI's abilities? They become obsolete or get hired by AI while waiting to become obsolete.

Having recognized the limitations of preparing students for tasks AI cannot perform, we must now explore how to cultivate the uniquely human qualities that will set them apart.

We're not just biological machines waiting to be outperformed.

Beyond the Gaps

There is another way that doesn't mean we become the humans of those shrinking gaps.

We're not just biological machines waiting to be outperformed. We're fundamentally different from AI and it's time we started acting like it.

Instead of viewing humans and AI as competitors in a zero-sum game,[5] we need to recognize the unique value humans bring. That value is not a skill or a set of knowledge; it's the fact that we are humans.

📢 Leadership Voice

"We must not lose sight of ourselves. For our own health and mental well-being, we must continue to care about the difference between the real and the virtual worlds. To understand ourselves is to understand both."

—*Tom Rogerson, Headteacher,*
Cottesmore School, England

This doesn't mean we should ignore the reality of AI advancements—far from it. We need to prepare our students for a world where AI is ubiquitous but not by placing them in the gaps where AI can't perform.

We must shift the focus from what our children *can do* to who they *can be*. Instead of asking, "What jobs will be left for humans?" we should ask, "What kind of world do we want to create, and how can we empower our children to shape it?"

This is a call to action. We need to change our education systems so that they aren't merely churning out more workers but cultivating rounded human beings ready to lead.

The future may see AI agents with the power to hire and pay humans. But

---

5. In this context, a zero-sum game refers to a mindset where humans and AI are seen as competing for the same limited resources, opportunities, or roles—where any benefit AI gains is perceived as a loss for humans, and vice versa.

it's up to us to ensure that our children enter this world not as mere gap-fillers but as confident, skilled individuals ready to work alongside AI in ways we may not yet imagine.

We need to ensure that all our children know their value.

The Value Creation Imperative

How do we translate this into practical education?

Much like today, in an AI-saturated world, the primary driver of success will be the ability to create genuine value. Our educational institutions must become centers of value creation, not remain as mere repositories of information. The skillset of value creation can be summed up in one word: entrepreneurship.

It's important to realize that entrepreneurial skills are not just for business people. They are the tools of human survival.

Our educational institutions must become centers of value creation, not remain as mere repositories of information.

DRIVERS

I have developed the **DRIVERS** entrepreneurial skills framework. A set of skills that, when unlocked in your students, will serve them for the rest of their lives. They are:

	Developing value proposition	e.g., Building a personal brand
	Relationship building	e.g., Building a community that likes the value you bring
	Influencing the world	e.g., Digital writing, communication and marketing
	Value delivery	e.g., Being able to sell your value
	Engaging with others	e.g., Building a network to learn from
	Resolving problems	e.g., Building products and services that help people
	Securing trust	e.g., Sustaining what you have built

Learning and teaching these skills to your students will transform their chances of success.

Those Who Offer Value Thrive

We have become used to thinking of school as a springboard to propel young people toward their aspirations. This isn't invalid, but if we want them to succeed in life, we should focus more on school as a place for them to discover their value.

The value we offer the world is the primary driver of success. Our education system has lost sight of this essential principle. Learning to gain knowledge or skills should serve the building of a value proposition. Many systems put the cart before the horse. It's about time we focused on helping our young people become value creators. For their sake and the sake of society.

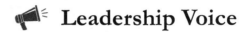 **Leadership Voice**

"We will stop looking to assess whether students have learned something and instead, look to how they have improved something or created something new."

—Heather Gold, Ed. D. and Adrian Peer,
Gateway Community Charters School, California, USA

In the face of AI's relentless advance, the question becomes: What value will our young people offer the world when AI can perform the skills and provide the knowledge we currently teach them?

The fact that most educational institutions have not been quaking in their boots indicates that they either do not see education as a process of forming value creators, misunderstand the implications of AI, or perhaps both.

We are on the brink of a paradigm shift and our education system seems blissfully ignorant and stagnant in its outdated methodologies. Education cannot lag without severe consequences to future generations' employability and adaptability. As educators, mentors and guides to our future generations, we must ask ourselves three pivotal questions:

1. What value do we offer to our students?

2. What value can they provide to the world?

3. How are we preparing them to provide that value?

The answers to these questions are crucial. They will redefine the trajectory of our education system.

The fact that most educational institutions have not been quaking in their boots indicates that they either do not see education as a process of forming value creators, misunderstand the implications of AI, or perhaps both.

We need to be more than just conduits of knowledge; we need to be catalysts for value creation. We must ensure that our students not only amass knowledge but also understand how to apply it meaningfully and effectively.

In this age of AI, the value our young people will need to offer the world is not just knowledge or skills but the uniquely human ability to connect, empathize, innovate and inspire.

Preparing our students to offer this kind of value will require a radical rethinking of our education system and people brave enough to speak up about it.

We must create an environment that encourages curiosity, embraces failure as a learning opportunity and celebrates diversity. We must rise to the occasion, acknowledge the shortcomings of our current education system and work tirelessly to shape it anew.

Our curriculum should not be limited to traditional subjects. It should encompass various disciplines, encouraging interdisciplinary learning and fostering a deep understanding of complex problems from multiple perspectives.

In the AI era, students need to be comfortable at the intersection of various fields and able to analyze and solve complex, multifaceted problems. These skills will enable them to offer value in a world where AI systems can easily handle isolated tasks but falter when faced with complex challenges.

We must inspire students to use AI ethically and responsibly to create technologies that align with our human values and societal goals. They need to understand that artificial intelligence is not just a tool to be wielded but a powerful force that needs to be guided and directed with responsibility and ethical considerations.

We must always remember that education's ultimate goal is to prepare students for the job market and life. Our education system should aim to cultivate well-rounded individuals equipped with knowledge and skills, empathy, integrity and wisdom to work for the betterment of society. I am privileged to work with leadership teams worldwide to develop strategic approaches to this innovation.

We must rise to the occasion, acknowledge the shortcomings of our current education system and work tirelessly to shape it anew.

Reframing the Human-AI Relationship

The key to thriving in this new world lies not in competing with AI but in collaborating with it. Imagine a future where AI handles the routine, the repetitive and the computationally intensive, freeing humans to focus on the creative, the empathetic and the ethically complex. This isn't science fiction. It's the world we're living in right now.

Our educational systems will need to prepare students not to work for AI but to work with AI. This means developing:

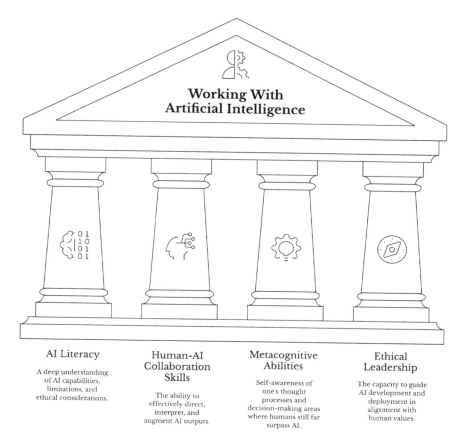

Working With Artificial Intelligence

AI Literacy	Human-AI Collaboration Skills	Metacognitive Abilities	Ethical Leadership
A deep understanding of AI capabilities, limitations, and ethical considerations.	The ability to effectively direct, interpret, and augment AI outputs.	Self-awareness of one's thought processes and decision-making areas where humans still far surpass AI.	The capacity to guide AI development and deployment in alignment with human values.

By cultivating these competencies, we empower the next generation to shape the AI-human relationship rather than being passively shaped by it.

From Knowledge Conduits to Value Catalysts

For too long, educators have seen themselves primarily as conduits of knowledge. In the AI era, this role has become increasingly obsolete. Information is now abundant and instantly accessible. What's scarce is the wisdom to apply that knowledge meaningfully and the creativity to synthesize novel solutions.

Educators will need to evolve into catalysts of value creation. This means:

- Inspiring curiosity and a love of lifelong learning

- Fostering critical thinking and discernment in an age of information overload

- Nurturing emotional intelligence and empathy

- Cultivating an entrepreneurial spirit and problem-solving mindset

- Instilling a robust ethical framework for navigating complex decisions

By focusing on these areas, we prepare students for the job market and life itself. We equip them to be architects of their destinies and societal contributors, regardless of how AI reshapes the economic landscape.

The Human Adventure Begins

As we look down the emerging path ahead, it's natural to feel a sense of vertigo. The future is uncertain and the pace of change can be dizzying. But we must resist the urge to retreat into a defensive posture, frantically trying to carve out a diminishing human niche in an AI-dominated world.

The future belongs not to those who can outperform AI but those who can most effectively harness its power while remaining unapologetically human.

Instead, let us embrace this moment as the beginning of a grand human adventure. Artificial intelligence allows us to redefine what we mean by being human. This is not a time for fear but for bold vision and decisive action.

The transformation required in our educational systems is not incremental but foundational. This is a call to action for all stakeholders:

- **Policymakers**

  Overhaul outdated educational standards and invest in innovation.

- **School Leaders**

  Foster cultures of experimentation that support infinite education.

- **Teachers**

  Embrace new pedagogies that prioritize creativity, critical thinking and value creation.

- **Parents**

  Advocate for education that prepares your children for an AI-integrated future.

- **Students**

  Take ownership of your learning journey and cultivate your uniquely human qualities.

The future belongs not to those who can outperform AI but those who can most effectively harness its power while remaining unapologetically human.

As we guide the next generation into this brave new world, let our mantra be not "Humans of the Gaps" but "Humans of the Infinite." For it is not in the shrinking spaces between machine capabilities that our future lies but in the boundless realm of human potential, amplified and augmented by the very technologies we create.

The choice is ours. Will we prepare our children to work for AI or empower them to create a future where AI works with us? As we tuck our children into bed each night, let us be filled not with worry about whether they'll work for AI but with excitement for the world they'll help create alongside it.

The era of AI is not the twilight of human relevance but the dawn of unprecedented possibility. Let us meet it with courage, creativity, and an unwavering belief in the power of the human spirit.

Ultimately, it is not the gaps that define us but the bridges we build across them.

5 Questions for Infinite Minds

1. How might we redesign our curriculum if we assumed AI could master and teach all traditional academic subjects? What uniquely human elements would remain essential?

2. In what ways are we inadvertently preparing our students to compete with AI rather than to harness its potential? How can we pivot towards a more symbiotic educational model?

3. If entrepreneurship is the new literacy, how do we transform our school culture to nurture 'value creators' rather than just 'good students'? What sacred cows might we need to sacrifice?

4. How can we evolve assessment to measure a student's ability to navigate ambiguity, synthesize novel ideas and create meaningful impact - skills that transcend AI capabilities?

5. If our goal is to cultivate "Humans of the Infinite" rather than "Humans of the Gaps," what radical changes in mindset, pedagogy and school structure are required? Are we brave enough to implement them?

Download the interactive Infinite Education Playbook to complete this task in the playbook and access more accompanying activities for you and your accelerator group.

TL;DR

- The "Humans of the Gaps" approach is a losing game: Preparing children only for areas where AI currently struggles ignores AI's rapid evolution and undermines human potential.

- Value creation is the new currency: In an AI-saturated world, entrepreneurial skills and the ability to generate unique value will be critical for success and fulfillment.

- Education needs a paradigm shift: It must move from knowledge transmission to cultivating adaptable, creative thinkers who can leverage AI for innovation.

- The AI revolution redefines human work: As AI potentially becomes the employer, humans must transition from competing with AI to directing and collaborating ethically.

- Embracing "Humans of the Infinite": Rather than fearing obsolescence, we should view the AI era as an unprecedented opportunity to explore and expand the boundaries of human potential.

Chapter 8

BARRIERS TO INNOVATION

The imperative for educational innovation has never been clearer. Change is no longer optional; it is a necessity. If our educational institutions continue to operate on a 20th-century model, we risk leaving our students unprepared for the realities of the 21st century.

New generations value collaboration, creativity and flexibility over traditional metrics of success. The world thrives on connectivity and the constant flow of information, with cultural dynamics evolving faster than ever before. Global markets demand adaptability and lifelong learning. With its rigid structures and outdated curricula, traditional education often fails to foster the qualities most in demand today. As the skills required by employers continue to evolve, education must become a catalyst for economic prosperity, not a barrier to it.

Reconnecting With the "Why"

Amidst this backdrop of rapid change, it's crucial for us to reconnect our school with its fundamental "why." This is the core reason we are committed to education in the first place. In chapter 13 we'll explore how to practically do this and craft a new purpose based on Ikigai, if it needs updating.

In earlier discussions, we explored how our educational system was largely built to serve the needs of the Industrial Revolution. This outdated structure no longer serves our students, leaving them unprepared for the demands of the modern world. Although the future is uncertain, embracing exploration and curiosity is essential.

📢 Leadership Voice

"We established a dedicated committee to meticulously review and consider our school's mission, vision, and core learning principles. This review helped us to tailor our approach to AI integration in a manner that supports and enhances our foundational educational objectives. From this, we developed a specific AI philosophy and set of guidelines that not only respect but also promote our commitment to fostering a forward-thinking and inclusive educational environment."

—*Maryam Ferdosi, Director of Technology,*
Berlin Brandenburg International School, Germany

In this new AI-driven world, the need for more humanity, empathy and creativity becomes even more important. We must consider humanity's place alongside advanced AI and find purpose in contributing uniquely human qualities. Reconnecting with our "why" reminds us that the purpose of education is not simply to fill young minds with knowledge but to equip them for a future we can barely predict.

Passion is essential for enduring the challenges of innovation. The best reason to start something is when you feel so compelled by an idea that you can't imagine not pursuing it. This deep sense of purpose fuels us through the inevitable challenges of building something new. Passionate leaders can inspire and attract talented individuals to join their mission.

A compelling "why" also helps gain external support. When a mission resonates with others, it's easier to garner support from investors, partners and stakeholders. People are likelier to rally behind a venture that aims to solve a meaningful problem. Reconnecting with the "why" can reignite motivation.

How do we reconnect with our "why"?

Reflect on the problem you're solving and its impact. Remember why you wanted to be a leader and the positive change you're bringing to the world. Engage with those who have been through your school system. Imagine if every year, schools gathered previous students who graduated ten years earlier and asked them three simple questions:

- Which parts of the curriculum have been helpful in your life?

- What parts of the school experience prepared you for success after you left formal education?

- What could the school have done to help you become more successful?

Then, they refined their practices annually to maximize their impact on student success. Doing this meaningfully for just five years could revolutionize schooling. Revisit your educational institution's original goals and aspirations to remind yourself of the initial vision. This can help you refocus and regain clarity.

When a mission resonates with others, it's easier to garner support from investors, partners and stakeholders.

Overcoming Psychological Barriers to Innovation

The Detrimental Impact of Procrastination

Despite understanding the urgency and our passionate "why," many struggle to take the first steps toward true innovation. Procrastination often stands in our way. It's not merely a time management issue; it's a self-regulation failure. According to psychological research, procrastination leads to higher stress levels, lower well-being and ultimately, subpar work.

The Zeigarnik Effect—a psychological phenomenon where unfinished tasks linger in our minds more than completed ones—suggests that by simply starting a project, even if we don't finish it immediately, we're more likely to return to it and eventually complete it. As Joel Snape notes, starting triggers this effect, making it more likely that we'll follow through.

The Innovator's Role as a Decisive Leader

Innovation requires decisive leadership. Leaders need to be comfortable making tough decisions and taking action quickly. Sam Altman, when he was President of Y Combinator, explained that innovations should be actions that "You can't not do." This deep sense of purpose compels us to act, even when faced with competing priorities or the possibility of disappointing stakeholders. The importance of "doing" over "talking" cannot be overstated. We need action over endless planning or theorizing. Leaders need to start building, experimenting and learning through direct engagement with their teachers, students and community.

Capitalizing on the "Why Now?" moment is crucial. Innovators have a compelling answer to why their ideas are relevant and timely. Understanding that great ideas often look bad initially can help us overcome initial skepticism. Disruptive ideas may appear unappealing or impractical initially, but that doesn't diminish their potential.

By acknowledging the psychological factors at play, we can employ strategies to mitigate their impact.

Psychological Barriers to Starting New Projects

Several psychological obstacles commonly prevent people from starting new projects:

- **Fear of Failure**

  Procrastination can be a form of self-sabotage, a subconscious attempt to protect our ego by attributing failure to a lack of effort rather than a lack of ability.

- **Perfectionism**
  The fear of not meeting impossibly high standards can paralyze us, leading to endless planning without action.

- **Lack of Motivation**
  We often prioritize immediate gratification over long-term rewards, making it difficult to muster the motivation to begin tasks that may not seem enjoyable in the present.

- **Emotional Dysregulation**
  Procrastination is often driven by a desire to regulate negative emotions, such as stress or anxiety. Delaying tasks offers temporary relief but exacerbates stress in the long run.

- **Lack of Clarity or Confidence**
  Uncertainty about the path ahead can lead to hesitation and a reluctance to commit.

Understanding these barriers is the first step toward overcoming them. By acknowledging the psychological factors at play, we can employ strategies to mitigate their impact.

Where to Start?

We've explored how important it is to start this journey of innovation, but where do we begin? Part two of this book will guide you through the practical four-step process, but before we get there, it is important to explore the potential of artificial intelligence in education so that we can focus our efforts.

The World Economic Forum's (WEF) report, "Shaping the Future of Learning: The Role of AI in Education 4.0," provides valuable insights into how we can harness AI's potential in education. Let's explore five high-level focal points where AI can begin to benefit education.

Addressing Systemic Challenges

AI offers solutions to longstanding educational issues, including the global teacher shortage, administrative overload, assessment inefficiencies and the digital skills gap. The WEF report highlights that:

> UNESCO projects that an additional 44 million teachers will be needed by 2030 to fulfill the ambitious targets set forth by Sustainable Development Goal 4, which aims to ensure inclusive and equitable education and promote lifelong learning opportunities for all.

AI could help bridge this gap by providing scalable, personalized learning experiences and automating routine tasks. This may allow teachers to focus on high-value activities like personalized instruction and mentoring.

📢 Leadership Voice

"The absence of a comprehensive AI policy, coupled with the bureaucracy typical of large institutions, has slowed the pace of technology integration. This hesitancy is often rooted in concerns about liability, student data privacy, and the potential risks associated with new technologies."

—Jess Baron, Ottawa Carleton District School Board, Canada

Redefining Educator Roles

AI empowers teachers to evolve their roles from lecturers to facilitators of personalized learning journeys. The WEF report emphasizes that "by freeing educators from routine tasks, AI empowers them to focus on building relationships, understanding individual student needs and fostering motivation. This synergy improves teaching effectiveness and underscores the indispensable human element in education."

This shift may enhance human interaction in education and open up opportunities for continuous professional development, ensuring teachers remain at the forefront of educational innovation.

Personalizing the Learning Experience

AI enables unprecedented levels of educational customization. The WEF report states, "AI can provide materials that match students' strengths, weaknesses and knowledge levels, and align with learning objectives, thereby enhancing the relevance of the educational content for each learner."

This personalization extends to adaptive learning paths, real-time feedback and multimodal learning experiences that cater to diverse learning abilities. The report further notes, "Customizable interfaces and adaptive technologies are particularly valuable for neurodiverse students and those with varying physical abilities."

Fostering Collaboration and Global Learning

AI could break down traditional education barriers to inclusivity and overcome language barriers. The WEF report highlights the potential of AI in creating more inclusive and accessible learning environments:

> Through AI technology, classroom lessons can be captioned for students who have auditory impairments, allowing them access to any classroom rather than relying on the availability of human sign language assistants; this helps teachers and learners engage in faster and more personalized communication.

Preparing Students for an AI-Driven Future

AI in education goes beyond using AI tools; it's also about teaching students about AI. The WEF report emphasizes the importance of AI literacy: "Integrating AI into education presents an opportunity to not only utilize AI tools in teaching but also to educate students about AI concepts and their broader societal impacts."

This includes understanding AI's capabilities and limitations, ethical AI use and developing human-AI collaboration skills. The report further stresses, "Teaching about AI not only equips students with the ability to recognize disinformation and misinformation but also fosters their development into responsible future AI developers."

Understanding and leveraging these potentials will be crucial as we move toward a more innovative, AI-integrated education system.

The Consequences of Delayed Action

The longer we delay innovation, the greater the skills gap becomes. Students are leaving schools without the ability to thrive in the new economy. The mismatch between what is taught and what is needed leaves them ill-equipped, widening the chasm between education and employment.

With outdated curricula that fail to resonate with students, engagement is plummeting. Learning must feel meaningful and connected to the world beyond the classroom to motivate our students. As some schools move to modernize their provision, those that cling to outdated models will inevitably fall behind, weakening their economic and potentially their social fabric in the process.

The longer we delay innovation, the greater the skills gap becomes.

The Ripple Effect of Immediate Innovation

Educational innovation means preparing students not just for today's jobs but for tomorrow's unknown challenges. It means cultivating creativity, resilience and a mindset geared toward lifelong learning—qualities that will empower the next generation to tackle whatever comes their way.

Innovative education creates broader societal benefits. By reducing educational inequality, we provide opportunities for all, leveling the playing field and fostering a more engaged, civically minded populace. An inclusive education system can reduce poverty rates and create more cohesive communities.

There's a direct correlation between educational innovation and economic prosperity. A workforce equipped with the skills of the future—not the past—will drive economic growth, create jobs and sustain global competitiveness. The link between modern education and economic health cannot be ignored.

Overcoming Fixedness

Despite the clear benefits of innovation, progress is often hindered. We are stuck in a finite system. I want to find out why, by exploring two kinds of fixedness:

Structural fixedness refers to rigid adherence to established structures and systems, such as standardized testing and traditional classroom layouts.

Functional fixedness is the tendency to see objects and concepts only in their traditional roles. It limits creative problem-solving by preventing us from considering alternative uses for familiar tools and ideas.

The Implications of Fixedness in Education

Both forms of fixedness contribute to the persistence of outdated educational practices that fail to meet the needs of modern learners. The traditional lecture-based classroom model, for example, may not effectively engage all students, yet structural fixedness keeps this model in place. Similarly, functional fixedness can prevent educators from leveraging technology in transformative ways.

In Tony McCaffrey and Jim Pearson's Harvard Business Review article "Find Innovation Where You Least Expect It" (2015), they demonstrate functional fixedness with the story of the Titanic: Crew members saw the iceberg solely as a threat, not as a potential life-saving platform. Imagine how many more might have lived if crew members had thought of the iceberg not just as the cause of the disaster but as a life-saving solution where they could transport passengers to wait for further support. Could we in education be overlooking innovative solutions because their function is too engrained in traditional frameworks? Instead of class time periods being a function of the fixed schedule, what if they were a function of the learning needs of the students? Instead of gaming consoles being for a student's home life, what if they could be used to learn spatial awareness and strategic problem-solving?

Strategies to Overcome Functional Fixedness

Embrace Cross-Disciplinary Learning

Functional fixedness often stems from viewing subjects in isolation. Promoting cross-disciplinary learning helps students see connections between different fields. For instance, integrating art with science can inspire creative problem-solving and a deeper understanding of both subjects.

Utilize the Generic Parts Technique

As discussed in "Find Innovation Where You Least Expect It," the generic parts technique involves breaking down objects into their most basic components and considering alternative uses. "When handed a product and asked to create a new design or variation on it, people tend to fixate on the features of the current design." In education, this technique can encourage students and teachers to deconstruct familiar tools and concepts, exploring new ways to use them in learning.

Foster a Vuja De Mindset

Inspired by comedian George Carlin's concept of "vuja de," educators should strive to see familiar situations with fresh eyes. Carlin used that perspective to develop a style of observational, questioning humor that could be considered the "why" school of comedy. This perspective shift can reveal opportunities for innovation that were previously overlooked. For example, reimagining a textbook not just as a source of information but as an interactive tool for collaboration and creativity.

Practical Applications

Consider a practical application in the classroom. Imagine a science teacher struggling to engage students in a lesson on photosynthesis. Structural fixedness might lead the teacher to rely solely on textbook explanations and lectures. However, by overcoming this fixedness, the teacher could redesign the lesson to include a hands-on experiment in a school garden, allowing students to observe and document plant growth firsthand.

Functional fixedness might initially prevent the teacher from seeing the potential of digital tools in this lesson. By applying the generic parts technique, the teacher could break down the components of photosynthesis and use AI tools, such as interactive simulations, to create an immersive learning experience. These tools can make the lesson more engaging and relatable, helping students grasp complex concepts through interactive and personalized learning.

A Strategic Outlook for Leading Change

As we conclude part one of this book by accepting the urgency of educational innovation, it's time to shift our focus toward the practical methods of leading this change. The next section will dive into strategic approaches, providing a roadmap for educational leaders ready to take bold steps. We'll explore actionable strategies for implementing change, managing resistance and building a coalition of support—all essential components for transforming our educational landscape. Together, we will unpack how to envision and lead the change that our schools and communities so urgently need.

5 Questions for Infinite Minds

1. How are we aligning our educational practices with the core purpose of preparing students for an unpredictable future?

2. What internal barriers—such as fear or procrastination—hinder innovation and how can we overcome them to lead decisively?

3. How can we leverage AI to address systemic challenges and personalize learning in our institution?

4. In what ways are we constrained by outdated structures or mindsets and how can we break free to foster true innovation?

5. What immediate actions can we take to prevent the skills gap from widening and ensure our students are equipped for the 21st century?

Download the interactive Infinite Education Playbook to complete this task in the playbook and access more accompanying activities for you and your accelerator group.

TL;DR

- Traditional education models are outdated, making urgent innovation necessary to prepare students for an AI-driven world.

- Reconnecting with the core purpose of education ignites passion to equip students for an unpredictable future.

- Overcoming psychological barriers like fear and procrastination is crucial for leaders to initiate decisive change.

- Leveraging AI can transform education by personalizing learning and addressing systemic challenges.

- Delaying innovation widens the skills gap, so overcoming fixed mind-sets is essential to revolutionize education immediately.

Chapter 9

SURVIVING THE LIMINAL SPACE

W e are all wandering into this new era, but not all who wander are lost.[1]

In a talk in May 2024, the former chief business officer for Google X, Mo Gadwat, put it in a more brutal way when he compared us to frogs in a pot being slowly boiled without realizing it.[2]

There is a lot of uncertainty among educators. Interestingly, the same level of uncertainty seems to not exist in the minds of those creating the frontier AI

1. Tolkien, J. R. R. (2009). The Fellowship of the Ring (The Lord of the Rings, Book 1). HarperCollins UK.
2. Mo Gawdat. "Mo Gawdat on AI: The Future of AI and How It Will Shape Our World." YouTube, 17 Sept. 2024, www.youtube.com/watch?v=HhcNrnNJY54.

models with which we are presented.[3] Instead, there is confidence. In his book *The Coming Wave*, Mustafa Suleyman, the co-founder of the artificial intelligence research laboratory DeepMind, explains that AI and synthetic biology will dramatically reshape our world, offering unprecedented potential for growth and innovation.[4] OpenAI CEO Sam Altman recently wrote that AI will revolutionize society, amplifying human potential and ushering in an era of unparalleled innovation and productivity.[5]

Many who are aware of the water heating up (to extend Gadwat's analogy) have concerns about where this technology might lead us. New technologies have always been met with apprehension. It is no different as we peer into a future of ubiquitous artificial intelligence. Questions about the purpose of education in this new world are becoming more prominent. Questions about the effects of AI on society and our children's development are being wrestled with daily.

Be under no illusion; humanity has been through this before—regularly. Throughout history, each technological revolution has cast us into uncertainty, but each time, we have found a way to adapt and progress as a society.

We are wanderers again, but history reassures us that we are not lost.

Throughout history, each technological revolution has cast us into uncertainty, but each time, we have found a way to adapt and progress as a society.

Historical Fears

In the 5th century BCE, the Greek philosopher Plato feared written language for its potential to diminish true wisdom and memory. He wrote:

---

3. Frontier AI models here refers to cutting edge AI at the forefront of current capabilities.
4. Suleyman, Mustafa, and Michael Bhaskar. The Coming Wave: Technology, Power, and the Twenty-first Century's Greatest Dilemma. First edition. New York, Crown, 2023.
5. "The Intelligence Age." Ia, 23 Sept. 2024, ia.samaltman.com. Accessed on Sep 23, 2024.

If men learn this, it will implant forgetfulness in their souls; they will cease to exercise memory because they rely on that which is written, calling things to remembrance no longer from within themselves, but by means of external marks.[6]

In the 2nd century BCE, the playwright Plautus lashed out against the sundial:

The gods confound the man who first found out how to distinguish hours! Confound him too who in this place set up a sundial to cut and hack my days so wretchedly into small portions! When I was a boy, my belly was my sundial.[7]

The fear of technology's impact on traditional skills and wisdom has deep historical roots. In the 1600s, coffee houses were blamed for a decline in serious learning, as noted by Oxford academic Anthony Wood: "Why doth solid and serious learning decline and few or none follow it now in the University?" he asked. "Answer: Because of Coffea Houses, where they spend all their time."[8]

6. Plato. Plato: Phaedrus. Cambridge UP, 1972.
7. Mitman, Carl W. "The Story of Timekeeping." The Scientific Monthly, vol. 22, no. 5, 1926, pp. 424–27. JSTOR, http://www.jstor.org/stable/7652. Accessed 22 Sept. 2024.
8. Higgitt, Rebekah. "We have always been modern, and it has often scared us." The Guardian, 9 May 2017, www.theguardian.com/science/the-h-word/2013/jun/24/technology-history-moderni-ty-speed-fears#:~:text=As%20Standage%20writes%2C,they%20spend%20all%20their%20time.%22. Accessed 22 Jan. 2024.

In the 1800s, there were fears that reading books and newspapers led to widespread vision deterioration. Some Victorians predicted that without appropriate care and attention, Britain's population would become blind.[9]

The telephone was also a target by Mark Twain, who wrote a Christmas card in 1890 stating:

> It is my heart-warm and world-embracing Christmas hope and aspiration that all of us-the high, the low, the rich, the poor, the admired, the despised, the loved, the hated, the civilized, the savage-may-eventually be gathered together in heaven of everlasting rest and peace and bliss-except the inventor of the telephone.[10]

Fears also arose with the advent of the VCR in 1982, likened by Jack Valenti of the Motion Picture Association of America to a threat as severe as the Boston Strangler.[11]

These historical examples underline a consistent pattern. New technological disruptions invariably bring about fears and resistance. It is now time for AI.

 Leadership Voice

"I want all the staff in our college community to feel confident and comfortable to play with AI in order to experience first hand its potential and limitations relevant to their own working context. I want to show staff it does not need to be complicated and that you can simply 'talk to AI' and learn organically how to extract what you need."

— Bryony Evett Hackfort, Director of Education,
Coleg Sir Gar Coleg Ceredigion, Wales

9. Almond, Gemma. "Why Victorians feared modern technology would make everyone blind." The Conversation, theconversation.com/why-victorians-feared-modern-technology-would-make-everyone-blind-107216#:~:text=In%20the%201800s%2C%20the%20rise,Britain's%20population%20would%20become%20blind. Accessed 23 Jan. 2024.
10. "Mark Twain's Christmas Wish." Carson Now, www.carsonnow.org/story/12/17/2012/mark-twains-christmas-wish#:~:text=%E2%80%9CIt%20is%20my%20heart%2Dwarm,except%20the%20inventor%20of%20the. Accessed 01 Dec. 2023.
11. Barro, Josh. "Thirty Years Before SOPA, MPAA Feared the VCR." Forbes, 24 Jan. 2012, www.forbes.com/sites/joshbarro/2012/01/18/thirty-years-before-sopa-mpaa-feared-the-vcr. Accessed 01 Dec. 2023.

Automation has been changing industry for decades, but new frontier AI goes beyond challenging our hands to confront our minds. White-collar workers are tasting the uncertainty blue-collar workers have long known. We wander in uncharted cognitive territories, but wandering is not the same as being lost. Just as Plato feared the written word would erode memory, we worry that AI might diminish our cognitive abilities today. Yet, history shows that such technologies can enhance human potential when embraced thoughtfully.

Will AI Take Our Jobs?

There is a lot of speculation about artificial intelligence replacing the work of humans.

 Leadership Voice

"We need to prepare our students to be critical thinkers, to use AI not as a replacement, but as a tool that will help them innovate, explore, and become effective problem-solvers in a world that desperately needs new ways of thinking and solutions."

— *Jess Baron, Ottawa Carleton District School Board, Canada*

This fear was fanned at the UK Government AI Summit when Tesla and SpaceX entrepreneur Elon Musk told UK Prime Minister Rishi Sunak that there "will come a point where no job is needed... you can have a job if you want a job... but AI will be able to do everything."[12]

Throughout history, technological progress has not replaced human work but redirected it. Understanding this pattern is crucial as we face significant

---

12. "'There will come a point when no job is needed,' says Elon Musk." BBC News, 2 Nov. 2023, www.bbc.co.uk/news/av/technology-67304427. Accessed 15 Sep. 2024.

technological disruption.

When Neolithic communities first cultivated crops, they didn't just abandon their daily hunting work; they changed their focus and ended up sparking civilization itself. Gatherers became city planners and artisans. Their focus shifted from daily survival to building lasting societies.

When the Sumerians and Egyptians invented writing, they didn't erase oral traditions. Instead, they focused this new technology on preserving and sharing knowledge. This shift enabled the creation of complex legal systems, rich literature and the foundations of scientific inquiry.

It won't replace us any more than the invention of written language replaced wisdom and memory. It will raise us to shift our focus as a species.

The steam engine didn't just threaten manual labor; it ignited the Industrial Revolution. Workers who feared for their livelihoods instead found new roles in industry. The focus shifted from individual craftsmanship to large-scale production and innovation.

Electricity transformed more than industry. It revolutionized healthcare, communication and education. Those who embraced it didn't just adapt; they thrived, finding new ways to harness its power for human advancement.

Even the much-maligned television proved its critics wrong. Far from being a fleeting distraction, it has become a powerful global awareness and education tool. It has shifted our focus from local concerns to a broader worldview.

The internet and smart devices have been the most transformative in recent times. They've democratized information access and connected humanity on an unprecedented scale. Our focus has shifted from consuming information to creating and sharing it globally.

Each of these developments initially sparked fear. Undoubtedly, there are growing pains associated with all technological advancements. We must try to mitigate these pains as much as possible. Progress is not black and white; there is nuance in the advancements outlined above. Yet each ultimately elevated human capability and redirected our focus to new, often unimaginable heights.

Will AI be different? No.

AI won't replace human value; it will redefine it. Just as calculators didn't replace mathematicians but allowed them to tackle more complex problems, AI will enable us to address challenges beyond our current reach.

It won't replace us any more than the invention of written language replaced wisdom and memory. It will raise us to shift our focus as a species. To what? Well, that's the million-dollar question.

A Liminal Space

Liminal: *occupying a position at, or on both sides of, a boundary or threshold.*[13]

We are in a liminal space. This makes it difficult to predict where our focus will land.

A world with advanced AI may enable us to pursue:

I'll just get my crystal ball...

- Personal creative endeavors
- Personal development and learning
- Relationships and community building
- Environmental stewardship
- Philosophical and ethical exploration
- Space exploration and research
- Health and wellness
- Global and community challenges

13. liminal meaning - Google Search. www.google.com/search?sca_esv=fd3ab408713f3899&s-ca_upv=1&sxsrf=ADLYWIJ1xcVNp7cq5oeCpBxHQPc7JzRDww:1727043173506&q=limin-al&si=ACC90nypsxZVz3WGK63NbnSPIfCB4CXhhYzyfueqW9LVXajp6tAUE4RXtq9Nls9-HDOnsvqeO-of1jJ7SMbiKivfaGbKiFHnIWw%3D%3D&expnd=1&sa=X&sqi=2&ved=2ahUKEwjqlvmWydeIAxXhX-UEAHQIUFgoQ2v4legQIHRAX&biw=1728&bih=992&dpr=2. Accessed 22 Sep. 2024.

- Deepening emotional intelligence and empathy
- Consciousness and mindfulness
- Biological augmentation
- New forms of governance

Instead of replacing us, technology may lift us to achieve more as a species.

Why? Because it always has.

Navigating liminal moments often brings discomfort and challenges. These moments happen when the old way falls apart, but the new way is still unclear.

The Liminal Space

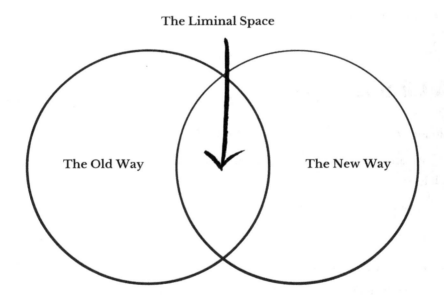

Liminal spaces are deeply rooted in human experience and have been studied by anthropologists like Arnold van Gennep since the early 1900s.[14] We still use rituals like graduations and weddings to navigate significant life transitions. These in-between states often feel unsettling due to their inherent uncertainty. Our brains evolved for survival and so crave predictability. They struggle with ambiguity. Just as our ancestors stayed alert for dangers like tigers, we experience

---

14. Arnold van Gennep is best known for his work on rites of passage, which he divided into three phases: separation, transition (liminality), and incorporation, significantly influencing anthropology and folklore studies.

stress in modern liminal situations—from finding a parking spot to navigating unemployment. However, liminality isn't inherently harmful. It's a neutral space of potential. It's a call to shift our perception from threat to opportunity. By doing so, we can learn to survive and thrive in these liminal periods, transforming our stress response into excitement for new possibilities.

In psychology, liminal spaces are notoriously challenging. They bring about anxiety, identity distress and even depression. However, they also offer an opportunity for profound transformation.

Liminal moments hurt because they can cause:

1. Existential Uncertainty

Liminal periods can provoke existential crises as individuals question their core values.

2. Social Fragmentation

Communities can divide over differing ideologies and narratives.

3. Adaptation Stress

This can lead to mental and physical exhaustion.

4. Historical Burden

It can lead to the bearing of heavy responsibility because of history-shaping decisions. Especially when leading institutional change.

5. Grief of the Past

Mourning the loss of past beliefs, traditions and ways of life can happen. This can trigger feelings of sadness, nostalgia and even anger.

A liminal space is not only a transitional phase. It's a time when our familiarity is losing meaning while what we move towards is yet to be created.

Breaking Through

In psychology, liminal spaces are notoriously challenging. They bring about anxiety, identity distress and even depression. However, they also offer an opportunity for profound transformation.

 Leadership Voice

"Students will use AI and we need to make sure we are using it too, so that we can guide and support them. You need to be agile and strong in your convictions as there is a lot of uncertainty surrounding how this topic will change and influence the sector moving forwards."

— Henry Exham, Head of Digital Learning,
Shrewsbury School, England

As educators navigating this uncertain terrain, we can draw upon valuable insights from the psychology of liminal spaces to help us survive and create the future of education.

We are not lost. We're explorers. We're finding our way to a future limited only by our imagination. As we navigate this great shift, we're not just adapting to change but authoring it.

An Opportunity to Evolve

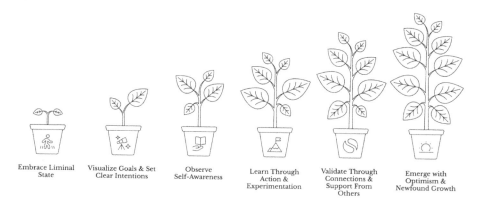

| Embrace Liminal State | Visualize Goals & Set Clear Intentions | Observe Self-Awareness | Learn Through Action & Experimentation | Validate Through Connections & Support From Others | Emerge with Optimism & Newfound Growth |

Here's my six-phase EVOLVE framework to help you thrive in this liminal space:

1. Embrace the Liminal State You're In

Embrace the unknown. By recognizing AI's challenges to traditional education, we can become aware of opportunities for growth and innovation. Just as explorers venture into uncharted territories, educators today must navigate this new landscape with courage and resilience.[15] Try going on a solo "disruption walk"—a walk through your school, a park, or even your city—thinking of how AI could disrupt each space you encounter. Use this time to reframe disruption as innovation, envisioning what could grow from these changes.

2. Visualize Your Goals and Set Clear Intentions

This involves creating a clear mental image of your desired outcome, providing direction amidst uncertainty. By visualizing your goals, you anchor your thoughts and actions, guiding you through ambiguity. This practice not only motivates you but also primes your mind to recognize opportunities that align with your vision, making change more tangible and achievable.[16] It might help to write a "future postcard" to yourself

15. Orman, Rob. "101. Being In-Between: Surfing the Liminal Space." Orman Physician Coaching, 31 Dec. 2023, roborman.com/stimulus/being-in-between-surfing-the-liminal-space.
16. Guthridge, Liz. "How to use liminal space for growth and development." Connect Consulting Group, connectconsultinggroup.com/how-to-use-liminal-space-for-growth-and-development.

dated five years from now, describing what your school will look like, how students are thriving and what you are most proud of. Stick it on the edge of your computer monitor and read it aloud to yourself each week as a grounding ritual.

3. Observe Self-Awareness

Reflect deeply on how these changes affect you, your students and your colleagues. By acknowledging discomfort in a transition, we can treat this as a step toward growth. By recognizing our fears and uncertainties, we can better manage them and find ways to thrive amidst change.[17] Try setting aside 10 minutes daily to close your office door, sit quietly and ask yourself: "What am I resisting today, and why?" Write down your answer and one step you can take to lean into that discomfort.

4. Learn Through Action and Experimentation

Actively gain insights through experimentation and reflection. Transform challenges into opportunities for knowledge acquisition. This stage encourages you to step out of your comfort zone, try new approaches and adapt based on your experiences. Learning in this context is both intentional and experiential, helping you develop new skills and perspectives that will serve you in your transformed state.[18] For an hour each week shadow a teacher or student using an AI tool. Immerse yourself in their experience, taking notes like an anthropologist observing a new culture.

5. Validate Through Connections and Support From Others

Build communities of educators who are navigating similar transitions. By sharing experiences and challenges, we can gain unique insights that can help us integrate AI. Collective wisdom and support can ease the burden of change and foster a collaborative spirit.[19] Why not start by hosting a dinner or virtual gathering with other school leaders to share stories, successes and struggles with integrating AI?

17. Amft, Theodora Blanchfield. "The Psychology Behind Liminal Space." Verywell Mind, 10 May 2023, www.verywellmind.com/the-impact-of-liminal-space-on-your-mental-health-5204371.
18. Phillips, Suzanne "The Space Between 'What Was' and 'What's Next': The Liminal Space." Psych Central, 22 Mar. 2017, psychcentral.com/blog/healing-together/2017/03/the-space-between-what-was-and-whats-next-the-liminal-space#1.
19. Orman, Rob. "101. Being In-Between: Surfing the Liminal Space." Orman Physician Coaching, 31 Dec. 2023, roborman.com/stimulus/being-in-between-surfing-the-liminal-space.

6. Emerge With Optimism and Newfound Growth

Transition from uncertainty to a new state of being. In this stage, you integrate the lessons learned and growth experienced during your journey. Emerging involves stepping into your transformed self with confidence and clarity. It's characterized by a sense of renewal and readiness to embrace new opportunities, armed with the wisdom gained from your liminal experience.[20] Why not start a bold new tradition for your school—a "Growth Day" where students, teachers and leaders reflect on their progress and share their visions for the future? Lead by example by sharing your own story of transformation, setting the tone for a culture of resilience and optimism.

This framework is not a linear journey. We move back and forth through these phases. Celebrate every success, no matter how minor. Recognize these moments as pivotal steps toward a more adaptive, personalized and effective educational model. Small victories can build momentum and confidence as we move forward.

---

20. Phillips, Suzanne "The Space Between 'What Was' and 'What's Next': The Liminal Space." Psych Central, 22 Mar. 2017, psychcentral.com/blog/healing-together/2017/03/the-space-between-what-was-and-whats-next-the-liminal-space#1.

A Catalyst for Change

Artificial intelligence can be a catalyst for change.

 Leadership Voice

"AI serves as a catalyst for creating inclusive, innovative, and equitable learning environments. It enables us to offer personalized learning at scale, automate administrative tasks, and thus allow our educators more time to focus on pedagogy. We are also mindful of the challenges such as the digital divide and privacy concerns, and are committed to providing training and support to our staff to navigate these issues effectively."

— Heather Gold, Ed.D. and Adrian Peer,
Gateway Community Charters, California, USA

In our wandering, we're not replacing ourselves but reinventing ourselves. The future belongs not to those who can outperform AI but to those who can dream with its capabilities.

We're the pathfinders. Our choices today will shape tomorrow's society. We grapple with profound questions: How do we ensure AI bridges divides rather than deepening them? How do we balance technological efficiency with essential human connection?

There's no map for where we're going, but there is a compass. We follow our unique human capacity for adaptation, creation and vision. AI isn't our destination; it's the ship we can sail to unimagined shores.

This wandering could be our greatest adventure. It demands courage and unwavering commitment to growth. We are not lost. We're explorers. We're finding our way to a future limited only by our imagination. As we navigate this great shift, we're not just adapting to change but authoring it.

Our task is monumental and the responsibility is profound. But so is the opportunity.

In our wandering, we will find our way.

5 Questions for Infinite Minds

1. Am I cultivating a culture of curiosity and adaptability that empowers my team to explore the unknown with confidence rather than fear?

2. What new purpose can our school embrace that aligns with an AI-driven future while honoring our core educational values?

3. How can I encourage educators and students to see AI as a collaborator in their learning journeys, enhancing rather than replacing human insight and creativity?

4. Am I building a resilient support network, within and beyond my school, that will help us navigate this transformation together?

5. How can I lead with vision and courage, demonstrating that the challenges of today are the stepping stones to a transformative future?

Download the interactive Infinite Education Playbook to complete this task in the playbook and access more accompanying activities for you and your accelerator group.

TL;DR

- Throughout history, every major technology has sparked fear and resistance. AI presents a unique challenge by reshaping not just tasks but how we think and create. School leaders must go beyond adapting to actively shape AI's role in education.

- AI challenges us to rethink the purpose of education. Rather than seeing it as a threat to jobs, leaders can view AI as a chance to elevate learning, focusing on creativity, critical thinking and lifelong skills that go beyond rote knowledge.

- Society is in a liminal space where the old systems are fading and the future remains uncertain. School leaders now face the challenge of managing today's uncertainties while crafting a bold vision for tomorrow's education.

- The EVOLVE framework provides a clear roadmap through change. By embracing uncertainty, setting clear goals, fostering awareness, experimenting, building support networks and emerging with purpose, leaders can guide schools confidently through this transformation.

- AI is a tool for reinvention, not replacement. The future belongs to those who can use AI to amplify human connection, creativity and problem-solving. School leaders have a profound opportunity to shape a future where education is defined by innovation and resilience.

PART 2

CREATING THE FUTURE

"The wish to preserve the past, rather than the hope of creating the future, dominates the minds of those who control the teaching of the young."

—Bertrand Russell

Chapter 10

WHY STRATEGY ALWAYS COMES FIRST

I often find that the word strategy is invoked but rarely understood. In staff meetings and professional development sessions, it's tossed around as a buzz-word. Social media and consultancy websites overflow with experts dispensing "strategy" advice. Yet, much of what's being offered isn't strategy at all. They're offering plans—usually, forward-thinking step-by-step guides on how to navigate the present. The distinction between strategy and a plan is profound: it's the difference between shaping and simply surviving the future.

The Misconception of Strategy

It's easy to conflate strategy with planning. Both involve thinking about the future, setting goals and allocating resources. However, whereas plans keep the lights on, strategy ensures a future worth illuminating. Plans are about the "how"; strategy is about the "why" and the "what if." Confusing the two is like mistaking the itinerary for the journey itself. One shows you the route and the other is the transformative experience that changes you.

Consider how many schools adopt new technologies in the classroom. They have detailed plans for integrating tablets, adopting learning management systems, or incorporating coding into the curriculum. These efforts are essential, but they aren't strategies. They are plans. They are responses to current trends aimed at improving existing processes.

At its core, strategy is about pioneering leadership and forward-thinking innovation. It's a blueprint for ensuring an organization's relevance and success well into the future. The plan comes afterward. True strategy requires a commitment to evolving with change, constantly assessing projects and initiatives to confirm they're building momentum for tomorrow's leadership. It's about staying ahead and continually positioning the organization to lead rather than follow. As my teacher Vijay Govindarajan states, "Strategy is innovation."[1]

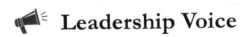 **Leadership Voice**

"We have developed a clear digital strategy aimed at positioning us as a leader in digital technology within the education sector."

—Rob Lea and Andrea Quantrill,
Heart of Yorkshire College Group, England

Strategy and Culture

You may have heard the saying, "Culture eats strategy for breakfast."[2] While catchy, it misrepresents the relationship between strategy and culture. Strategy must come before culture. Strategy is innovation. It sets the strategic direction that the culture must align with. Without a clear strategy, culture has no real direction—it's like a ship without a compass, adrift in the sea of organizational habits and norms.

---

1. I studied under Vijay Govindarajan while completing a postgraduate diploma in design thinking and innovation.
2. Often falsely attributed to the management consultant Peter Drucker, the exact source of this phrase is unclear.

Whereas plans keep the lights on, strategy ensures a future worth illuminating.

Strategy provides the vision and objectives that guide the development of culture. The foundational blueprint determines where the organization wants to go and what it aims to achieve. Culture is the collective behaviors, values and beliefs that support and accelerate the journey toward that strategic destination.

If you focus solely on culture without a clear strategy, you risk cultivating an environment that, while potentially positive and engaging, lacks purpose and alignment. The culture may promote values like collaboration or innovation, but these efforts can be scattered and ineffective without strategic direction.

The Art of Future Crafting

Strategy is the art of future crafting. It's not a static document or a downloadable PDF on your website. It's a dynamic process that evolves with new information and changing circumstances. At its core, strategy revolves around:

- **Essence**
  Your organizational North Star. What are the fundamental purpose and values guiding every decision?

- **Focus**
  A long-term, adaptable vision that senses opportunities before they fully emerge.

- **Timeframe**
  A horizon that stretches years, even decades, into the future. An infinite mindset.

While plans deal with the known, strategy navigates the unknown. In an era where technological advancements occur at an unprecedented pace, predicting technology's capabilities even five years into the future is nearly impossible. Yet, it's precisely this navigation of the unknown that we need. That's what part two of this book is about.

If you focus solely on culture without a clear strategy, you risk cultivating an environment that, while potentially positive and engaging, lacks purpose and alignment.

Building an Integrated Strategy

Developing a strategy requires making integrated choices that position your organization to lead. This involves:

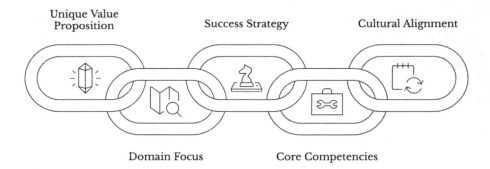

Unique Value Proposition   Success Strategy   Cultural Alignment

Domain Focus   Core Competencies

- **Unique Value Proposition:**
  What unique value will you offer in the future educational landscape transformed by AI?

- **Domain Focus:**
  Decide which domains of education you will focus on and which you will consciously avoid.

- **Success Strategy**

  Articulate how your school will ensure that your students succeed.

- **Core Competencies**

  Recognize the essential competencies you need to develop or enhance to execute your strategy.

- **Cultural Alignment**

  Ensure your organizational culture supports and accelerates your strategic goals.

The Interplay Between Strategy and Culture

While strategy comes first, culture is essential for execution. A well-defined strategy without a supportive culture is unlikely to succeed. Once the strategic direction is established, the culture must be developed or adapted to align with it. This involves:

- **Communicating the Strategy Clearly**

  Ensure that all organization members understand the strategic goals and why they matter.

- **Modeling Desired Behaviors**

  Leadership must exemplify the values and behaviors that support the strategy.

- **Reinforcing Through Systems and Processes**

  Align organizational systems, such as performance management and rewards, to encourage behaviors that support the strategy.

- **Engaging Employees**

  Involve staff at all levels in discussions about how the culture can support the strategy fosters ownership and commitment.

We will explore this more deeply and with practical examples in this book's influence and alignment chapters.

Moments That Matter

In my experience, pivotal moments in an organization's journey disproportionately impact outcomes. Getting these moments right creates a multiplier effect on other activities, embedding new norms and behaviors that support your strategic intent. These include:

- **Strategy Development**
  Involve a diverse group of stakeholders in crafting the strategy fosters inclusivity and collaboration, traits you may wish to strengthen in your culture.

- **Critical Conversations**
  Open dialogues about performance, expectations and aspirations help align individual goals with the strategic direction.

- **Crisis Management**
  How you handle crises can reinforce your cultural values and demonstrate commitment to your strategy.

- **Launch of New Initiatives**
  Introduce new programs or technologies in a way that exemplifies your strategic goals and cultural values reinforces both.

An essential aspect of strategy is the ability to detect weak signals—subtle indicators of significant future trends.

Creating a Common Language

To effectively connect strategy and culture, developing a common language is essential. This means ensuring that terms like "innovation," "collaboration," and "excellence" have understood shared meanings within your organization. It also involves bridging gaps between different teams—such as educators, administrators and IT professionals—so that everyone is aligned in understanding and executing the strategy.

Weak Signal Detection

An essential aspect of strategy is the ability to detect weak signals—subtle indicators of significant future trends. Others might overlook early signs of change because they lack widespread acceptance or supporting data. Spotting these signals requires vigilance, open-mindedness and a willingness to challenge conventional wisdom.

For instance, when AI technologies first appeared in education, many dismissed them as novelties. Those who recognized the potential began to explore how AI could personalize learning, enhance student engagement and transform educational outcomes. They positioned themselves as innovators and leaders by acting on these weak signals. We will explore this in-depth in the upcoming chapter on scope.

Opportunism and Agility

Opportunism in strategy is about being prepared to seize unexpected opportunities. It's not about exploiting situations unethically but about cultivating readiness and agility. When circumstances change, opportunistic organizations can pivot quickly, turning potential disruptions into advantages.

In the years leading up to the COVID-19 pandemic, I had worked tirelessly to integrate virtual learning platforms into my high school. When lockdowns were announced and we knew that most students would have to stay home, we were in a perfect position to pivot to fully online learning within hours. Readiness allows you to transition smoothly. Strategic opportunism enables you to thrive amid disruption.

Evolving Core Competencies

Your organization's core competencies are its unique strengths and abilities. In a rapidly changing world, these competencies must evolve. What sets you apart today may not suffice tomorrow. Continuous development and adaptation are essential.

Core competencies in a school are the unique, knowledge-based strengths that distinguish it. They represent collective expertise. Govindarajan's book *The Three Box Solution: A Strategy For Leading Innovation* (2016) uses the example of the car manufacturer Honda. Honda's expertise in small engines allows it to excel across diverse applications, from motorcycles to power tools, illustrating how a well-developed core competency fuels versatility and innovation.[3]

Students and parents may not directly see a school's core competency, but they can sense it in the quality of education and the learning environment. For example, a school's core competency might be its ability to collaborate. Notice that competency isn't a single skill but a collection of skills the team shares. A core competency of collaboration might help a school excel at external partnerships, community engagement and student voice. This would empower students to excel in both academic and social areas. By identifying and nurturing these competencies, schools can build a lasting edge, strategically guide resource allocation and lay a strong foundation for current success and future leadership.

Readiness allows you to transition smoothly. Strategic opportunism enables you to thrive amid disruption.

---

3. Govindarajan, V. (2016). The three box solution: A Strategy for Leading Innovation.

Strategy vs. Plan: Understanding the Difference

Strategy

Plan

To truly grasp the difference between strategy and plans, consider these distinctions:

Strategy	Plan
Makes integrated choices to shape the future	Outlines steps to navigate the situation as we know it now
Embraces uncertainty and explores possibilities	Seeks to control variables and execute tasks
Asks "What unique position will we hold?"	Answers "How will we execute these tasks?"
Focuses on the infinite game of long-term wins	Focuses on the finite game or completing projects on time and budget

Plans are vital. They are finite games that support the infinite game of strategy. Let's not confuse them. The second part of this book is designed to develop strategy first. To focus on the infinite game of education. We will connect this to subsequent plans; however, these plans will emerge from the strategy.

Lifting another school's plan or a plan from a website or book is tempting. This might get you some finite wins and keep your head above level in the short term, but it is not the mentality of those we want to lead.

Our choices today will determine the learning experiences of generations to come. Are we content with continuing the finite game, or are we ready to reimagine education in ways that prepare students for a world we can hardly predict?

Let's craft strategies that don't just adapt to the future but actively shape it. Let's create educational environments where innovation thrives, where culture aligns with visionary goals and where our colleagues are empowered to contribute to a legacy of excellence.

The road ahead is uncertain, but it's also filled with unprecedented opportunities. With a clear strategy and a supportive culture, we can navigate the unknown, seize emerging possibilities and evolve our core competencies to meet the demands of tomorrow.

The following chapters will explore specific models and frameworks to develop and implement effective strategies in your educational institution.

Our choices today will determine the learning experiences of generations to come. Are we content with continuing the finite game, or are we ready to reimagine education in ways that prepare students for a world we can hardly predict?

---

5 Questions for Infinite Minds

1. How am I actively shaping the future of my school beyond maintaining current operations?

2. In what ways does our school's culture align with and reinforce our long-term strategic vision?

3. How prepared is our school to seize unexpected opportunities and adapt to disruptions effectively?

4. How have we established a common language that unites different teams and ensures alignment with our strategic goals?

5. How are we continuously evolving our core competencies to maintain a strategic advantage in a rapidly changing educational landscape?

Download the interactive Infinite Education Playbook to complete this task in the playbook and access more accompanying activities for you and your accelerator group.

TL;DR

- Strategy goes beyond planning by focusing on shaping the future and driving innovation instead of maintaining current operations.

- A clear and visionary strategy must lead and align the organizational culture, ensuring that values and behaviors support long-term goals.

- Visionary leadership and agility are essential for anticipating changes, detecting weak signals and adapting to seize opportunities.

- Developing a robust strategy involves defining unique value propositions, strategic focus areas and continuously evolving core competencies.

- Aligning daily operations with the strategic vision and effectively managing critical moments ensures cohesive execution and sustained success.

Chapter 11

THREE BOXES THAT WILL CHANGE THE WAY YOU THINK ABOUT INNOVATION

"The past is no longer precedent. Thus, the innovator's job cannot be to deliver a proven result; it must be to discover what is possible, that is, to learn, by converting assumptions into knowledge as quickly and inexpensively as possible."[1]
—Vijay Govindarajan

How can we prepare students for a future we can barely comprehend? The answer lies in a deceptively simple yet profoundly powerful framework called the Three-Box Solution.[2] This three-pronged approach has been a compass for many companies worldwide and can now help us in our educational transformation efforts.

Why are we using a business strategy in education? The answer is short.

---

1. Vijay Govindarajan, Chris Trimble (2013), The Other Side of Innovation: Solving the Execution Challenge. p. 18
2. First articulated in Govindarajan, V. (2016). The Three Box Solution: A Strategy for Leading Innovation.

Businesses strategize to gain or maintain leadership within a competitive market. Education faces competition the likes we've never seen before. Ignoring this competition and maintaining the status quo further places us behind where we need to be. Let's learn from how businesses have been innovating for years.

What does strategy have to do with innovation?

Everything.

Strategy is innovation. Leadership tomorrow and into the future requires new ways of thinking and a bold reimagining of what we are doing in education.

The Three-Box Solution offers a practical framework for the strategic innovation discussed in chapter 10, providing a roadmap for overcoming the barriers highlighted in previous chapters.

The strategic outlook in this chapter will enable us to honor our present commitments while boldly charting a course toward the future. By balancing the maintenance of current educational practices, the selective forgetting of outdated methods and the creation of innovative future-oriented strategies, we can effectively navigate the complexities of an AI-augmented world.

| **Box 1** Performance Engine | **Box 2** Forgetting the Past | **Box 3** Creating the Future |

Education faces competition the likes we've never seen before. Ignoring this competition and maintaining the status quo further places us behind where we need to be.

Understanding the Three-Box Solution

As my teacher Vijay Govindarajan wrote, "The three boxes must be understood each on its own terms as well as in relation to the others."[3] This insight underscores the interconnected nature of the Three-Box Solution. While each box has a distinct focus, they are not isolated silos. We must understand how the boxes influence and support each other to achieve strategic fitness.

Strategy is innovation.

Reimagining Education in the AI Era

The challenge before us is monumental. To reimagine education for an age where artificial intelligence complements and transforms human capabilities. This reimagining is not about settling for incremental improvements or adorning traditional methods with superficial technological enhancements. Instead, it is about forging an educational paradigm that genuinely prepares students and educators for the multifaceted complexities of a future deeply intertwined with AI.

 Leadership Voice

"We have no doubt that AI will continue to be rapidly adopted in every other segment of society and see it as our responsibility not just to keep up but to shape how that happens."

—Anna Haney-Withrow, Interim Director,
Institute of Innovative and Emerging Technologies,
Florida SouthWestern State College, USA

---

3. Ibid., 214.

Govindarajan's Three-Box Solution provides a strategic framework to address this transformation, ensuring we balance maintaining current educational practices with fostering innovation and discarding outdated methods.

Box 1: The Present

Innovation in Box 1 is about enhancing the effectiveness of existing educational approaches. This represents linear innovation, where the focus is on the efficiency and efficacy of current systems without fundamentally altering the educational paradigm.

Some schools can be very effective at implementing linear innovation. In recent years, it has almost become the rai·son d'ê·tre (reason for being) of some to streamline their schooling methods and become super efficient at maximizing traditional education. Facilitated by books such as Teach Like a Champion, educational leaders worldwide have oiled their performance engines to achieve better finite goals such as exam grades.

In some ways, linear innovation in a rigid education system is the most obvious way to innovate. It's what we have the most control over. It also helps us reach the standards required of external quality control organizations. The problem comes when external factors threaten to make our Box 1 irrelevant. This does not have to be a technological threat; it could be a change in area demographics or new government policy. Whatever it is, if we treat Box 1 as the be all and end all then we are playing the finite game. When finite education is seen as the end, we leave ourselves weak. Innovating a finite system in an infinite world is shortsighted and leaves schools open to irrelevance.

Because it is the most obvious way to innovate, it is where we see the most use of artificial intelligence in schools. AI tools are a way to make teachers and leaders more efficient. As someone who works with schools on AI integration, it is also where the most appetite is from school leaders. How can we use this new technology to do what we've always done faster and more efficiently? And who can blame them?

Leadership Voice

"Reducing workload for teaching staff is going to be a massive area in the next few years. AI could customize planning and preparation to a specific teacher and their own subject area."

—Michael Armstrong, Breda Academy, Northern Ireland

So, let's start with Box 1 innovation. How can AI help us right now? Here are some ideas from the organizations I've worked with recently:

1. Enhancing Curriculum Delivery

Utilize AI tools to personalize learning experiences. For example, many teachers use 'teacher-tuned' AI chatbots to assist students in their learning journey. These can be adaptive and can analyze student performance in real time.

2. Operational Efficiency

AI tools to help with administrative tasks are a low-hanging fruit for this technology. They can reduce the workload of teachers and support staff, allowing them to focus on more pressing parts of their jobs.

3. Supporting Students

AI is being used to provide additional resources and support for students. AI tools that close the feedback loop without the teacher present are helping students progress in their learning. Differentiating materials is also becoming a fast process due to text-generating AI.

4. Leadership and Culture

Leaders are using research AI tools to help them digest the masses of information thrown their way. They are also using them to streamline their learning and the learning of their colleagues by training AI bots to coach them and help them think through decisions.

Although Box 1 innovation cannot be the end goal, it must remain a focus. Abandoning our Box 1 system ensures that our schools fail to function in the current system. This emphasizes that while organizations should allocate resources to future-oriented activities, they cannot neglect the core business. Maintaining focus and efficiency in Box 1 is essential for generating the resources to push further innovation.

Linear innovation in a rigid education system is the most obvious way to innovate.

Box 2: Forgetting the Past

Box 2 activities involve the crucial task of shedding practices, methodologies and structures that no longer serve us or our students' future needs. This involves critically evaluating traditional approaches and a willingness to abandon what is no longer effective.

Leadership Voice

"I think a cultural shift is necessary. And it involves dismantling some prized assumptions about the teacher-student relationship, the value of assessment strategies, and student agency. We are keeping these assumptions in mind during our faculty professional development and trying to create a safe and even uplifting space for them to question them, re-evaluate their own practices, and create a new vision of the possibilities in education."

—Anna Haney-Withrow, Interim Director,
Institute of Innovative and Emerging Technologies,
Florida SouthWestern State College, USA

Box 2 plays a crucial role in clearing the path for future innovation. By letting go of the past, organizations create the space and mental freedom to explore new possibilities.

What might Box 2 activities look like? Here is what I have done and witnessed in my work:

1. Challenging Assumptions

Questioning longstanding educational norms and practices to identify those that may hinder innovation and adaptability. This includes reevaluating standardized testing, rigid curricula and hierarchical administrative structures that may stifle creativity and critical thinking.

2. Dismantling Obsolete Structures

Removing or revising curricula, teaching methods and administrative processes that are no longer relevant. For example, integrating interdisciplinary studies that combine technology, humanities and sciences can better prepare students for complex real-world challenges.

3. Letting Go of Past Successes

Recognizing that past educational achievements may not guarantee future success and being willing to pivot as necessary. This mindset shift is crucial for embracing new educational paradigms that align with evolving societal and technological landscapes.

4. Leadership and Culture

Leaders in Box 2 must be courageous and resilient, making tough decisions about what to abandon. They must foster a culture that embraces change and encourages continuous improvement, ensuring the organization remains agile and forward-thinking. This requires transparent communication, stakeholder engagement and a clear vision for the future.

By letting go of the past, organizations create the space and mental freedom to explore new possibilities.

Box 2 is often the most difficult to manage due to the inherent resistance to change and the emotional attachment to traditional practices. Overcoming inertia and confronting deeply held beliefs require strong leadership and a clear vision for the future. Educators and administrators may feel nostalgic for tried-and-true methods, making transitioning to new approaches a delicate process.

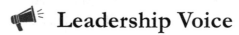 **Leadership Voice**

"Over the last decade our traditional education model, which largely focuses on preparing students for a knowledge directed linear examination, has become more and more irrelevant to what students require to be successful global citizens when they leave school."

—Henry Exham, Shrewsbury School, England

Building upon the need to let go of outdated practices in Box 2, we now explore how Box 3 encourages us to create the future through bold innovation.

Box 3: Creating the Future

This is where true innovation takes place. Non-linear innovation. This box is dedicated to generating breakthrough ideas and developing new services and models that will define the future of education in your school.

Creating the future is essential for ensuring that education remains relevant and responsive to the world's evolving demands.

The power of the Three-Box Solution lies in achieving a dynamic balance between managing the present, selectively forgetting the past and creating the future. Box 3 embodies the creation of a forward-thinking educational landscape that anticipates and shapes future trends. It's what the upcoming four steps outlined in this book will help you to do. It involves:

1. Identifying Emerging Trends

Monitoring and analyzing weak signals and emerging technologies that could present future opportunities for education. This includes staying abreast of advancements in AI and other technologies.

2. Experimenting With New Ideas

Encouraging the exploration of unconventional methods, interdisciplinary studies and AI-driven educational tools that challenge existing paradigms. Piloting programs, hackathons and innovation labs can serve as incubators for new educational concepts.

3. Developing New Competencies

Investing in building skills and capabilities necessary for educators and students to thrive in the world as it is, not how we want it to be. This includes training teachers in digital literacy and the ethical use of AI and equipping students with critical thinking, creativity and adaptability.

4. Visionary Leadership

Leaders must be visionary, possess a long-term perspective and tolerate risk and uncertainty. They must inspire and motivate teams to pursue ambitious goals, fostering a culture of creativity and critical thinking. These leaders champion experimentation and are willing to embrace failures as learning opportunities.

Creating the future is essential for ensuring that education remains relevant and responsive to the world's evolving demands. It enables institutions to anticipate and shape future trends rather than merely reacting to them. By fostering a culture of Box 3 innovation, educational institutions can develop new models of education that better prepare students for an uncertain and rapidly changing future.

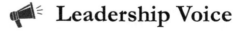 **Leadership Voice**

"AI is not 'the new calculator' and it is not 'the new world wide web'. AI is much more culturally significant than calculators and even the internet; AI challenges the very essence of what it means to be human."

—*Tom Rogerson, Headteacher, Cottesmore School, England*

The Interplay of the Boxes

While each box requires a distinct approach, their interplay is critical for achieving strategic fitness in education. The Three-Box Solution provides a clear framework to navigate uncertainty and make informed decisions in complex environments, such as modern educational systems grappling with AI integration.

Educational institutions must allocate resources proportionately across all three boxes. Overemphasizing Box 1 can lead to neglecting the school's future, while focusing solely on future initiatives without maintaining current operations can destabilize the organization. A balanced approach ensures that present operations are efficient, outdated practices are eliminated and future innovations are actively pursued.

 Leadership Voice

"As a college, it's imperative that we remain attuned to the needs of both present and future learners. Failure to anticipate and embrace the technologies and skills demanded by upcoming generations could undermine our role in preparing students for the evolving workplace and meeting employer expectations."

—Andrea Quantrill & Rob Lea,
Heart of Yorkshire College Group, England

Establishing a specialized team for each box can ensure each area receives the necessary attention and expertise. Collaboration between these teams fosters a cohesive strategy integrating present management and future creation.

Motivation Behind the Strategy

Being a Box 1 leader is sufficient in our current system. You can lead incremental improvements to grades and standards, move to another school to do it again and then retire on a decent pension. So why should you even consider Box 2 or 3?

Dustin Moskovitz, co-founder of Facebook and Asana, offers a cautionary perspective against the simplistic notion of leading change for the sole aim of "doing it better."[4] While this mindset may seem appealing, especially for those who have experienced frustration with our current systems, Moskovitz argues that it often overlooks the complexities involved in effective leadership and innovation.

Consider the difference between two schools: one aiming to "do it better" by making their online learning platforms the best of any school in their district and another driven by a mission to democratize education through accessible and personalized learning. The latter is more likely to create transformative change because it is motivated by a deeper purpose, leading to more innovative and impactful solutions.

Ultimately, Moskovitz argues that the desire to create a better solution should stem from a deep passion for solving a problem that truly matters, not just from a sense of frustration or a belief that you can outsmart existing players. Do it because it is the only thing you can do. Prioritize initiatives that genuinely enhance students' successes and prepare them for future challenges rather than simply seeking to optimize current practices.

We can create an education system that doesn't merely react to the AI era but actively shapes it.

---

4. Dustin Moskovitz on why starting a company usually isn't the best way to achieve your goals. Start-up Archive. https://www.startuparchive.org/p/dustin-moskovitz-on-why-starting-a-company-usually-isn-t-the-best-way-to-achieve-your-goals

Benefits for the School

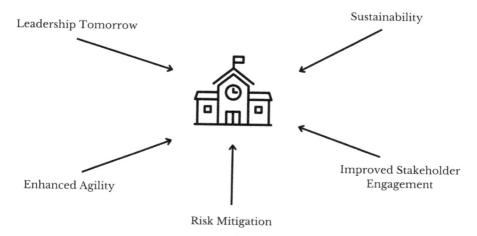

Leadership Tomorrow

Sustainability

Enhanced Agility

Improved Stakeholder Engagement

Risk Mitigation

1. Leadership Tomorrow

As an innovator and as a school, you demonstrate your leadership capabilities. You prove yourself as more than a caretaker manager to someone leading into the future. As a school, you prove that you have no interest in doing it because that's how it has always been done; you become a center of excellence.

2. Sustainability

Balancing current operations with future innovations ensures long-term viability and adaptability. Educational institutions can maintain high education standards while continuously evolving to meet future challenges.

3. Enhanced Agility

Becoming more responsive to emerging opportunities to prepare students for success. This agility allows you to pivot quickly in response to disruptive advancements and shifts in educational demands.

4. Risk Mitigation

Diversifying focus reduces dependency on a single business model, mitigating potential disruption risks to Box 1. Institutions can navigate uncertainties more effectively by maintaining robust current operations, eliminating outdated practices and fostering innovation.

5. Improved Stakeholder Engagement

A balanced approach fosters greater stakeholder engagement, including educators, students, parents and community members. By addressing present needs, eliminating barriers and creating future opportunities, institutions can build stronger relationships and a more supportive community.

Benefits for Students

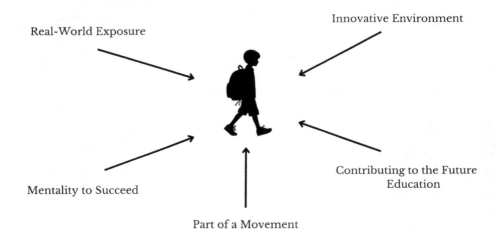

If students are included in the innovative processes and are empowered to contribute, then they will benefit in these ways:

1. Innovative Environment

Where opportunities replace boundaries, students will grow curious and be empowered to problem-solve. This approach builds the resilience and creativity essential for navigating an unpredictable world. Qualities that transform them into proactive, agile learners.

2. Part of a Movement

Attending an infinite school is more than an education. It's a call to be part of something bigger. Students learn that they're change-makers, shaping the future alongside visionary educators. This sense of purpose deepens their engagement and can instill a lifelong commitment to positive impact.

3. **Contributing to the Future of Education**

   In an innovative school, students actively participate in evolving education, providing feedback that directly informs future practices. This experience empowers them to see their voices as valuable and impactful, making them partners in a system committed to continual improvement.

4. **Real-World Exposure**

   Students bridge the gap between theory and action through direct connections with the world beyond the school building. Real-world projects and partnerships give them hands-on insights that prepare them to lead, solve problems and confidently approach the challenges of the modern workplace.

5. **Mentality to Succeed**

   An innovative school fosters a growth mindset and perseverance, teaching students that challenges are opportunities. This resilience and adaptability create a success-driven mentality that will serve them well in future pursuits.

Challenges and Considerations

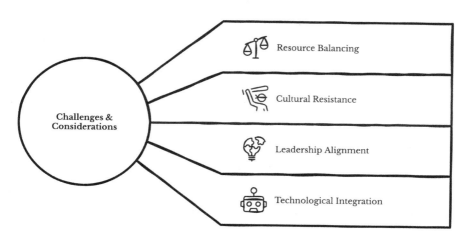

1. Resource Balancing

Allocating resources effectively across Box 1 and Box 3 is difficult, especially when most schools barely have the means to keep their Box 1 going. I am not advocating for an equal balance between linear and non-linear innovation; this will be impossible for most schools. In the next chapter, I will explain how I help schools build capacity for creating the future.

2. Cultural Resistance

Shifting organizational culture to embrace change and innovation may encounter resistance from colleagues accustomed to existing processes for many years or those who need help seeing past Box 1. Overcoming this resistance requires transparent communication, inclusive decision-making and the demonstration of the tangible benefits of transformation. We will look at strategies for this when we explore Step 3 further in this book.

3. Leadership Alignment

Ensuring all leaders are aligned and committed to the Three Box framework is crucial for its successful implementation. Misalignment can lead to fragmented efforts, conflicting priorities and inefficiencies, undermining the overall strategy.

4. Technological Integration

Integrating AI and other advanced technologies into educational systems requires careful planning and execution. Institutions must address technical challenges, ensure data security and privacy and provide adequate training to educators and students to maximize the benefits of technology.

Vijay Govindarajan's Three-Box Solution offers a strategic framework for leading innovation and shaping educational strategy in an AI-driven world. By understanding and managing the distinct characteristics of each box, educational institutions can build a path toward adaptability.

The future of education is not some distant abstraction; it is being written now through the decisions we make and the innovations we choose to embrace or dismiss. We can create an education system that doesn't merely react to the AI era but actively shapes it. We can nurture a generation of learners who approach challenges with curiosity, creativity and critical thinking and are equipped to navigate and lead in a rapidly evolving world.

Will we rise to this occasion, reimagining learning for a new age? Or will we allow our educational systems to become relics, increasingly disconnected from the world our students will inherit? The choice is ours and the stakes could not be higher. Let us approach this task with the gravity and vision it deserves, forging an educational future that unleashes the full potential of human intelligence in a world of ubiquitous artificial intelligence.

I propose this strategic framework as a focal point. A mindset that underpins all our efforts. With the Three Boxes at the heart of what we do, who will lead?

5 Questions for Infinite Minds

1. What assumptions underlie our current practices and how might we reimagine them with AI to better prepare students?

2. Which cherished traditions are holding us back and how can we create a safe space for staff to challenge them?

3. What future skills are our students missing and what bold steps could we take now to equip them for an AI-driven world?

4. How do we prioritize present needs without neglecting future growth and what criteria guide our resource allocation?

5. How might we turn resistance into resilience, inspiring our community to embrace the vision of a reimagined education?

Download the interactive Infinite Education Playbook to complete this task in the playbook and access more accompanying activities for you and your accelerator group.

TL;DR

- Education must adopt a strategic approach to innovation by balancing current needs, discarding outdated practices and creating future-focused models.

- Vijay Gobvindarajan's Three Box Strategy teaches us that our Box 1 activities focus on enhancing current systems. Using AI in our current systems will normally lead us to tools that help us reach our existing goals more efficiently.

- Box 2 activities require letting go of outdated practices that no longer prepare students for an AI world, creating space for meaningful progress despite resistance to change.

- Box 3 activities are about creating the future with bold, non-linear innovation by embracing emerging trends and experimenting with new methods to prepare students for an AI-driven world. It is a movement from finite education to infinite education.

- Success lies in balancing all three boxes to ensure agility and resilience, managing present demands, clearing obsolete practices and inventing tomorrow's education.

Chapter 12

A SMALL GROUP OF PEOPLE WHO WILL CHANGE YOUR SCHOOL

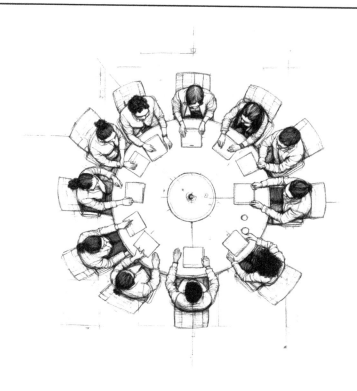

Committees or task forces won't shape the future of education. A different breed of innovators will forge it—a carefully curated team of visionaries, mavericks and experts who understand that transformation isn't just about adapting to change; it's about creating it.

The people are the foundation of how you create the future. People are key.

What is the Accelerator Group?

Imagine a startup thriving within your school's ecosystem. Not bound by "we've always done it this way" thinking, but propelled by "what if?" and "why not?" Rather than functioning as a traditional administrative committee, this group serves as an institutional catalyst for change and a conduit to transformative educational innovation.

The Accelerator Group operates with the agility of a startup company while leveraging the wisdom and resources of an established institution. It's where bold ideas find sanctuary and failure isn't feared but embraced as the stepping stone to breakthrough innovations. This group isn't an island of innovation. It's the yeast in the dough. It should cause a rise in creative thinking and transformative practices throughout your organization.

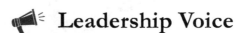

Leadership Voice

"We've assembled an Edtech and AI working party made up of staff members representing diverse subjects and key stages, including our heads of department. This group believes strongly in gathering perspectives from across the school."

—*Jess Baron, Ottawa Carleton District School Board, Canada*

They are united by the purpose of assuring your school's future leadership. They will foster new educational models and innovative ways to prepare students for success.

The group meets weekly to brainstorm ideas, pilot new programs and review progress, maintaining open communication with school leadership to align initiatives with the school's strategic goals.

Imagine a startup thriving within your school's ecosystem. Not bound by "we've always done it this way" thinking, but propelled by "what if?" and "why not?"

The group's mission is clear and comprised of four main areas:

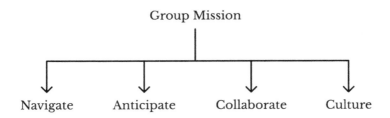

Group Mission

Navigate   Anticipate   Collaborate   Culture

- **Navigate**

  Generate ideas and transform them into tangible practices. This requires a skill set and mindset distinct from the day-to-day operations of running a school.

- **Anticipate**

  Refrain from reacting to AI and other disruptions. Anticipate them. Cultivate new competencies, experiment relentlessly and adapt swiftly.

- **Collaborate**

  While the accelerator group operates differently, it doesn't work in isolation. It taps into the school's existing expertise and resources, creating a symbiosis between innovation and tradition.

- **Culture**
  The group's impact ripples far beyond its projects. Championing new ideas and challenging norms sparks a cultural shift toward agility and future readiness across the organization.

Invite a visionary parent, a local innovative business leader, a young local politician and even a student or two.

To achieve this, your accelerator group needs the right mix of minds. These might be people in your school you have never given responsibility to. Your best leaders might be proficient Box 1 managers but lack Box 3 vision. So you might find this group is not the kind of group you have traditionally gathered together. The Accelerator Group primarily focuses on Box 3 activities—creating the future—while collaborating with those managing Box 1 and Box 2 to ensure a cohesive strategic approach.

I also encourage you to go beyond the educators at your school. Invite a visionary parent, a local innovative business leader, a young local politician and even a student or two.

Who Is the Accelerator Group?

In the group, it is essential to have the following:

- **Diversity**
  Assemble a team that's a microcosm of your community and beyond. Different backgrounds, experiences and viewpoints are your safeguard against blind spots.

- **Visionaries**
  Seek out those rare individuals who can spot paradigm shifts before they

happen. They're your early warning system for change.

- **Youth**

  Don't underestimate the power of those new to the profession. Those less entrenched in how things are done often see possibilities others miss.

- **Career Experts**

  Include experts who understand emerging careers and student aspirations. They'll keep your innovations relevant and future-focused.

- **Technologists**

  Edtech coaches, IT professionals and digital strategists are essential guides.

- **Business Minds**

  Finance, marketing and business development professionals ensure your innovations are groundbreaking and sustainable.

- **Education Leaders**

  Both internal experts and external stakeholders bring crucial context and credibility.

- **Mavericks**

  These are your wild cards. The ones whose ideas make others squirm. They're essential for true innovation.

In assembling this team, you're not just filling seats. You're igniting a transformation that will ripple through your entire institution and beyond. The accelerator group is your catalyst for change, your compass in uncharted waters and your bridge to the future of education.

The question isn't whether you can afford to create such a group. In a world of relentless change and increasing competition, the real question is: Can you afford not to?

Having established the importance of assembling a diverse Accelerator Group, it's crucial to understand the support they require to thrive within the institution.

What Your Accelerator Group Needs in Return

There are certain freedoms the accelerator group will need so that it doesn't starve of oxygen. Without these, the initial burst of enthusiasm will wither on the vine.

They will need:

- **Leadership Commitment**
  Secure Buy-In: Secure commitment from top management and key stakeholders, including board members, administrators, teachers, parents and students. Leadership must champion the Three Box framework and communicate its importance clearly and consistently.

 ## Leadership Voice

"We have strategically involved our principals and other key administrative leaders in our AI committee. This inclusion ensures that decision-makers are well-informed and directly engaged in shaping the AI strategy for our school. Leadership must be proactive in advocating for and supporting AI initiatives."

—Maryam Ferdosi, Director of Technology,
Berlin Brandenburg International School, Germany

 ## Leadership Voice

"Our initial goal was to persuade the school's leadership team that this significant shift in educational technology was crucial and needed to be embraced by the entire Northlands community."

—Jennifer Verschoor, Northlands, Argentina

- **Defined Roles and Responsibilities**

  Clearly define roles and responsibilities for managing each box. Assign dedicated teams or leaders to oversee the activities within Box 1, Box 2 and Box 3, ensuring that each area receives the necessary attention and resources.

- **Integration of the Framework**

  Incorporate the Three Box framework into the organization's strategic planning process. Develop a comprehensive plan that outlines how each box will be addressed and integrated into the institution's overall strategy.

- **Budgets and Resources**

  Allocate budgets and resources to support activities across all three boxes. Ensure sufficient funding is available to maintain current operations and invest in innovative initiatives.

- **Training and Development**

  Invest in training and development to build capabilities aligned with each box. Provide educators and staff with the necessary skills and knowledge to effectively utilize AI and other emerging technologies.

- **Regular Reviews**

  Review progress in each box regularly. Conduct periodic assessments to evaluate the effectiveness of current practices, the success of transformation initiatives and the impact of innovative projects.

- **Flexibility**

  Adjust strategies based on performance data and evolving market conditions. Stay agile and responsive to changes, ensuring the institution remains on track to achieve its strategic goals.

- **Communication**

  The promotion of open communication between teams managing different boxes. Facilitate regular meetings, workshops and collaborative sessions to share insights, challenges and successes.

- **Sharing of Success**

  The willingness to share successes and lessons learned across the organization to promote a unified approach. Celebrate achievements and use setbacks as opportunities for learning and growth.

Once you have the group assembled, it's time to begin the four steps.

The question isn't whether you can afford to create such a group. In a world of relentless change and increasing competition, the real question is: Can you afford not to?

---

5 Questions for Infinite Minds

1. What unconventional voices or perspectives have I overlooked that could unlock new possibilities for my school's future and how can I actively bring them into the fold?

2. How can I foster a school environment where the accelerator group's bold ideas and potential failures are embraced as catalysts for meaningful change?

3. How can I prepare my school to respond to and lead in the face of educational disruptions like AI and what competencies are essential to this vision?

4. What role should I play in sustaining the accelerator group's momentum and commitment and how can I align this with our school's long-term vision and goals?

5. How can I communicate the value of the accelerator group's work in a way that shifts our entire school culture toward future readiness and continuous innovation?

Download the interactive Infinite Education Playbook to complete this task in the playbook and access more accompanying activities for you and your accelerator group.

TL;DR

- The Accelerator Group is a powerhouse of change within the school, designed to challenge old norms and drive transformative innovation.

- With a startup mindset, this group brings bold ideas to life, embracing failure as an essential part of breakthrough success.

- They are dedicated to steering change, anticipating future needs, collaborating across roles and building a school culture primed for agility and growth.

- Diverse talents, including visionaries, career experts, technologists and mavericks, fuel the group united to create future-ready education.

- Success relies on unwavering leadership support, defined roles, ample resources and open communication, giving the group the strength to thrive and inspire lasting impact.

Chapter 13

STEP 1–SCOPE

"Mediocrity can talk, but it is for genius to observe."
—Benjamin Disraeli

Based on my work, I have collated and adapted the following practical activities to help you and your accelerator group in your scope process. They are mechanisms designed to enable meaningful observation, recording and analysis of your current state of play.

It's tempting to dive headfirst into new ideas. Yet, taking time to scope the current landscape is a strategic necessity. Understanding and analyzing the present state sets a foundation for meaningful change. It's about unearthing insights that reveal where our real opportunities lie. We can direct our efforts with purpose by exploring what's working, identifying what's stalled and finding hidden potential.

Understanding the present is also a defense against risk. Patterns, cultural dynamics and past lessons give us a playbook to avoid known pitfalls. Real innovation doesn't happen in isolation. It emerges from a clear grasp of our current environment. By tuning into this, we're not only preparing for change but also ensuring it can succeed in a context that's ready for it.

The scoping activities in this chapter will help you create a crucial anchor point. Documenting our current status allows us to track progress, celebrate milestones and adjust courses when needed. I have also included AI prompts to assist your accelerator group in collaborating with AI.

It's tempting to dive headfirst into new ideas. Yet, taking time to scope the current landscape is a strategic necessity.

Assessing Your Readiness

To be truly ready for AI integration is to stand at the precipice of a new educational paradigm. AI integration involves not just adopting new technology but reimagining the purpose and process of learning in a world where human and artificial intelligence coexist.

The most visionary educational leaders recognize that AI readiness is a catalyst for addressing age-old challenges. It's an opportunity to shatter the industrial-age model of schooling and craft an approach that honors individual potential, fosters creativity and prepares students for an uncertain future. These leaders see AI not as a tool to optimize existing systems but as a means to redefine what's possible in education.

This isn't just about staying relevant; it's about catalyzing a renaissance in human learning and achievement.

Here are some vital questions that you will need to ask your school to start this journey successfully:

Readiness Checklist

1. Does your leadership team possess an understanding of AI, its potential benefits and its potential pitfalls in education?

2. Have you identified key challenges within your school that AI could effectively address?

3. Is your infrastructure prepared for successful AI implementation?

4. Is a professional development plan in place to train staff on AI tools and methodologies?

5. Have you secured sufficient funding for AI initiatives, including initial investments and ongoing support?

6. Are there established policies and guidelines to ensure the ethical and responsible use of AI in your school?

7. Have you involved all relevant stakeholders, including teachers, students, parents and community members, in initial discussions about AI integration?

8. Have you set up your dedicated accelerator group to manage and oversee AI projects from inception to completion?

9. Do you have metrics and evaluation strategies in place to measure AI's impact on educational outcomes and overall school performance?

10. Have you conducted a thorough risk assessment to identify potential challenges and developed mitigation plans for AI integration?

11. Have you been informed about the latest advancements in AI tools for education and do you have a framework for assessing and adopting these technologies?

You may want to send this to your colleagues as an anonymous survey and discuss the results in the first accelerator group meeting.

Supporting AI Prompt

Collect responses in a Google Form, open them in a Google Sheet and download them as a CSV file. Then upload the file to your ChatGPT conversation and use this prompt:

"Analyze the uploaded survey spreadsheet, focusing on:

- Key Trends: Summarize recurring themes or patterns.

- Sentiment: Assess general sentiment (positive, neutral, negative).

- Category Insights: Group responses by main topics (e.g., curriculum, staff well-being) with insights for each.

- Strengths & Improvement Areas: Identify strong points and areas needing attention.

- Recommendations: Suggest actionable steps for school leadership based on feedback.

- Unique Perspectives: Highlight any valuable outliers or innovative ideas.

Present the analysis in a structured format for clear, actionable insights."

Your Hopes and Fears

There is a powerful activity that can help your accelerator group during their first session together. It's called Sailboats and it is a powerful task to do with your accelerator group during the first session. I also like to do this with the leadership team when I work with schools. I then share the results with the accelerator group so they can understand the leadership's hopes and fears.

In this exercise, a sailboat represents AI in education. The group identifies various elements using sticky notes:

- **Wind**: Positive forces propelling the project forward (strengths and opportunities).

- **Rocks**: Risks or challenges that could impede progress.

- **Anchors**: Factors that slow the project down (obstacles and weaknesses).

The process involves drawing a sailboat scene on a large whiteboard. Participants write their thoughts on sticky notes and place them in the appropriate areas: wind near the sails, rocks under the water and anchors at the bottom of the boat. The team then discusses each note, grouping similar ideas to identify common themes.

This exercise can provide powerful insights into your school's readiness to adapt and change in the age of AI. It will also give you early indicators of what will motivate colleagues and what issues you must solve along the way.

Supporting AI Prompts

1. After completing the board, take a photo with your cell phone. Then, write this prompt and attach the photo: "This is a board of sticky notes that show the positives, risks and obstacles of integrating AI into our school. Analyze the results and summarize the information."

2. "What other positives, risks and obstacles would you add that we haven't included on our board?"

Understanding these hopes and fears provides valuable insights as we revisit our school's core purpose.

Stay Rooted in Your Purpose

It's easy for schools to lose sight of their north star. Shiny new AI tools can lead us astray. Chasing trends rather than serving our students. The schools that will thrive are those that remain firmly anchored to their core purpose.

Your purpose is the beating heart of your institution. The reason you open your doors to your students each morning. It's your promise to them and their families—your commitment to your community.

Purpose gives you...

- Clarity in Decision-Making
- Sense of Direction
- Goal Setting Framework
- Resilience in Adversity

It will provide you with:

- **Clarity in Decision-Making**
  A clear purpose acts as a compass, guiding you through complex choices by aligning decisions with your core values and goals.

- **Sense of Direction**
  Purpose infuses all you do with meaning, providing motivation and a clear vision of where you're headed.

- **Goal Setting Framework**
  Your purpose helps define long-term aspirations, informing shorter-term, actionable objectives.

- **Resilience in Adversity**
  When faced with challenges, a well-defined purpose reignites passion and determination, reminding you why you started.

Being rooted in your purpose does not mean being static.

The most successful schools will be those that can simultaneously hold fast to their core values while reaching toward a rapidly evolving future. They'll ask: How can AI help us better fulfill our purpose? How can we use these new tools to serve our students and community more effectively?

The task before us is not to simply bolt AI onto existing systems. It's to reimagine education from the ground up. This reimagining must always serve our deepest values and aspirations for our students.

Need to Update Your Purpose?

It's not out of the realm of possibility that the implications of AI mean your purpose needs updating. You can use the purpose framework from chapter 6 to quickly assess the relevance of your purpose:

- **Help Students Discover Their Passion**

  Is there a focus on helping students identify and pursue their interests and passions?

- **What the School is Good At**

  Is there a focus on the school's strengths, such as academic excellence, the arts, sports, or innovative teaching methods?

- **What the World Needs**

  Is there a focus on addressing the community's and society's needs, such as educational gaps, inclusivity and future challenges?

- **What Helps the School Be Sustainable**

  Is there a focus on ensuring long-term sustainability through financial stability, community support and effective resource management?

To survive is to react, but to succeed is to redefine the game.

Five Forces You Need to Get a Grip Of

In education, as in business, survival and success are rarely the same. To survive is to react, but to succeed is to redefine the game. It's a finite versus infinite game. This distinction is critical for schools navigating the uncharted waters of AI-driven transformation. The question isn't whether competition exists but whether you can be unmatched by what you offer. To do this, we don't play the same game but set a new standard altogether.

Michael E. Porter's Five Forces Model, widely respected in business strategy, offers a powerful framework for analyzing and adapting to market dynamics. Adapting it for education can become a strategic tool for school leaders, illuminating where competitive pressures are building, where opportunities are emerging and how your school can remain relevant and essential.

The classic Five Forces are:

- Competitive Rivalry
- Supplier Power
- Buyer Power
- Threat of Substitution
- Threat of New Entry

I have reframed them for educational institutions in an AI-powered world:

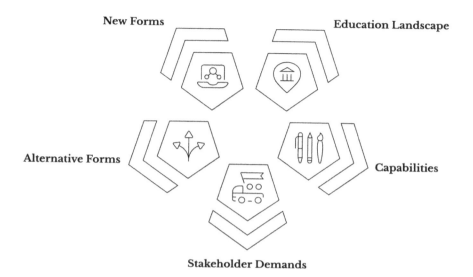

New Forms **Education Landscape**

Alternative Forms **Capabilities**

Stakeholder Demands

1. Education Landscape

Your competition now extends beyond the other schools in your town. Global online platforms, AI-enabled learning models and tech-driven educational networks are rewriting the rules of engagement. This means grappling with a larger, often invisible set of rivals whose reach and resources transform expectations.

Here are some factors to consider:

- **Global Competition**

  Options such as Minerva Virtual Academy[1] or new innovative home-schooling packages are pioneering alternative learning models that transcend borders, offering differentiated, flexible and personalized education experiences. These platforms are reshaping what students and parents expect from educational institutions.

- **AI as a Differentiator**

  Schools that embrace AI to provide personalized learning, adaptive assessments or predictive analytics can gain a distinct competitive edge.

1. https://www.minervavirtual.com/

- **Data-Driven Positioning**
  Advanced analytics can help schools better understand market shifts, monitor competitor moves and make data-driven decisions that place them ahead of the curve, rather than reacting to it.

2. Capabilities

The capabilities that schools develop—or lack—determine their future. AI has renewed relationships with technology providers for many schools, making them essential partners. Not all capabilities need to come from outside. Schools that build unique internal capabilities can stand out from the crowd.

Here are some factors to consider:

- **Internal vs. External Expertise**
  Deciding which competencies to cultivate internally (e.g., teacher training in AI tools, project-based learning or virtual learning methods) versus which to source externally (e.g., complex data systems) can help schools maintain adaptability and independence.

- **Scalability and Return on Investment**
  School leaders must balance scalability with measurable returns when choosing investments. Tools that support adaptive learning and administrative efficiency aren't just tools; they're strategic assets.

- **Supplier Influence**
  Suppliers hold greater power if the pool of AI vendors is limited or if switching costs are prohibitive. By scrutinizing vendor options for cost-effectiveness, innovation and alignment with school goals, leaders can ensure they aren't just at the mercy of technology but actively driving its implementation.

3. Stakeholder Demands

Everyone has a vested interest in advancing innovation in schools, from students and parents to employers and government entities. Adopting new technology, such as AI, introduces new demands as each group brings its expectations.

Here are some factors to consider:

- **Diverse Expectations**
  While students may prioritize interactive and engaging experiences, parents might look for improved outcomes and employers may value skills adaptability. Meeting these diverse expectations is essential to building trust and loyalty among stakeholders.

- **Feedback Loops**
  Initiatives in education must be adaptable. Continuous stakeholder feedback provides the insights needed to refine and align AI's role in meeting evolving needs.

- **Transparency and Communication**
  Clear, ongoing communication about how initiatives enhance learning can reassure stakeholders and underscore the school's commitment to staying relevant and effective.

4. Alternative Forms

With flexible, affordable and highly accessible learning platforms, alternative educational models are not just an option but will become legitimate competition. Schools need to understand what makes these models appealing to effectively respond to or integrate aspects of them into their offerings.

Here are some factors to consider:

- **Direct-to-Student Services**
  Platforms like Duolingo, self-guided AI tutors or VR-based training don't replace schools directly but offer powerful alternatives. Schools integrating these options can retain students who might otherwise turn to external solutions.

- **Flexibility and Accessibility**
  Alternative models thrive on offering flexible schedules, personalized pacing and cost-efficiency. Understanding which aspects make these

models appealing can guide how traditional schools approach AI and innovation in their services.

5. New Forms

The barriers to entry for education are changing. The traditional structures that defined and guarded the field are giving way to new competitors, ranging from micro-schools to tech-enabled education startups. Schools must remain vigilant and adaptive.

Here are some factors to consider:

- **Emerging AI Startups**
  Specialized AI startups are creating solutions to address unique educational needs, such as AI-driven social-emotional learning, real-time language translation or even AI-enabled project-based learning. As new players enter the field, schools should identify ways to set themselves apart or partner strategically with these innovators.

- **Partnerships Lowering Entry Barriers**
  With tech companies and educational providers teaming up, new options for learners are proliferating.

- **Strategic Flexibility**
  As new entrants bring AI-enhanced learning to the forefront, established schools can maintain a competitive edge by embracing flexibility in adopting new models and avoiding rigidity in their operational structures.

The power of the Five Forces isn't just about identifying risks but seizing opportunities. For school leaders, it means looking beyond immediate challenges to understand and act on the broader forces at play.

Success won't come from controlling these forces but from adapting to them with agility, insight and strategic foresight. Using this framework, you can pinpoint threats and opportunities, setting your institution on a course to survive and lead in a transformed educational landscape.

How to Understand Eachother

Empathy mapping cuts through the noise of AI hype, revealing the human at the heart of our assumptions.

I love leading this session when I work with schools. It brings students and educators together. You can even invite parents, school board members and local government officials to participate.

Imagine a classroom buzzing with energy as students map their teachers' thoughts on AI while educators do the same for their pupils across the hall. This isn't just an exercise; it's a revelatory experience that shatters assumptions and builds bridges.

Students uncover their teachers' hidden fears about job security and excitement for personalized learning. Teachers glimpse their students' anxieties about being left behind and their hunger for ethical AI guidance. When parents and administrators join in, the picture deepens further.

The magic happens when these groups then share their maps. Lightbulb moments crackle through the air. The teacher who thought her students didn't care about AI discovered their deep curiosity. The student who saw his teacher as a technophobe learns of her eagerness to innovate if she had more support.

This process improves communication. It's a strategic necessity. Schools that truly understand all stakeholders will thrive. The insights gained here will shape policies, guide AI implementation and nurture a culture of collaboration essential for navigating this new frontier.

Empathy mapping reminds us that education's core is human connection, even in an AI-driven world. By strengthening these bonds, we create resilient learning communities ready to harness AI's potential while staying true to education's deepest values.

Understanding each other is the key to ensuring that AI enhances rather than replaces the beautifully human act of learning.

In the end, this simple exercise does more than bridge divides. It lays the foundation for an educational future where technology and humanity work harmoniously, each amplifying the other's strengths. And that's a future worth building, one empathy map at a time.

Empathy mapping reminds us that education's core is human connection.

Five Red Flags to Look Out For

The path to meaningful change may involve challenges that need careful navigation.

As we embark on this journey, we must first acknowledge a fundamental truth: without strong leadership, even the best ideas will wither. Leaders, your unwavering support isn't just important; it's the foundation upon which all innovation stands.

With that in mind, let's explore five red flags that could derail your efforts.

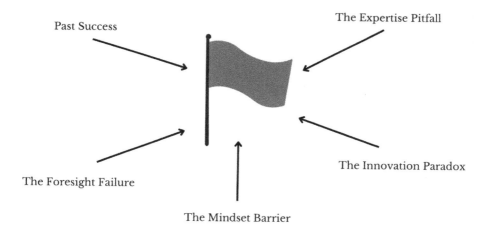

Past Success

The Expertise Pitfall

The Foresight Failure

The Innovation Paradox

The Mindset Barrier

1. Past Success

Previous achievements can blind us to future challenges. When test scores are high and accolades are plentiful, believing we've cracked the code of effective education is tempting. This complacency is dangerous.

In our data-driven world, it's easy to fixate on short-term metrics. We celebrate improved standardized test scores as the ultimate measure of learning. In doing so, we risk creating students who excel at tests but struggle with real-world problems.

The world beyond our classrooms evolves rapidly. New technologies emerge, industries transform and the skills our students need change constantly. We'll miss these crucial shifts if we're too focused on past successes.

To avoid this trap, we must redefine success. Value growth over grades. Curiosity over conformity.

---

5 Questions to Help You Discover This Red Flag

1. How might our current success metrics limit our vision for the future?

2. In what ways could our past achievements be hindering our ability to innovate?

3. How would our approach change if we prioritized adaptability over consistency?

4. What blind spots might our reputation for excellence be creating?

5. How are we balancing short-term gains with long-term educational impact?

---

2. The Expertise Pitfall

Knowledge is vital in education, but it can also hold us back. When we've spent years honing our craft, relying on that expertise is natural, but this can lead to dangerous rigidity.

This pitfall manifests in our reluctance to learn new skills, dismissal of emerging teaching methods and fear of technologies that challenge traditional roles. We risk becoming experts in outdated practices, perfectly adapted to a world that no longer exists.

To overcome this, we must become learners again. We must improve our practices and model lifelong learning for our students.

5 Questions to Help You Discover This Red Flag

1. How often do we challenge our expertise and seek perspectives from outside education?

2. In what ways might our collective experience be stifling new ideas?

3. How do we ensure our hiring practices don't simply reinforce our existing paradigms?

4. What assumptions about learning are so ingrained in our institution that we rarely question them?

5. How might we be unconsciously dismissing innovative ideas due to our established expertise?

3. The Innovation Paradox

Innovation disrupts the status quo, creating a paradox: How do we move forward without losing what already works well? This fear of loss often breeds resistance to change.

We cling to familiar curricula, resist new technologies and push back against progressive teaching methods. It's as if we're trying to sail to new horizons while keeping one anchor firmly lodged in familiar shores.

To resolve this paradox, we must reframe our thinking. Innovation isn't about discarding everything we know but building upon it. Let's use our educational heritage as a foundation for growth, not a barrier to progress.

Our established thought patterns can become our greatest obstacle to innovation.

4. The Mindset Barrier

Our established thought patterns can become our greatest obstacle to innovation. We get trapped in cycles of conventional thinking, unable to envision alternatives to the status quo.

In this mental prison, creativity withers. A "that's not how we do things here" mentality often stifles new ideas. And when innovative thoughts emerge, they may be lost in translation between different stakeholders in the educational ecosystem.

To break free, we must actively cultivate creativity and open dialogue. Let's create environments where new ideas are welcomed, failure is seen as a learning opportunity and diverse perspectives are valued. By challenging our assumptions, we open doors to new possibilities.

5 Questions to Help You Discover This Red Flag

1. How might our organizational culture be inadvertently stifling creativity?

2. In what ways could our decision-making processes be reinforcing conventional thinking?

3. How do we ensure that dissenting voices are not just heard but valued?

4. What unspoken rules or norms in our institution might be limiting innovative thinking?

5. How might our leadership style be inadvertently discouraging risk-taking and experimentation?

5. The Foresight Failure

In the rush of daily educational challenges, it's easy to miss subtle signals of impending change. This blindness to emerging trends can leave us unprepared for the future our students will face.

We risk focusing so intently on current practices that we miss technological advancements, evolving workforce needs or global events that will reshape education. This shortsightedness can leave our students ill-equipped for their futures.

To sharpen our foresight, we must become keen observers of the world beyond our institutions. Let's engage with industries, stay abreast of technological advancements and remain attuned to societal changes. By anticipating future needs, we can prepare our students not just for the world as it is but as it will be.

5 Questions to Help You Discover This Red Flag

1. How might our current success be blinding us to future challenges?

2. In what ways are we preparing for educational needs that don't yet exist?

3. How effectively are we translating global trends into local educational strategies?

4. What potential disruptors to education are we not paying enough attention to?

5. How might our planning processes reinforce short-term thinking at the expense of long-term vision?

These five pitfalls aren't just obstacles to avoid. They're challenges to overcome. Recognizing and addressing them, we transform potential stumbling blocks into stepping stones for meaningful change.

Challengers of Convention

In the pursuit of innovation, our most valuable resources often go unnoticed. They are the quiet revolutionaries within our institutions and the visionaries beyond our walls. If we knew where to look and how to listen, these pioneers would hold the keys to transforming education.

The pioneers are out there, both within your schools and beyond.

Inside Your Institution

Start by examining your organization closely. Who are the educators that students gravitate towards, even if their methods don't fit the traditional mold? These educators often fly under the radar of official recognition, yet their classrooms buzz with engagement and genuine learning.

Look for the people whose proposals initially raise eyebrows. Their seemingly radical ideas might be what your school needs to leap into the future. Don't overlook the support staff either–librarians, counselors and technicians often have unique insights into student needs and innovative solutions.

These internal pioneers are your early warning system for the inevitable educational changes. They've already begun adapting to the future, often out of necessity or a deep understanding of student needs.

Beyond the Fence

Now, cast your net wider. The world outside education is rich with insights that can revolutionize learning.

Beyond their products, tech companies offer valuable workflow, collaboration and problem-solving lessons—skills crucial for the modern classroom. Game designers are masters of engagement and motivation, with much to teach about keeping learners invested in their growth.

Don't stop at the obvious. Chefs pioneering sustainable practices, architects reimagining spaces and behavioral economists unraveling human decision-making all offer profound lessons for education. Their seemingly unrelated fields can spark ideas transforming how we approach teaching and learning.

The Power of Diverse Perspectives

By engaging with diverse perspectives, we uncover new possibilities for education. This diversity is crucial in preparing students for a future we can barely predict. Combining internal expertise and external innovation provides a robust foundation for meaningful change.

Identifying these pioneers is just the beginning. The real challenge lies in translating their insights into actionable changes in our schools.

This isn't about blindly adopting every new idea. It requires discernment to recognize truly transformative concepts, courage to experiment with them and wisdom to adapt them to our specific educational contexts.

We must be willing to question our fundamental assumptions about teaching and learning. This means embracing the possibility of failure as a step towards success. It means having the audacity to envision an education system that doesn't just react to the world but helps shape it.

The pioneers are out there, both within your schools and beyond. Their ideas are the seeds of educational transformation. Your task is to find them, listen to them and nurture those seeds into a thriving ecosystem of innovation.

The future of education is not a distant concept. It's being shaped right now by our actions and the voices we choose to heed. Will you have the courage to listen to the pioneers?

The transformation journey starts with a single step: opening our eyes and ears to the innovators already among us.

Practical Steps Forward

1. Identify your internal pioneers. Look for those who consistently think outside the box, even if their ideas initially seem unconventional.

2. Create platforms for these innovators to share their ideas. This could be through regular innovation meetings, a dedicated online forum, or an annual "ideas festival."

3. Establish connections with industries outside of education. Attend conferences, workshops, or seminars in technology, design, or business to gain fresh perspectives.

4. Implement a system for testing and evaluating new ideas. Not every innovation will succeed, but each attempt provides valuable learning opportunities.

5. Foster a culture that values experimentation and sees failure as a stepping stone to success. This mindset shift is crucial for meaningful innovation.

6. Regularly reassess your school's practices and be willing to discard approaches that no longer serve your students, no matter how long-standing they may be.

Your Unique Strengths

Leveraging your school's unique strengths is vital.

These competencies are the distinctive capabilities that set your school apart. They're not just what you do well but what you do exceptionally well—better than most. These aren't surface-level skills or resources but deep-rooted strengths woven into your institution's fabric.

Identifying Your Competencies

Gather a diverse group, including leadership, teachers, students, parents and community partners. Create an environment for open, honest dialogue and ask:

1. What do we consistently excel at compared to other schools?

2. What unique approaches have we developed over time?

3. What aspects of our school receive the most positive feedback?

4. In what areas do other schools seek our advice?

As you explore these questions, patterns will emerge. You may excel at communicating with parents, integrating technology, or fostering exceptional student leadership. Perhaps your strength lies in community engagement or nurturing students' emotional intelligence.

Competencies aren't just about academic excellence. They could be rooted in your school culture, problem-solving approach or teacher development methods.

Evaluating Potential Competencies

Once identified, test your potential competencies against these criteria:

1. It provides significant value to students and stakeholders.

2. It's difficult for other schools to replicate quickly.

3. It can be leveraged across different areas or into new educational ventures.

For example, if your school excels at developing student-led sustainability initiatives, this competency adds value by teaching real-world skills. It's hard to replicate because it's deeply embedded in your culture and can be applied across subjects and grade levels.

Leveraging Competencies for Innovation

Your competencies are not static assets but dynamic tools for innovation. Use them as springboards, not constraints.

If project-based learning is your strength, how can you push boundaries? Consider developing a program where students tackle real community issues with AI, partnering with local businesses and government agencies. This enhances your competency while opening new avenues for student growth and community engagement.

If technology integration is your forte, look for cutting-edge applications. Could you pioneer a virtual reality language immersion program or develop an AI-assisted personalized learning platform?

The key is to think expansively. Your competencies give you a unique vantage point. Use it to spot opportunities others might miss.

Practical Steps for Innovation

1. Cross-Pollinate

Apply your strengths in new contexts. Extend that beyond traditional roles if you're great at fostering student leadership. Create programs where students mentor peers in academic subjects or life skills.

2. Collaborate

Partner with other schools, universities or businesses that complement your strengths. These partnerships could lead to groundbreaking initiatives.

3. Involve the Community

Your teachers, students and parents can offer fresh perspectives on applying your competencies in new ways.

4. Iterate and Evolve

Regularly reassess your competencies. What sets you apart today might become standard practice tomorrow. Be prepared to develop new strengths.

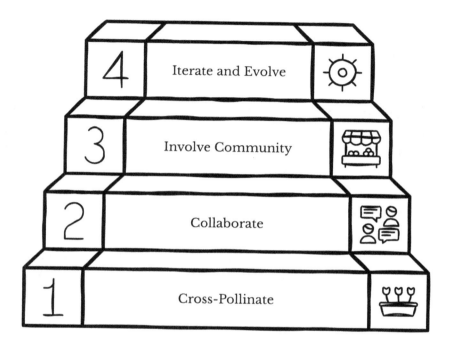

Identifying and leveraging your competencies is about knowing who you are as a school and using that self-knowledge to chart a course toward innovation and excellence. It's about being proactive rather than reactive, shaping the future of education rather than merely responding to it.

Your competencies are your school's superpowers. By recognizing them, nurturing them and creatively applying them, you can transform challenges into opportunities.

The goal isn't to become a different school but to become the best version of your school. Your unique strengths are the key to unlocking this potential. Use them wisely and you'll navigate the changing educational landscape and help shape it.

Ad Astra's Competencies

When Josh Dahn co-founded the Ad Astra school at SpaceX, one of the stand-out features was the innovative "synthesis classes." These classes, designed for the children of employees, focused on problem-solving tasks to enhance students' collaboration and communication skills. The unique combination of expertise and creativity that Josh and the Ad Astra team brought to these sessions became a defining element of the school's educational approach.

The synthesis classes at Ad Astra were more than just lessons; they were immersive experiences where students tackled real-world problems, encouraging them to think critically and work together effectively. This hands-on, problem-solving methodology was highly effective in nurturing essential life skills, setting a new standard for educational excellence. The synthesis classes became a major competency of the Ad Astra school.

Based on these classes' success, Josh Dahn founded his online school, Synthesis. He leveraged the competencies developed at Ad Astra, making problem-solving tasks the foundation of all classes. The focus remained on enhancing collaboration and communication skills among students.

Synthesis has since achieved remarkable success, attracting families from around the globe. By emphasizing practical, skills-based learning, Josh Dahn has created an educational model that prepares students for academic success and equips them with the tools needed for future challenges.

5 Questions for Infinite Minds

1. How well do we understand our school's current landscape in terms of AI integration and what hidden opportunities or challenges might we be overlooking in this initial assessment?

2. How can we align our purpose and vision with AI's potential, ensuring that new technologies serve our core mission rather than becoming distractions or superficial enhancements?

3. As we prepare for an AI-driven educational transformation, how can we create feedback loops with diverse stakeholders (students, parents, teachers and community members) to ensure their needs and concerns shape our AI strategy?

4. How might we leverage our school's unique strengths (competencies) to stay resilient and adaptable in a competitive landscape that increasingly includes global online platforms and AI-driven educational models?

5. What indicators of potential red flags, such as reliance on past successes or resistance to change, should we actively monitor as we pursue innovation and how can we address these proactively to foster a culture open to growth and adaptation?

Download the interactive Infinite Education Playbook to complete this task in the playbook and access more accompanying activities for you and your accelerator group.

TL;DR

- Scoping the current landscape creates a strong foundation for change and helps school leaders understand what is working, what needs improvement and where new opportunities may lie. This allows for strategic and informed decision-making.

- AI readiness represents a chance to rethink traditional educational models, helping leaders transform outdated approaches and design learning environments that celebrate individual potential, creativity and future preparedness.

- Involving all stakeholders in AI transformation ensures that AI initiatives align with community needs, build trust and foster a shared vision that keeps students, parents and teachers engaged in the school's evolving direction.

- Identifying and leveraging a school's unique strengths provides a competitive advantage. It allows leaders to build on what they do best and create distinctive educational experiences that set the school apart from other AI-driven models.

- Staying vigilant for pitfalls like complacency and resistance to new ideas fosters a culture of growth and adaptability, enabling sustainable, meaningful change in an educational landscape increasingly shaped by AI.

Chapter 14

STEP 2–SHAPE

"I'm here to build something for the long term. Anything else is a distraction."

—Mark Zuckerberg

To effectively shape our strategy, we must envision the future while addressing the present. This is not an exercise in prediction—put your crystal balls away. It is the act of shaping a vision and then making it a reality.

Our scoping activities in Step One have not ended. They continue to form part of our ongoing practice as we shape our strategy: Our leadership in the future.

To effectively shape our strategy, we must envision the future while addressing the present.

You've explored the weak signals of change. The opportunities both inside and outside your institution. Now, we must weave these threads into a coherent vision. To stand in the future, we must shed our current assumptions. This allows us to ask bold questions, for example:

- What if competency, not age, determined student progression?

- How might schools serve as community hubs, integrating education with health and social services?

- What if the line between schooling and real-world experience blurred completely?

These questions aren't academic exercises. They're catalysts for innovation, challenging us to rethink education at its core.

The shaping activities set out in this chapter will help you hone your vision and craft your strategy. You will plant your flag in the future and begin to reverse-engineer your way there. As you work through this chapter with your accelerator group and the wider community, you will rewrite your story and uncover the innovation gaps you will fill.

You will plant your flag in the future and begin to reverse-engineer your way there.

Stepping Into the Future

Speculative Design gives school leaders a powerful tool to envision the future of education. Reacting to immediate challenges is no longer enough in today's fast-changing world. Leaders must shape long-term strategies that prepare students for what lies ahead. Speculative Design invites you to explore "what if" scenarios and consider paths forward not as predictions but as possibilities.

What is Speculative Design?

Unlike traditional design, which often aims for practical solutions, Speculative Design looks beyond current needs. It creates concepts and products for imagined futures. It began with Critical Design at the Royal College of Art, where designers Anthony Dunne and Fiona Raby used design to question the status quo[1] Speculative Design builds on this, asking leaders to consider what might happen if we reimagined education.

Every bold step starts with a question. Speculative Design pushes leaders to examine the current education system and ask, "Why do we do things this way?" Today, education relies on standardized testing, rigid curriculum structures and teacher-centered classrooms. But is this approach preparing students for the future? Speculative Design encourages a deeper look at these assumptions. Imagine a future where curriculum changes to suit AI-powered classrooms and students take charge of their learning journeys.

Speculative Design doesn't just invite us to dream about the future; it offers practical ways to start building it.

Imagine Future Possibilities

With questions come possibilities. Leaders can use Speculative Design to picture different futures for their schools. Think of possible, probable and preferred futures. A possible future might see AI guiding every student. A probable future could mean personalized learning for all. A preferred future might involve inclusive education, where every student learns independently. By exploring these paths, leaders shape strategies that are adaptive and resilient.

Speculative Design opens up rich conversations. It's a chance to bring teachers, parents and students into discussions about the future. Imagine presenting the idea: "What if physical schools became unnecessary?" or "What would learning look like with AI teaching assistants?" These conversations can inspire insights, prompt new ideas and build a shared vision for the future.

Speculative Design isn't just about new ideas—it's about responsible ones. Ethical considerations matter, especially with technology in schools. Leaders must ask hard questions. What happens to student privacy when AI collects data? Who benefits from these technologies? Speculative Design lets you explore these issues before they arise, making it easier to make choices that align with school values.

1. Dunne, A., & Raby, F. (2013). Speculative Everything: Design, Fiction, and Social Dreaming. MIT Press.

Practical Ways to Use Speculative Design in Schools

Speculative Design doesn't just invite us to dream about the future; it offers practical ways to start building it. Four approaches stand out for school leaders: Scenario Building, Artifacts From the Future, Storytelling and Interdisciplinary Exploration. These methods allow you to move from abstract possibilities to tangible plans, engaging your team and your community in shaping the future of education.

Let's explore these methods:

1. Scenario Building

Create scenarios that explore different futures. Look at current trends in education, technology and society. Imagine how these could evolve. Build scenarios around questions like, "What if AI handles daily teaching tasks?" or "What would schools look like if virtual reality (VR) became our primary learning tool?" These scenarios don't predict the future; they prepare you for various possibilities, making your strategy flexible and resilient.

Activity: "Future School Snapshots"

Objective: Envision various futures for the school, driven by trends in artificial intelligence.

Step 1
Begin by briefing the group on a certain aspect of artificial intelligence (e.g., AI-assisted learning or virtual tutors). Discuss these trends and any assumptions they hold about the future.

Step 2
Divide the group into smaller teams and assign each team a timeline (e.g., 5 years, 10 years, 20 years into the future).

Step 3
Each team creates a "snapshot" of what a school day might look like in their assigned future. Encourage them to consider aspects like school infrastructure, classroom setup, teacher-student interactions, curriculum and school culture.

Step 4

Each team presents its snapshot in a short skit or visual storyboard. After each presentation, have a brief Q&A during which the larger group questions or challenges assumptions.

Reflection: Facilitate a discussion on the differences and commonalities across the future snapshots. What insights emerged about how we might need to prepare for these futures?

Outcome: By imagining different timelines, participants gain a clearer understanding of how trends might shape the school environment and they identify potential priorities for innovation.

2. Artifacts From the Future

Create physical " artifacts " to bring imagined futures to life. These could be models of a redesigned curriculum, prototypes of AI-assisted learning tools, or mock-ups of future classrooms. Tangible artifacts allow staff, students and parents to interact with future concepts, making abstract ideas feel real. When people can see and touch the future, they understand it better and engage with it more deeply.

Activity: "Tomorrow's Tools"

Objective: Design a tangible artifact representing a potential future learning tool, policy or classroom setup.

Step 1

Begin by brainstorming some "what if" questions related to future education (e.g., "What if all learning materials were adaptive to each student's pace?" or "What if students could choose VR or in-person classrooms?")

Step 2

Each group selects one question and creates an artifact representing this future scenario. It could be a prototype of an AI-powered desk or a mock-up of a personalized learning app.

Step 3

The artifact must include a visual component explaining how it functions and a use case showing how it benefits students, teachers or the school community.

Step 4
Display the artifacts in a "Future Education Gallery Walk." Each group presents their artifact while others ask questions or provide feedback.

Reflection: Discuss what each artifact suggests about potential needs or challenges, like student data privacy or the need for tech-based teacher training.

Outcome: Creating tangible "artifacts" helps participants move from abstract ideas to concrete applications, revealing practical implications and generating innovative, actionable insights.

3. Storytelling

Stories connect us to ideas. Craft narratives that bring your future vision to life—a "Day in the Life" of a student in 2035, for example. Show how they learn, interact with technology and solve problems. Let teachers, students and parents step into this future through storytelling. A vivid narrative can help everyone feel the potential of the future you're creating and inspire them to become part of it.

Activity: "A Day in the Future School"

Objective: Use storytelling to vividly imagine daily life in a future school setting, helping to humanize and relate to abstract ideas.

Step 1
Have the group brainstorm aspects of future schooling (e.g., how students learn, classroom activities, teacher roles). Give each small team one aspect to focus on.

Step 2
Each team crafts a narrative for "A Day in the Life" of a student, teacher, or parent in a future version of your school. Encourage them to focus on realistic and relatable details like schedules, routines and relationships.

Step 3

Teams can bring the story to life through a written story, an illustrated storyboard, or even a short video or audio recording.

Step 4

Teams present their narratives then discuss how each vision might impact current school practices and values.

Reflection: Reflect on how these stories highlight potential benefits or challenges. Ask, "What would need to change now for this future to be possible?" or "Are there aspects we'd want to avoid?"

Outcome: By immersing themselves in detailed narratives, participants gain empathy and insight into how future changes might affect different school community members, helping prioritize ideas that foster positive change.

4. Interdisciplinary Exploration

Future-focused education requires perspectives beyond education alone. Invite voices from technology, philosophy, social sciences and more. This interdisciplinary input enriches your understanding and brings fresh, often surprising, ideas into your strategy. Collaboration across fields strengthens your approach, ensuring your vision for the future is well-rounded and considers all facets of a changing world.

Activity: "Innovation Crossroads"

Objective: Combine perspectives from multiple fields to examine the impacts of educational trends on schools.

Step 1

Invite teachers or professionals from different disciplines (e.g., technology, social sciences, philosophy and environmental studies) to provide short "trend briefs" on how changes in their field could impact education.

Step 2

Assign teams, each with a mix of expertise or interest areas, to focus on one trend (e.g., climate change, AI ethics or neurotechnology).

Step 3

Each team discusses how their trend could transform learning, teaching and school operations. They then brainstorm and record three potential challenges and three opportunities they present.

Step 4

Ask teams to summarize their findings and potential solutions or experiments schools could consider in response to these interdisciplinary insights.

Reflection: Have a closing discussion on how the interplay of different disciplines enriches our understanding of future challenges. Ask, "How can we better prepare for these cross-disciplinary issues?"

Outcome: This activity encourages diverse viewpoints, revealing insights that single-discipline perspectives might miss and creating well-rounded, future-focused strategies that acknowledge broader societal impacts.

These are valuable activities to do with students, wider stakeholders and your accelerator group. You can even prepare a presentation and experience evening for the community to explore speculative design ideas.

A forward-thinking school encourages students, teachers and staff to question, imagine and innovate.

Speculative Design builds more than strategy; it builds culture. A forward-thinking school encourages students, teachers and staff to question, imagine and innovate. It cultivates a mindset that sees challenges as opportunities. By asking "what if," leaders inspire others to look ahead with curiosity and courage. Schools that think this way lead the way.

Speculative Design turns the unknown into a playground for ideas. It gives school leaders the tools to shape the future, not just adapt to it. This isn't about preparing for change. It's about creating it.

Having explored practical methods of Speculative Design, we now turn to a storytelling framework that can help craft compelling future scenarios.

The Four-Part Scenario Builder

To truly stand in the future, we need a structured approach to envisioning possibilities. Pixar's fourth rule of storytelling is a powerful tool for crafting compelling future scenarios. Also known as the "Story Spine" framework, it offers a deceptively simple yet powerful blueprint for storytelling. By guiding storytellers to ground their audience in a relatable setting, introduce characters with purpose and then disrupt the familiar with a catalyst, this structure sets a story in motion with clarity and direction.

This is the simple structure:

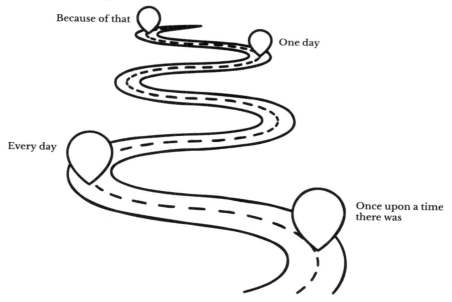

1. Once upon a time, there was
2. Every day,
3. One day
4. Because of that,

Each sentence to be finished isn't just a step in the plot but a chance to deepen tension, reveal character and build momentum. When used effectively, the Story Spine doesn't just create a story—it crafts an emotional journey that draws the audience in, making the resolution satisfying and deeply resonant.

This simple framework can help you step into the future and create vivid, actionable visions. Here's how to apply it to educational foresight:

1. Once upon a time, there was

Set the stage with current realities. What defines your institution today? This grounds your scenario in recognizable truths.

2. Every day,

Describe the status quo. What patterns and practices characterize daily life in your institution? This establishes a routine that's ripe for disruption.

3. One day

Introduce a catalyst for change. For example, this could be the technological breakthrough of generative AI or a policy overhaul. It's the spark that ignites transformation.

4. Because of that,

Explore the effects of this change. How does it reshape your practice? Try to imagine what the scenario looks like.

Here's an example:

1. Once upon a time, there was Oakridge High School, a traditional institution proud of its academic rigor and focus on college preparation.

2. Every day, teachers assign written work to measure students' learning progress and meticulously grade them to push students to higher exam grades.

3. One day, generative AI tools became sophisticated enough to produce high-quality, seemingly original essays on any topic. This made the teachers question their students' skills to succeed.

4. Because of that, Oakridge transformed how it measures students' progress. Students now orchestrate complex projects, seamlessly blending AI tools with their own critical insights. Digital communication and ethics classes help students master the art of using AI to a high standard. Teachers, liberated from grading rote assignments, now mentor students in the nuanced

skills of curating, synthesizing and critically evaluating information from both human and AI sources. The school's annual showcase celebrated AI-human synergy, featuring student-led innovations that leverage AI to address real-world challenges in their community and beyond.

By creating scenarios like this, your accelerator group can explore various potential futures, preparing them to innovate proactively rather than merely react to technological changes. These visions serve as beacons, guiding us toward educational models that don't just accommodate new technologies but harness them to unlock human potential in unprecedented ways.

Remember, the goal isn't to predict the future accurately. It's to expand our vision of what's possible and prepare for various outcomes. These scenarios become launching pads for strategic planning, helping us chart a course toward the future we want to create. They are also simple ways to communicate a vision to the rest of your organization.

Supporting AI Prompt

"Act as a screenwriter from Pixar Studios. Assess my draft story below and craft it into a concise, compelling and insightful story spine in the style of Pixar's fourth rule: (Insert draft story)."

Embracing Uncertainty

The path to this future isn't linear or predictable. Uncertainty is inevitable. Rather than fearing it, we must see uncertainty as fertile ground for innovation.

The goal isn't to predict the future accurately. It's to expand our vision of what's possible and prepare for various outcomes.

This mindset shift turns us into explorers of education's frontier. Each challenge becomes an opportunity to adapt and create. As we craft these futures, we bear a great responsibility. Our visions will shape generations of learners. We must ensure they're not just ambitious but equitable and inclusive.

We must constantly ask:

1. Who benefits from these changes?
2. Who might be left behind?
3. How can we expand opportunities for all?

These questions keep our innovations grounded in ethical considerations.

By mastering the art of standing in the future and acting decisively, we become the architects of educational change.

Other Tasks That Will Help

1. What? So What? Now What?

You can do this exercise to transition your accelerator group from Scope to Shape. It is a reflective discussion that will work well if the group is given time beforehand to think about the questions and time during the exercise to write down their ideas and share them with the group.

What?: Reflect on observations and data from the scoping activities, noting key points without interpretation. This stage grounds the group in shared experiences.

So What?: Analyze the observations to understand their significance. Discuss patterns, assumptions and why these findings matter.

Now What?: Use the insights to develop early beliefs about the way ahead. Strategic goals may also be discussed and objectives identified to make these goals a reality.

This reflection from Liberating Structures helps teams reflect on their understanding and plan effective actions based on their insights.[2]

2. Lipmanowicz, K. M. H. (n.d.). Liberating Structures - 9. What, So What, Now What? W3. https://www.liberatingstructures.com/9-what-so-what-now-what-w/

2. Nine Whys

As a follow-up to the previous exercise, another Liberating Structures activity is the Nine Whys.[3] This can help the group justify their vision.

1. Split everyone into pairs.

2. Each person will take turns asking their partner about the vision in pairs.

3. They then follow up with "Why is that important to you?" up to nine times or until the fundamental purpose is revealed.

4. These are then shared with the main group and the whys are synthesized so that they can be used to justify intent.

Crafting Your Statement of Intent

A well-crafted statement of intent serves as your school's guiding light. Unlike broad mission statements, a strategic intent crystallizes your aspirations into a focused, energizing declaration. It's your north star, illuminating the path forward and igniting the passion to pursue bold innovations.

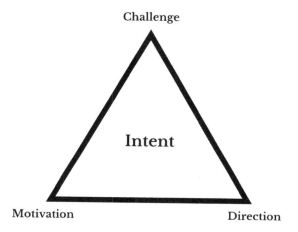

---

3. Lipmanowicz, K. M. H. (n.d.-a). Liberating Structures - 3. Nine Whys. https://www.liberatingstructures.com/3-nine-whys/

To forge an effective statement of intent, envision it in three parts[4]:

1. Direction

Paint a vivid picture of your desired destination. Don't get bogged down in the minutiae of how you'll get there. Instead, articulate a clear, compelling vision that sparks imagination and propels your team forward. Your statement should be a rallying cry, not a roadmap.

2. Motivation

Infuse your intent with emotional resonance. It should strike a chord within your organization, kindling a fire of purpose in every employee. When people feel their work contributes to something meaningful, their passion becomes unstoppable.

3. Challenge

Embrace audacity. Your statement should stretch the boundaries of what seems possible, creating a thrilling tension between your current reality and your ambitious goals. This gap fuels innovation, driving your team beyond the status quo.

Consider the assistive technology company Texthelp's declaration: "We want to help everyone to understand and be understood. By 2030, we want to have advanced the literacy and understanding of 1 billion people around the world." You can be in no doubt of their intention and the challenge, motivation and direction that lies within:

Challenge: Improving Global Literacy and Understanding: The primary challenge is to enhance the literacy and understanding of a significant portion of the global population.

Motivation: Desire to Facilitate Communication: This goal aims to help everyone understand and be understood, emphasizing the importance of clear and effective communication in bridging gaps between people.

Direction: Ambitious Target by 2030: The direction is to work towards advancing the literacy and understanding of one billion people by 2030,

4. Govindarajan, V., & Tangri, M. (2020). The Three-Box Solution Playbook: Tools and Tactics for Creating Your Company's Strategy. Harvard Business Press. 39-44.

setting a clear and measurable goal to guide efforts and track progress.

As you craft your statement, avoid the trap of being too narrow. Your intent should be a springboard for diverse innovations. Regularly reassess your statement against the shifting landscape of education and the world.

There is a tension between ambitious dreams and current realities.

A potent statement of intent doesn't just describe a future; it summons it into being.

Supporting AI Prompt

"You are an expert consultant helping our school craft a powerful statement of intent to guide their future innovation of AI and strategic direction. This statement should be concise yet impactful, incorporating three key elements:

1. Direction: A clear, compelling vision of the school's desired future state.

2. Motivation: An emotionally resonant purpose that inspires passion in staff and students.

3. Challenge: An audacious goal that stretches the boundaries of what seems possible.

Create a statement of intent that:

- Articulates a bold vision for the school's future

- Inspires and motivates the school community

- Presents a significant yet achievable challenge

- Aligns with the school's values and strengths

- Is broad enough to spark diverse, innovative ideas

- Considers the evolving landscape of education and technology

- Maximum of 50 words"

Identifying Your Innovation Gap

There is a tension between ambitious dreams and current realities. This tension is normal. It's the catalyst for meaningful change. But how do you transform lofty aspirations into tangible progress?

The key lies in understanding and strategically addressing your innovation gap. Where you want to be, minus where you are, equals your innovation gap.

Your Starting Point

Before charting a course, you must accurately assess your current position. This requires an honest, clear-eyed evaluation. The Scope stage of this journey will have given you insights such as:

- How are teachers and students are currently using AI?

- What digital tools are in place and how effectively are they utilized?

- What is the current level of AI understanding among staff and students?

- Is there any eagerness or reluctance towards AI adoption?

Document these realities objectively. This is your baseline. The foundation for your AI journey.

Your AI Vision

You have articulated your school's intent concerning AI innovation. This will be ambitious but realistic. Start to gather ideas from your accelerator group about:

- What specific AI tools will enhance teaching and learning?

- How could AI change assessment, personalization and administrative tasks?

- What new skills will your graduates possess?

Your Pixel Fourth Rule exercises will have helped you clearly envision where you want to be in three to five years. This vision will guide your innovation efforts.

Measuring the Gap

Your innovation gap is the distance between your current state and your envisioned future. Break it down into key components:

1. **Technology:** What new tools and systems are needed?

2. **Skills:** What competencies must be developed?

3. **Culture:** How must attitudes and practices evolve?

4. **Operations:** Which processes need reimagining for AI integration?[5]

Where possible, quantify these gaps. Express them in terms of specific tools, training hours, or operational changes needed.

Be prepared to adapt your vision as AI technology evolves.

---

5. This is adapted from Govindarajan, V., & Tangri, M. (2020). The Three-Box Solution Playbook: Tools and Tactics for Creating Your Company's Strategy. Harvard Business Press.

The Dual Approach to Innovation

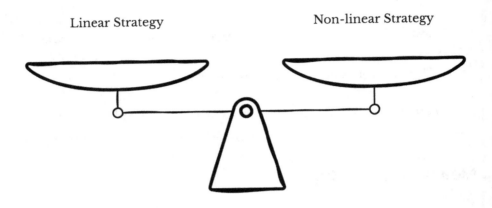

Linear Strategy   Non-linear Strategy

Bridging your gap requires a balance.

1. Linear

How will your existing educational model naturally evolve? How will planned improvements move you toward your vision? How will you optimize your performance engine?

2. Non-linear

Identify the bold shifts needed to realize your AI vision fully. What experiments or radical changes are necessary? How will you create the future? This is the space where true innovation must occur.

Building Your Case for Change

With a clear understanding of your gap, craft a compelling narrative for all stakeholders. Include:

1. Why AI innovation is crucial for your school's future

2. The specific innovations needed to bridge your gap

3. The concrete benefits awaiting on the other side

Your goal isn't to discard educational foundations but to evolve them for the future.

Practical Steps Forward

1. Prioritize: Identify the most impactful AI initiatives to tackle first.

2. Experiment: Start small, learn fast. Run pilot programs to test AI integrations.

3. Upskill: Invest in training for staff and students.

4. Collaborate: Partner with tech companies, universities or other schools on projects.

5. Measure: Establish clear metrics to track progress in closing your innovation gap.

Continuous Evaluation

Analyzing your innovation gap isn't a one-off task. As you implement initiatives, regularly reassess your position and adjust course. Be prepared to adapt your vision as AI technology evolves.

Overcoming Challenges

Expect resistance and setbacks. Common hurdles include:

- Budget constraints: Prioritize high-impact, low-cost initiatives initially.

- Technical difficulties: Start with user-friendly AI tools, gradually increasing complexity.

- Staff reluctance: Showcase early wins and provide ample support and training.

- Ethical concerns: Develop clear guidelines for responsible AI use in education.

The schools that will thrive in the AI age won't necessarily be those with the biggest budgets. They'll be the ones who clearly understand their innovation gaps and persistently work to bridge them.

Supporting AI Prompt

Use this prompt to begin collaborating with ChatGPT or other text-generating AI tools on the measurement of your innovation gap and solutions to bridge that gap:

"Help me measure the innovation gap that exists in my school. We currently (explain briefly your current approach). We want to (insert your statement of intent). What is the innovation gap and what steps will we need to take to narrow this gap?"

Touch Point Innovation

While setting ambitious goals is essential, achieving them often involves incremental steps. Working with schools on every continent, I encounter the same common issues: poor teacher retention, decreasing budgets and increasing workloads. Taking large strides toward innovation is difficult when you're worried about keeping the current system on track.

Setting Fire to Camels

In 1398, the Mongol conqueror Timur faced a powerful enemy. The sultan's army in Delhi stood ready. War elephants led their lines. These animals were huge and intimidating. Their tusks dripped with poison and armor protected their thick skin. Timur knew these beasts could break any ordinary force.

Timur saw a way through. He used the camels his army had. His men packed the camels with wood. They lit the wood on fire. The burning animals ran toward the elephants, who panicked. The elephants stampeded back, crushing their own ranks. The sultan's army fell into chaos.

Timur's soldiers acted fast. They attacked, knowing their moment had come. The sultan's army, now disordered, could not hold. Timur claimed victory.

Timur showed genius in that battle. He didn't think "outside the box"; he worked with what he had and thought "inside the box." His decision to use camels changed the battle's course. He made an unexpected choice, yet it worked perfectly.

Working with what you already have innovatively can have a huge impact. Remember Yaacov Hecht and his City Schools? He uses the expertise that already exists in the community to teach his students. Here are a few more examples:

- **Lockdown Classes:** Before COVID, many schools already had access to video conferencing platforms and used them for some meetings. Many also used platforms like Google Classroom or Microsoft Teams to post student resources. Innovative teachers in those early days of lockdown realized that those tools, already at their disposal, could be an answer.

- **School Library Spaces:** In Scotland, school libraries are being transformed into innovation hubs by repurposing the existing spaces and materials. Projects funded by the Scottish Library and Information Council support creative initiatives within school libraries, encouraging the use of current resources to drive innovation across the school.[6]

- **Open Development:** The OER4Schools program in sub-Saharan Africa focuses on teacher professional development using existing educational resources (OER). By employing freely available materials and fostering peer collaboration, schools that use them enhance teaching practices without incurring additional costs.[7]

- **Playing With Time:** High Tech High in San Diego has taken a unique approach to innovating within the constraints of a traditional school schedule by implementing flexible class periods. Rather than adhering strictly to a fixed-period schedule, the school allows teachers to extend or shorten class times as needed, depending on the specific demands of each project or the needs of the students.

- **Students Teaching Students:** Matthew Moss High School in Rochdale, UK, has implemented several initiatives that promote peer-assisted learning, where students support and teach one another. A notable example is the D6 Saturday School program. D6 offers an open invitation to all pupils to attend four hours of extra study on Saturdays, starting at 9:00 am. This program emphasizes social learning in a relaxed environment. Students determine their learning needs and form study groups, fostering a culture of self-reliance and collaboration.[8]

Left untested, even good ideas can turn into blind spots.

---

6. Tulloch, P. (2023, March 16). How libraries can drive innovation across a school. Tes Magazine. https://www.tes.com/magazine/analysis/general/how-libraries-can-drive-innovation-across-school

7. OER4Schools. Wikipedia. https://en.wikipedia.org/wiki/OER4Schools

8. For more information visit https://www.mmhs.co.uk/our-school/d6-saturday-school/

Compiling Your Touch Points

This powerful exercise allows you to start with small steps and achieve meaningful innovations with what you already have. To innovate with what you have, you need to know what you have. We begin by mapping out each touch point a member of your community has with you. Touch points are moments when key people interacting with your organization come into meaningful contact with your offering.

These touch points may already form regular parts of our thinking and planning. For example, your marketing lead will work on your branding for recruitment, or your teachers will hone their skills in classroom management. But how often do we look at them as a journey? A journey that can be atomized and adjusted, parts of the whole process that can be innovated to affect the future of the whole process.

Touch points for a student can range from initial enrollment to post-graduation reflection. Take the high school experience: By breaking it down into distinct steps, from orientation to college applications, you can identify multiple opportunities for innovation at each stage.

As educational innovators, the key lies in understanding the unique aspects of school design. Map out your school's touch points and identify pain points and opportunities. Don't be afraid to challenge conventions. Every interaction, no matter how small, contributes to the overall experience.

Every experiment matters. Every pivot has a purpose. Each win or loss is a building block. This is how lasting strategies form—not from perfection but from persistence, creativity and a shared commitment to innovation.

You will need to do this for your own school, but here is an example touchpoint list to get you started:

Students	Teachers	Parents	Local Businesses
An open evening	Job advertisement	Word of mouth	Word of mouth
Daily social interactions	Job application form	School advertisements	Offering work experience
Homework	Interview process	Open Evening	Mentoring students
Word of mouth in elementary school	Onboarding and orientation	Purchasing school supplies	Participating in a career fair
The application form	Interactions with students	School committees or events	Guest lectures or workshops
The acceptance email or letter	Student assessment and grading	Their child's homework	Providing donations
Parent-teacher conferences	Communication with parents	Parent-teacher meetings	Advertising in a school publication
After school clubs	Parent-teacher conferences	Daily drop-off and pick-up	Sponsoring a school event
The daily experience in their classrooms	Meeting with their department for the first time	Receiving and reviewing progress reports	Participating in school board meetings
The orientation day	Job offer email	Application form	
Their first day	Staff meetings	Acceptance email	
Career guidance	Working with colleagues	Communication with teachers	
Exams			
Field trips	Professional development and training	Supporting children's preparation for exams	
Report cards			
Graduation	Extracurricular involvement		
Alumni network			

Supporting AI Prompt

"Map out all the points of contact that a (name the stakeholder) will have on their journey with high school."

Applying Systematic Inventive Thinking

Once we have identified our touch points, we must determine which ones we can innovate. Systematic Inventive Thinking (SIT) offers a radical yet practical approach.[9] For schools with few resources, SIT challenges us to innovate using only the resources at hand. It's "inside the box" thinking.

At its core, SIT flips our usual thinking on its head. Instead of only considering grand visions, it challenges us to begin with what exists. This "function follows form" principle isn't just a clever idea—it's an essential approach for resource-strapped schools.

This is where your user touchpoint lists come in. We can apply the SIT methods below to our developed user experience touch points.

The Five SIT Methods

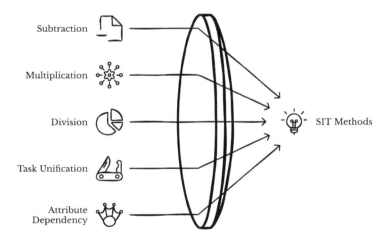

---

9. This is an innovation method first set out in Boyd, D., & Goldenberg, J. (2013). Inside the box: The creative method that works for everyone. Profile Books.

1. Subtraction: Remove to Improve

This technique involves removing what seems to be a crucial element from a system or process. By doing so, we challenge our assumptions and often discover innovative ways to deliver value with fewer components. What if certain student classes were removed in favor of AI-driven tutoring that students access from anywhere and anytime? What if elements of parent-teacher communication were removed in favor of a real-time AI-driven parent chatbot that can answer questions about student progress? By stripping away what we assume is essential, we force ourselves to rethink the fundamentals. This isn't about loss but discovering what truly matters in education.

2. Multiplication: Diversity Through Replication

This method identifies a key component within the system and then creates multiple versions. Each copy is given a unique twist, opening up new avenues for value creation. What if a teacher creating one resource with AI can now generate multiple personalized resources, each tailored to different student's needs? What a local business owner presenting at a career fair now becomes an interactive AI-driven avatar that can answer student questions throughout the year. By creating variations of what we have, we serve diverse needs without demanding more resources.

3. Division: Rearrange for Change

We break down an existing structure into its basic parts and then rearrange these elements to create new benefits or enhance existing ones. This process often reveals hidden potential within familiar systems. What if prospective students could have an orientation of the school through a VR experience before they ever set foot in the building? What if work experience is brought into every class as AI enables them to explore the context of the knowledge they are learning? We could create more effective and meaningful school touch points by dissecting and reassembling the components.

4. Task Unification: Double the Impact

In this approach, we assign additional responsibilities to one component. With the help of AI, what if student progress could be measured in real-time while they are learning in class, making end-of-year exams non-essential? What if the alumni network used AI to connect former and current students exploring career choices? By merging previously separate functions, we often uncover surprising efficiencies and synergies.

5. Attribute Dependency: Create Smart Connections

This technique involves creating new connections between previously unrelated attributes or features. As one aspect changes, it triggers a corresponding shift in another, often leading to novel and valuable interactions. What if the curriculum automatically changed for each student depending on the measurements of their progress and interests? What if, during the application process, parents were automatically added to parent social media groups or planning committees based on their interests? By linking different aspects of the school experience, we create a more responsive, effective learning environment.

By embracing SIT, we're not just redesigning schools. We're redefining the very process of educational innovation.

As we grapple with preparing students for an uncertain future, SIT offers a powerful toolkit for educational reinvention. It reminds us that the most profound changes don't always require more money or resources. They often start with a simple shift in perspective—a willingness to see our familiar educational landscape with fresh, inventive eyes.

By embracing SIT, we're not just redesigning schools. We're redefining the very process of educational innovation.

Supporting AI Prompt

"Taking into account all the points of contact that (stakeholder type) will have with my school. Can you suggest ways to innovate on any of these, using Boyd and Goldenberg's work on Systemic Inventive Thinking."

The TRAP Roadmap

It's time to create your strategic plan.

Clarity is paramount. The TRAP Framework—Targets, Results, Approach and Procedures—offers a straightforward yet powerful tool for navigating this complex terrain.

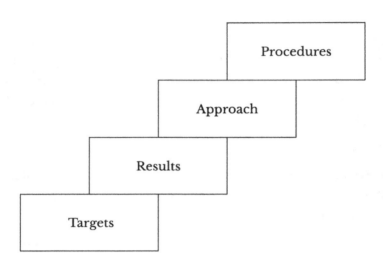

Targets: Defining Your Vision

Targets are the compass points guiding your journey. They answer the fundamental question: What are we trying to achieve with AI in education?

Results: Measuring Success

Results transform abstract aspirations into concrete, measurable outcomes. They answer the question: How will we know we've succeeded?

Approach: Charting the Course

Your approach outlines the general strategy for achieving your targets and results. It answers the question, "What's our overall plan to get there?"

Procedures: Taking Action

Procedures are the specific, actionable steps that bring your approach to life. They answer: What exactly will we do?

Let's look at an example:

Target

Develop comprehensive AI literacy among all students, enabling them to understand, critically evaluate and effectively utilize generative AI.

Results

- AI-literate students across all grade levels at an appropriate level

- Students demonstrate proficiency in leveraging AI tools for academic pursuits, creative projects and problem-solving

- Students engage with AI-related extracurricular activities, fostering a culture of innovation

- Students graduate with a nuanced understanding of AI ethics, capable of navigating complex AI-related societal issues

- Students have advanced critical thinking skills, particularly in evaluating AI-generated information and outputs

- Students are well-prepared for AI-infused higher education and job markets

- The school district is a pioneer in AI education, attracting partnerships and resources

Approach

Integrate AI literacy across the curriculum, combining dedicated courses with practical application in various subjects.

Procedures

- Develop age-appropriate AI literacy curriculum for elementary, middle and high school levels

- Train teachers across all subjects on integrating AI into their lessons

- Implement hands-on AI projects in science, math and computer science classes

- Establish an "AI Ethics Council" comprised of students to discuss and debate AI-related issues

- Partner with local tech companies to provide real-world AI exposure through field trips and guest speakers

- Create an annual "AI Innovation Challenge" where students develop AI-powered solutions to community problems

- Integrate AI literacy assessments

- Develop a mentorship program pairing AI-proficient high school students with younger learners

- Host regular parent workshops on AI to ensure family support for AI literacy initiatives

TRAP Integration

The true strength of TRAP lies in the alignment of its components:

- Targets keep you focused on the big picture.

- Results ensure accountability and measurable progress.

- Approaches provide a strategic roadmap.

- Procedures translate plans into action.

When these elements work harmoniously, they create a robust framework for implementing AI in education effectively and purposefully.

All Ideas Are Bad...Initially

Every idea starts flawed. Many ideas require refinement before they reach their full potential. The best concepts need refining. Left untested, even good ideas can turn into blind spots. Early testing transforms weaknesses into strengths and reveals what truly works. The faster ideas face the real world, the sooner strengths and weaknesses show. Quick experiments get you closer to what works. The goal isn't a perfect plan on paper. It's a strategy that evolves through trial and discovery.

Innovation demands movement. Needs shift. Costs of technology changes.

Standing still isn't an option. Only constant testing and adjusting keep you relevant. Experiment often. Make small changes based on real feedback. Each experiment drives you forward. Each adjustment keeps you aligned with your purpose. Innovation doesn't come from staying put. It thrives in the energy of movement and discovery.

True innovation requires a culture of learning. Embrace risks with your accelerator group and let mistakes teach you. Encourage a focus on real problems, not theories. Ideas that don't work should be abandoned without regret. This isn't about giving up. It's about clearing space for ideas that solve real issues. Speed of learning should beat precision. Teams that own their work innovate faster and better. Your accelerator group should have freedom but also be responsible for their work. When people feel trusted, creativity flows. They test. They improve. They will make your school stronger.

In this culture, every experiment matters. Every pivot has a purpose. Each win or loss is a building block. This is how lasting strategies form—not from perfection but from persistence, creativity and a shared commitment to innovation.

Avoid These Common Pitfalls

As you implement TRAP, be mindful of these potential stumbling blocks:

- **Vague Targets**
  Ensure your vision is clear and specific. Avoid setting ambiguous goals that can lead to confusion and misalignment.

- **Unrealistic Results**
  Set ambitious yet achievable goals to maintain motivation and focus. Goals that are too far out of reach can lead to frustration and wasted resources.

- **Falling in Love With Ideas Too Early**
  Be open to evolving ideas rather than becoming overly attached. This flexibility allows for innovation and adaptation as you gather insights and data.

- **Overcomplicated Approaches**
  Keep your strategy straightforward and focused. Complexity can make it hard to implement, manage and communicate effectively.

- **Disconnected Procedures**

  Ensure every action and tactic aligns with your overall target, maintaining cohesion and purpose across all efforts.

- **Not Testing Ideas Quickly and Cost-Effectively**

  Test and validate ideas early to identify what works. Quick, low-cost testing helps refine approaches without major time or financial investments.

- **Spending Too Much Time Planning Instead of Experimenting**

  Balance planning with action. Excessive planning can slow momentum, while real-world experiments often provide clearer guidance.

- **Ignoring Feedback and Market Realities**

  Stay responsive to input from your community. When innovating for technology such as AI, the greatest mistake you can make is to think you understand it because of its current state. Stay alert to progress. Ignoring these can lead to outdated strategies that fail to meet actual needs.

Lightning Demos

The "lightning demo" technique originated from the Design Sprint methodology developed by Google Ventures. This method involves team members conducting quick, focused presentations of existing solutions or ideas to inspire and inform the design process. By sharing these concise demonstrations, teams can gather a diverse range of concepts and approaches.[10]

For us, it can be a powerful, time-efficient exercise that can inspire items for your roadmap.

At its core, the lightning demo is about expanding horizons. For 45 minutes, your accelerator group becomes explorers, venturing beyond the familiar territory of education to discover how AI is reshaping other industries. This cross-pollination of ideas is the key to unlocking new innovative solutions.

The process:

1. Research (20 minutes): Participants search for 2-3 examples of innovative

---

10. You find out more about design sprints at https://www.thesprintbook.com/

AI use, regardless of industry.

2. Present (15 minutes): Each person shares their findings, focusing on core concepts and potential applications.

3. Synthesize (10 minutes): The group categorizes and prioritizes ideas, identifying the most promising for their context.

The power of the Lightning Demo lies in its ability to:

- Break mental barriers: By looking outside education, participants free themselves from preconceived notions of what's possible.

- Accelerate ideation: Time constraints force quick, intuitive thinking, often leading to unexpected insights.

- Foster collaborative innovation: The sharing process allows ideas to build upon each other, creating a collective vision.

- Ground ideas in reality: The resulting concepts are inherently practical by starting with real-world applications.

The goal isn't to find perfect solutions but to spark ideas that can be adapted and refined. A customer service AI might inspire a new approach to student support. A predictive maintenance system could evolve into an early warning system for academic struggles.

As you guide your team through this exercise, encourage them to think boldly. The most transformative ideas often come from unexpected places. A lightning demo isn't just about finding solutions; it's about cultivating a mindset of innovative thinking that will serve your school well beyond this single exercise.

5 Questions for Infinite Minds

1. In reimagining our curriculum through Speculative Design, what ethical dilemmas could arise from AI-integrated learning environments and how will we ensure these advancements truly benefit every student rather than deepen existing inequities?

2. When envisioning preferred futures for our school, what deeply embedded traditions or values might we unintentionally overlook and how can we bring these perspectives to the surface to enrich our long-term strategy?

3. How can we leverage storytelling and tangible "artifacts from the future" to inspire a shared vision that resonates emotionally with stakeholders, ensuring they feel both seen in the present and motivated to journey with us toward a transformed future?

4. As we map our innovation gap, what "hidden resources" or overlooked touch points could serve as powerful tools for change, helping us achieve strategic goals in ways that might otherwise seem beyond our current means?

5. Imagine a future where student growth is measured by real-world skills and personal development rather than standardized tests. How might we redefine our metrics of success to reflect deeper, lifelong learning and adaptability?

Download the interactive Infinite Education Playbook to complete this task in the playbook and access more accompanying activities for you and your accelerator group.

TL;DR

- Speculative Design drives leaders to question the status quo and imagine bold new futures. It challenges leaders to think beyond today's limitations, envisioning possibilities where schools become hubs for community or where students progress based on skills rather than age. This approach empowers leaders to create change rather than react to it.

- Storytelling gives vision a powerful voice. Through vivid narratives, leaders can turn abstract goals into compelling stories that inspire action. A shared story helps every stakeholder see the future and feel part of the journey, making innovation a goal and a collective mission.

- The "innovation gap" reveals the difference between your school's reality and potential. By mapping where you are against where you want to be, you clarify the steps to take. This approach turns lofty goals into achievable milestones and helps every action feel purposeful.

- Systematic Inventive Thinking transforms limits into strengths. Instead of relying on more resources, SIT encourages leaders to rethink and reinvent what they already have. This method brings out innovative solutions that are practical and impactful, making meaningful change accessible.

- An agile culture of experimentation lets schools stay ahead. Testing ideas quickly and adapting to feedback fosters resilience. Instead of perfection, focus on progress and learning. This mindset ensures that every step forward builds a school's ability to thrive in a changing world.

Chapter 15

STEP 3–INFLUENCE

"The key to successful leadership today is influence, not authority."
—Kenneth Blanchard

In an era when artificial intelligence is reshaping industries and redefining societal norms, the role of school leaders is evolving. Beyond managing the status quo, leaders must guide institutions toward adaptability, innovation and future readiness. Achieving this level of organizational change requires more than decision-making authority. It demands influence.

Influence is the art of inspiring trust, empowering individuals and fostering a shared vision. In this chapter, we explore how you can build and wield influence to help your school navigate the complexities of a world increasingly dominated by AI and technology.

Many organizations will manage the scope and shape elements of strategy. But most stop there. It's because influence is difficult. But it is a skill you can develop.

The strategies and activities in this chapter will help you develop the relational influence needed to inspire trust, navigate resistance and align your school community around a shared vision. By fostering collaboration, addressing fears and leveraging purpose-driven motivation, you will empower your team to embrace change and drive meaningful innovation in an ever-evolving educational landscape.

Influence Versus Persuasion

Influence

Persuasion

For members of your accelerator group, understanding the distinction between influence and persuasion is a critical step toward shaping the broader culture of your school. Persuasion is a transactional process. It is focused on convincing someone to agree with a specific idea or take a particular action, often using arguments or data to back your case. Influence, by contrast, is relational. It grows from trust, credibility and alignment with shared values. The former CIA Intelligence Officer, Andrew Bustamente, describes influence as "what you have when you are not talking."[1] Influence empowers others to seek your perspective and engage with your vision willingly, even when they may initially disagree.

The ability of the accelerator group to wield influence will define your capacity to drive meaningful, lasting change in your school. Sometimes, convincing colleagues to adopt an idea through persuasion might be appropriate, but this will only work when delivered through a skilled line manager. The accelerator group will need to work on their ability to influence their colleagues so that they are inspired to become advocates of that idea themselves. The latter is not about exerting authority but about earning trust, fostering collaboration and creating a shared sense of purpose.

Influence is the art of inspiring trust, empowering individuals and fostering a shared vision.

1. The Diary Of A CEO. (2024, July 29). Former CIA Spy Reveals How They're Controlling You! - Andrew Bustamante [Video]. YouTube. https://www.youtube.com/watch?v=P_A8XElrAqA

In educational leadership, this paradigm shift matters deeply because you're transforming practices and shaping the attitudes and mindsets that will prepare students for a rapidly evolving world.

The ability of the accelerator group to wield influence will define your capacity to drive meaningful, lasting change in your school.

Influence vs. Persuasion Task

Here is a one-hour activity you can do with your accelerator group to develop an understanding of these distinctions:

Objective: Help the accelerator group understand and practice the difference between influence and persuasion by collaboratively tackling a real-world school challenge.

Step 1: Define the Challenge (10 minutes)
As a group, identify a shared school challenge
Map the stakeholders' key needs, focusing on trust and alignment opportunities.

Step 2: Develop Two Approaches (15 minutes)
Split into two teams:

1. Persuasion Team: Create a pitch using evidence, arguments and direct appeals to gain buy-in.

2. Influence Team: Design an approach based on building trust, shared goals and fostering collaboration.

Use simple sketches, sticky notes or quick outlines to prototype each pitch.

Step 3: Present and Test (20 minutes)

Teams present their pitches to the other team.

The Persuasion Team focuses on convincing the audience through logic and evidence, while the influence team focuses on trust-building and relational alignment.

Questions to reflect upon during the presentations: What elements feel more engaging? Which inspired more long-term buy-in?

Step 4: Reflect and Act (15 minutes)

Discuss as a group:

- What were the strengths and limitations of each approach?

- How can influence create deeper, more sustainable change?

- Write down one actionable strategy to build influence in your school. Assign each member a small, related task to try in the coming weeks.

This concise activity ensures participants experience both approaches first-hand while focusing on practical, actionable takeaways to enhance their leadership within the school.

Supporting AI Prompt

"Design a comprehensive framework to help school innovators decide when to use persuasion versus influence while introducing new AI tools for teachers. Provide clear criteria, practical examples and actionable strategies to ensure the framework is easy to apply in real-world scenarios. The focus should be maximizing effectiveness and stakeholder alignment in educational settings."

How to Build Influence

Building influence is a key leadership skill. The foundation of influence lies in sense-making, a concept grounded in understanding how relationships evolve. Andrew Bustamente, who drew from his CIA training to decode influence, championed this framework, illuminating how leaders can transform initial skepticism into lasting trust and collaboration.

The Three Stages of Relationship Progression

Avoidance $\longrightarrow$ Competition $\longrightarrow$ Compliance

At its core, influence is about guiding relationships through three key stages:

1. Avoidance

Initially, individuals may resist engagement, often driven by uncertainty, fear of change, or past negative experiences. In schools, this can manifest as hesitation to adopt new teaching strategies or reluctance to embrace technologies like AI.

2. Competition

As interactions deepen, dialogue becomes more dynamic. Staff may express differing opinions or challenge ideas, leading to spirited debate. While this stage may feel contentious, it's a sign of investment in the relationship and a precursor to meaningful collaboration.

3. Compliance

Finally, relationships reach a stage where trust and understanding foster a willingness to collaborate or follow guidance, even if total agreement isn't present. In this stage, innovation begins to flourish as colleagues align on shared goals and act cohesively.

The progression from avoidance to compliance is the essence of influence. Creating an environment that prioritizes openness, dialogue and respect allows relationships to move naturally through these stages.

The Know | Like | Trust Framework

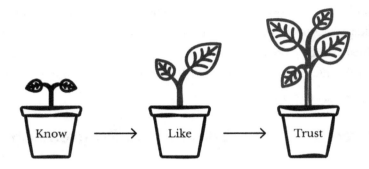

Influence cannot thrive without trust. Bustamente's CIA-inspired strategies bring us to the Know, Like, Trust framework, which emphasizes how trust develops incrementally:

1. **Know**

   Visibility and consistency are the first steps to influence. Leaders who are predictable in their actions reduce uncertainty, enabling others to feel secure in their presence. For example, consistently sharing updates about adopting AI tools and providing clear guidance helps staff feel informed and included.

2. **Like**

   While relational warmth strengthens bonds, professional trust doesn't require deep personal connection. Authenticity in interactions, such as actively listening to concerns and acknowledging contributions, cultivates mutual respect, which is often more critical than mere "liking."

3. **Trust**

   Trust emerges when leaders demonstrate reliability, transparency and follow-through on commitments. A school leader who promises professional development for new AI tools and delivers on that promise will earn the confidence of their team, transforming resistance into readiness.

By aligning your actions with this framework, you can transition from being perceived as a mere manager to becoming a partner in progress. This paves the way for innovation to take root.

Building Influence Task

Here is an activity you can do with your accelerator group to develop an understanding of these distinctions:

Objective: Systematically build influence by engaging colleagues and moving them through the stages of relationship progression.

Step 1: Map Your Influence Landscape

Make a list: Write down all the individuals or groups involved in or affected by your innovation initiative. Then, determine their current stage:

- Avoidance: Are they disengaged, skeptical or resistant?

- Competition: Are they voicing concerns or debating the initiative?

- Compliance: Are they supportive and willing to collaborate?

Tip: Use observation or direct feedback to gauge attitudes. For example, if teachers regularly miss meetings about AI, they're likely in avoidance. If they actively critique AI tools, they're in competition.

Prioritize key people: Identify the top 3-5 people whose buy-in is most critical to the success of your initiative.

Step 2: Create a Targeted Engagement Plan

Use the Know, Like, Trust framework to design specific actions for each group based on their current stage.

For Avoidance: Build Awareness (Know)
Action Ideas: Host a non-threatening informational session (e.g., "How AI is Simplifying Teacher Workloads"). Share quick, positive examples of similar innovations working in other schools. Offer anonymous surveys to understand concerns without pressure. The goal is to reduce uncertainty and show that you're approachable.

For Competition: Foster Dialogue (Like)
Action Ideas: Organize small-group discussions where colleagues can express their perspectives openly. Acknowledge valid concerns and reframe debates as opportunities for collaboration. Highlight small wins and invite people to participate in testing solutions. The goal is to respect differing opinions and align on shared goals.

For Compliance: Build Ownership (Trust)
Action Ideas: Delegate meaningful tasks (e.g., invite teachers to co-lead professional development sessions on AI). Regularly share progress updates to reinforce transparency. Deliver consistently on promises, such as providing training or tools on schedule. The goal is to deepen trust and create champions who advocate for your initiative.

Step 3: Implement Your Plan

Timeline: Assign clear deadlines for each action. For instance:

- Week 1-2: Build awareness with emails or presentations.

- Week 3-4: Facilitate discussions to address concerns.

- Week 5+: Deliver resources and measure buy-in.

Responsibilities: Assign specific tasks to team members.

Step 4: Measure Progress and Adapt

Evaluate Engagement:

- Are stakeholders attending sessions?

- Are they providing feedback?

- Are they showing reduced resistance (e.g., asking constructive questions or volunteering ideas)?

Gather Feedback: Use surveys or informal check-ins to learn what's working and what's not.

Adjust Strategies: If certain people remain stuck in avoidance or competition, revisit the Know, Like, Trust framework and adjust your tactics.

Step 5: Celebrate Wins

Share stories of early adopters and their successes to motivate others. Acknowledge the efforts of stakeholders who have moved to compliance, reinforcing their value in the process.

Example in practice:

Scenario: Teachers skeptical about AI integration in classrooms.

Avoidance

Send an email: "Did you know AI can save teachers three hours a week? Join us for a 15-minute demo."

Hold a voluntary Q&A session.

Competition

Facilitate a meeting where teachers can openly discuss fears about AI replacing jobs. Reframe concerns: "AI isn't here to replace, but to enhance your expertise."

Compliance

Assign a teacher to co-lead an AI pilot program. Deliver tools and training as promised. Share success metrics (e.g., "AI saved 15 hours of grading time last month").

This step-by-step approach empowers you and your accelerator group to effectively build influence, fostering an environment where trust and collaboration lead to lasting change.

Supporting AI Prompt

"I'm a school leader working to build influence and drive buy-in for an innovation initiative, such as integrating AI in classrooms. Help me:

- Map key stakeholders and assess their current stage of engagement.

- Design targeted actions for each stage to foster trust and collaboration.

- Create a timeline for implementation with clear milestones and team roles.

- Develop strategies to measure progress and adapt as needed.

- Plan ways to celebrate wins and motivate others through success stories.

  Tailor suggestions to a school setting, prioritizing trust-building and collaboration."

Building upon the foundations of influence and trust, we now explore the S.P.A.R.K. framework, which delves into the key motivators that drive individuals to embrace change.

Motivating Through Purpose

The S.P.A.R.K. framework provides a practical and human-centered approach to understanding what motivates people and aligning their interests with your vision.

The Five Motivators of S.P.A.R.K.

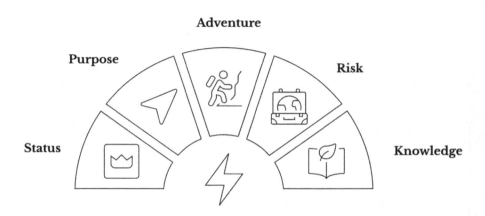

1. Status

Humans have a fundamental need to feel valued and respected. In the school setting, this could mean acknowledging educators' expertise, highlighting their achievements or positioning them as leaders of change. Status recognition reassures stakeholders that their contributions matter.

2. Purpose

People are most engaged when they see their work as part of a bigger picture. Linking initiatives to shared values or overarching goals, such as improving student outcomes or preparing learners for the future, can create an emotional connection to the mission.

3. Adventure

Novelty and exploration drive curiosity and enthusiasm. Rather than imposing changes, presenting challenges as exciting opportunities for growth shifts the narrative from obligation to opportunity.

4. Risk

Fear is one of the biggest barriers to influence. Risk includes not just failure but also uncertainty about change. Leaders who confront these risks directly, whether related to job security, workload, or the ethics of new technologies, cultivate trust and reduce resistance.

5. Knowledge

Growth-oriented individuals are motivated by the opportunity to learn and develop. Offering training, resources and continuous support fosters confidence and competence. This makes people more willing to embrace change.

Applying S.P.A.R.K.: An Example With AI in Education

If you're introducing artificial intelligence tools in your school or district, applying the S.P.A.R.K. framework might look like this:

1. Status

Create a "Pioneers of Progress" recognition program where educators who integrate AI effectively are celebrated as leaders in innovation. Share their successes in newsletters or staff meetings.

2. Purpose

Connect AI adoption to the mission of equipping students with future-ready skills. Show how these tools align with values like equity, personalized learning and career readiness.

3. Adventure

Invite educators to participate in a "Future of Teaching" pilot program. Frame it as an exploration of groundbreaking teaching strategies that could shape the future of education.

4. Risk

Address anxieties head-on by creating a transparent FAQ about AI, detailing how it complements rather than replaces educators. Host open forums to discuss concerns and co-create solutions.

5. Knowledge

Offer hands-on workshops, one-on-one coaching and access to online resources to demystify AI tools and build confidence in their use.

This approach builds influence and creates an atmosphere of shared excitement and trust.

S.P.A.R.K. Task

Objective: Equip your innovation group to apply the S.P.A.R.K. framework in a practical, step-by-step way to build influence for a specific initiative.

Step 1: Choose a Specific Initiative

Gather your group and choose a well-defined initiative to focus on. Examples include launching a digital learning platform, revising teaching methods, or starting a mentorship program. Ensure the initiative is relevant and timely for your school or district.

Step 2: Introduce the S.P.A.R.K. Framework

Briefly explain the five motivators of S.P.A.R.K.:

- Status: Recognizing contributions.

- Purpose: Aligning with shared values.

- Adventure: Creating excitement around innovation.

- Risk: Addressing concerns transparently.

- Knowledge: Offering opportunities for growth.

Step 3: Divide and Conquer

Split the group into five smaller teams or assign individuals to focus on one motivator each. This ensures each S.P.A.R.K. element is given dedicated attention. For smaller groups, participants can address multiple motivators.

Step 4: Brainstorm for Each Motivator

Give teams 15–20 minutes to brainstorm actionable strategies using the following prompts:

- Status: How will this initiative enhance stakeholders' recognition? Examples: Awards, titles, spotlighting success stories.

- Purpose: How does this initiative tie into shared goals or values? Examples: Connecting to the school's mission or students' future success.

- Adventure: What makes this initiative exciting or innovative? Examples: Framing it as a groundbreaking exploration.

- Risk: What concerns need to be addressed and how? Examples: Clarifying misconceptions or offering reassurances.

- Knowledge: What resources or training will support adoption? Examples: Workshops, online courses, or expert guidance.

Encourage teams to focus on actionable, specific ideas.

Step 5: Develop Mini Action Plans

Each team drafts 1–2 actionable strategies for their assigned motivator. Example outputs include:

- Status: Create a "Change Leader" badge for participants who adopt the initiative early.

- Purpose: Develop a compelling narrative about how this program supports long-term student success.

- Adventure: Organize a kickoff event with a "vision for the future" theme.

- Risk: Develop a list of FAQs and hold a Q&A session to address concerns.

- Knowledge: Schedule a professional development day dedicated to hands-on practice with the new tools.

Teams should also identify quick wins to implement early in the process.

Step 6: Present and Refine

Bring everyone back together. Each team presents their strategies, explaining how their ideas connect to the motivator they were assigned. As a group, discuss the following:

- Are there overlaps that can be streamlined?
- Are there any gaps in the overall approach?
- How can strategies be strengthened or adapted to fit stakeholders' needs?

Make adjustments based on group feedback.

Step 7: Execute and Track Results

Compile the strategies into a cohesive action plan and assign responsibilities for execution. Develop a timeline for implementation and identify simple metrics to evaluate success. Metrics could include:

- Attendance at training sessions.

- Survey feedback from stakeholders.

- Participation rates in related activities.

- Success stories from early adopters.

Commit to revisiting the plan regularly to assess progress and make adjustments as needed.

Following these seven structured steps, your team can confidently use the S.P.A.R.K. framework to build influence and drive meaningful change. This approach ensures every stakeholder feels heard, valued and engaged in the journey toward innovation.

At the heart of transformative leadership lies the ability to articulate a vision so bold, so unyieldingly clear that it challenges the status quo.

Supporting AI Prompt

"I'm working on building influence and fostering engagement for a specific initiative in my school. Here's the initiative we're focusing on: (Describe the initiative). I'd like your help in the following ways:

- Overview and Strategy: Provide a quick summary of how we can address the motivating factors of Status, Purpose, Adventure, Risk and Knowledge.

- Customized Brainstorming Prompts: Suggest specific, actionable questions or prompts that our team can use to generate ideas for each motivator.

- Action Plan Suggestions: Based on the framework, propose initial strategies or quick wins we can use to get started. Include examples for each motivator.

- Feedback Mechanisms: Help us identify simple metrics and feedback tools to track the success of our initiative and adjust as needed.

- Co-Creation Tips: Offer advice for facilitating team discussions and ensuring all voices are heard when applying this framework."

The Power of Polarity

We can shape the future of education through strategic vision and influential leadership. At the heart of transformative leadership lies the ability to articulate a vision so bold, so unyieldingly clear that it challenges the status quo. This often necessitates taking firm, even polarizing positions. This may seem counterintuitive in a domain where inclusivity is sacrosanct. Yet, this willingness to embrace polarity distinguishes leaders who drive change from those who merely maintain the status quo.

When wielded with intention and empathy, polarization is not about creating division. It is about sharpening focus. It demands leaders prioritize what truly matters, cutting through the noise to illuminate a path forward. By doing so, they draw in allies who share their passion and commitment while inviting even their skeptics to engage in meaningful dialogue. The process is not without friction, but this tension fuels innovation and catalyzes growth.

Consider a leader championing AI-driven personalization in education. A vision that promises to revolutionize how students learn and teachers teach. Inevitably, such a stance will encounter resistance. But a visionary leader doesn't shy away from the challenge. Instead, they articulate the transformative potential of AI with clarity and conviction, acknowledging fears while countering them with evidence and empathy. This is not a battle to be won; it is a forum where ideas clash, evolve and ultimately coalesce into progress.

Through thoughtful polarization, leaders galvanize their teams around a shared mission. They invite their communities to wrestle with big questions: What does the future of learning look like? How can we honor tradition while embracing innovation? This is not creating echo chambers but cultivating cultures of critical thinking and purposeful debate. It is about building environments where disagreement is a catalyst for discovery and where dissent, when welcomed and explored, becomes a tool for refining the vision.

We cannot avoid controversy, but we can navigate it with grace. Ignite the focused energy that drives change by embracing polarity, ensuring their teams are prepared for the future and actively shaping it.

We cannot avoid controversy, but we can navigate it with grace.

Polarity Exercise: Critical Conviction

Here's an exercise you can do to develop the skill of strategic polarization by refining your ability to take a bold stance while fostering dialogue and innovation.

Step 1: Identify a Core Belief
Select a bold, potentially polarizing belief central to your vision. Make this something transformative for your school's mission.

Example: "Project-based learning should replace standardized testing."

Step 2: Anticipate Resistance
List key stakeholders (teachers, students, parents, administrators) and outline:

- Their likely objections.
- The values, fears or assumptions driving their concerns.

Step 3: Create a Balanced Narrative
Develop a message that bridges your vision and their concerns:

- Highlight shared values and clear benefits.
- Acknowledge fears while explaining why change is vital.

Example: "Standardized tests provide structure, but project-based learning equips students with critical real-world skills."

Step 4: Pilot the Idea

Test your stance with a small group through a presentation, workshop or small-scale initiative:

- Encourage open dialogue, welcoming agreement and dissent.
- Note what resonates and what creates pushback.

Step 5: Reflect and Refine

After the pilot, reflect on the process by asking:

- What worked and what didn't?
- What did I learn from opposing perspectives?
- How can I clarify or reinforce my vision?

Step 6: Scale Strategically

Use insights from the pilot to refine your approach and roll out the idea to a larger audience, maintaining focus while fostering constructive tension.

This exercise builds a leader's confidence in championing bold ideas, understanding and addressing resistance and using tension to drive innovation and growth. It transforms polarization into an asset for progress.

Influential leaders take time to understand others. Small openings in conversations reveal people's deeper perspectives. These "windows and doors" offer insights into their thoughts and feelings.

Supporting AI Prompt

"List some bold, potentially polarizing beliefs central to my vision of (explain your vision). They should be transformative for our school's mission."

A Roadmap for Rapid Influence

You must act fast when guiding your school through change and fostering innovation. A short-term goal of proving your influence can build a solid foundation for developing your influence in the long term. Andrew Bustamante's Four Cs framework provides practical steps to build influence in large organizations.[2]

The four Cs are:

1. Consideration: Understand Perspectives

Influential leaders take time to understand others. Small openings in conversations reveal people's deeper perspectives. These "windows and doors" offer insights into their thoughts and feelings.

Recognize that everyone lives in their own "perception." Actively work to see the world through their eyes. Look for "windows" in conversations that expose deeper thoughts and motivations. Get quiet before important meetings or decisions. Clear your mind to sharpen your focus and improve your observational skills. Validate others' perspectives, even when they differ from your own. This builds trust and connection.

2. Consistency: Build Trust

Trust grows from reliability. People feel secure when they can predict your behavior. Consistency promotes confidence, even in situations where disagreements arise.

Ensure your actions and beliefs align consistently over time. This steadiness creates comfort for those around you. Understand that inconsistency quickly erodes trust and credibility. Acknowledge mistakes, but remain unwavering in your core values and principles. Remember, people don't have to like you to trust you. Reliability is more important than approval.

3. Collaboration: Create New Ideas

Collaboration moves beyond compromise. True collaboration combines ideas from all sides to create something better for everyone involved. It transforms challenges into opportunities for growth.

---

2. The Diary Of A CEO. (2024, July 29). Former CIA Spy Reveals How They're Controlling You! - Andrew Bustamante [Video]. YouTube. https://www.youtube.com/watch?v=P_A8XElrAqA

Shift from compromise to co-creation. Collaboration means bringing together different ideas to create a third, better outcome. Use the three stages of relationship progression framework, avoidance, competition and compliance, to guide collaborative efforts. Recognize that disagreements, handled collaboratively, can strengthen relationships. Treat conflicts as opportunities to find mutual benefits and shared goals.

4. Control: Lead With Purpose

Control is often misunderstood but essential for effective leadership. Leaders must act decisively to inspire followership, even when their decisions are not universally liked.

Capitalize on the trust you've built to guide your team toward meaningful goals. Accept that exercising control might make you less liked, but is necessary for true leadership. Understand that leadership requires action, especially in moments of uncertainty. Lead with conviction. Inspire others through your confidence and clarity, even in difficult situations.

Trust grows from reliability. People feel secure when they can predict your behavior. Consistency promotes confidence, even in situations where disagreements arise.

Putting the Four Cs Into Action

Each of the Four Cs strengthens your ability to influence and lead. By mastering these principles, you can create an environment of trust, innovation and progress. How will you use them to shape the future of your school?

The Rapid Influence Strategic Plan Activity

Here is a workshop you can lead with your accelerator group to help you create a rapid, actionable plan to influence your school organization and begin driving change using the Four Cs.

Step 1: Define the Goal (10 minutes)

Identify a specific challenge or goal (e.g., improving staff morale, introducing a new program). Write a simple statement describing what success looks like.

Step 2: Develop Strategies Using the Four Cs (20 minutes)

Break into four small teams. Each team focuses on one C.

1. Consideration

   Focus: Understand key stakeholders.

   List who is affected (teachers, students, parents, etc.).

   Write 3-5 questions to uncover their needs or concerns.

   Decide how to gather their input (e.g., surveys, meetings).

   Outcome: A plan for gathering and using stakeholder insights.

2. Consistency

   Focus: Build trust through reliable actions.

   Decide what messages and actions must stay consistent.

   Identify where things might get inconsistent.

   Create a simple timeline for clear communication.

   Outcome: A trust-building plan with reliable messaging.

3. Collaboration

   Focus: Engage others to create better ideas.

   List ways to involve stakeholders (e.g., brainstorming sessions, feedback forums).

   Decide how to handle disagreements constructively.

   Choose one collaborative activity to start.

   Outcome: A collaborative engagement plan.

4. Control

   Focus: Lead with confidence and purpose.

   Identify key decisions you'll need to make.

   Decide how to communicate decisions clearly.

   Plan how to take decisive action when necessary.

   Outcome: A leadership action plan for guiding the group.

Step 3: Combine and Finalize (20 minutes)

Share each team's plan with the group.

Combine ideas into one unified plan.

Assign roles and next steps for action.

Step 4: Commit and Act (10 minutes)

Each person chooses one immediate action to take this week.

Set a check-in date to track progress.

Outcome: A clear, practical influence plan that uses the Four Cs to achieve your goal.

Supporting AI Prompt

"We are a school innovation group working to create a rapid strategic plan for influencing our organization using the Four Cs framework: Consideration, Consistency, Collaboration and Control. Our goal is (insert your goal or challenge, e.g., improving staff morale, introducing new technology, etc.). Please help us with the following:

Consideration:

- Identify key stakeholders who this initiative will impact.
- Suggest questions or methods we can use to understand their perspectives and needs.
- Provide tips for uncovering deeper insights from stakeholders.

Consistency:

- Outline how we can create trust through consistent messaging and actions.
- Identify potential areas where inconsistencies could arise and how to avoid them.

- Suggest a communication strategy that keeps everyone aligned.

Collaboration:

- Recommend ways to engage stakeholders in a collaborative process.

- Provide strategies to handle disagreements constructively.

- Suggest tools or techniques to co-create innovative solutions.

Control:

- Guide us on how to take decisive leadership actions while maintaining trust.

- Suggest ways to balance control with openness to feedback.

- Provide tips for effectively communicating and implementing decisions.

- Help us integrate these ideas into a clear, step-by-step strategic plan. Keep the suggestions practical and focused on influencing our organization to achieve our goal."

Dealing With Resistance

Innovation will keep your school relevant in a changing world. Without it, even the most successful institutions risk falling behind. Resistance to change often arises not from laziness but from a force embedded in every organization's culture called dominant logic. This logic stems from past successes and shapes decisions, behaviors and beliefs. It feels safe, but it blinds leaders to new possibilities.

Past achievements don't guarantee future relevance; staying still in a moving world leads to being left behind.

Organizational Resistance

Organizations can fall into three common traps tied to dominant logic: complacency, cannibalization and overreliance on existing strengths.[3] Understanding these traps is vital for leaders who want their schools to evolve and thrive.

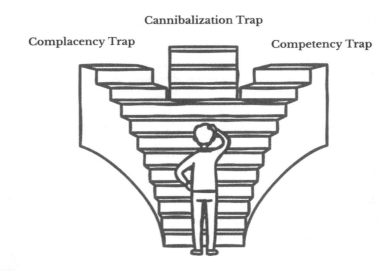

Cannibalization Trap

Complacency Trap

Competency Trap

1. Complacency Trap: Success Masks the Need for Change

Success feels reassuring. It encourages schools to stick with what has worked before. The complacency trap arises when leaders assume current approaches will remain effective no matter how the world shifts around them.

Blockbuster once ruled the video rental market. Its leaders believed customers would always want physical stores and late fees didn't matter. This mindset kept Blockbuster from adapting to the rise of streaming services like Netflix. By the time the company reacted, it was too late.

Schools that cling to traditional methods fall into the same pattern. High test scores, strong reputations and parent satisfaction can mask the need for innovation. Meanwhile, the world demands skills like collaboration, adaptability and digital fluency. Without new approaches, students risk leaving school unprepared.

Leaders must question what "good" means. Past achievements don't guarantee

3. Institute for Management Studies. (2022, December 5). Strategies for Leading Innovation with Dr. Vijay Govindarajan & Charles Good I TGLP #52 [Video]. YouTube. https://www.youtube.com/watch?v=QTStPtySRyM

future relevance; staying still in a moving world leads to being left behind.

2. Cannibalization Trap: Protecting the Present Risks the Future

New initiatives often feel like threats to what already works. The cannibalization trap emerges when schools avoid innovation because they fear it will undermine existing programs or their reputation.

Kodak invented the digital camera but hesitated to embrace it fully. The company feared it would lose film sales revenue. That hesitation allowed competitors to dominate the digital photography market, leaving Kodak irrelevant.

Schools face this trap when they avoid change to protect their identity. A school known for academic rigor might resist project-based learning, worrying it could hurt test scores. A district with strong teacher-centered instruction might avoid adopting personalized learning tools, fearing a loss of tradition.

Innovation expands opportunities. It's not about replacing what works but finding new ways to serve students. Schools thrive when leaders embrace change as a chance to evolve rather than a threat to their legacy.

3. Competency Trap: Overreliance on Strengths Limits Growth

Skills that bring success today may not meet tomorrow's challenges. The competency trap occurs when schools lean so heavily on current strengths they fail to develop new capabilities.

Nokia excelled at making mobile phones but ignored the growing importance of software. Its reliance on hardware expertise kept it from adapting to the rise of smartphones and the company lost its leadership position in the industry.

Schools often rely on traditional teaching methods, ignoring emerging trends like AI-driven learning tools or social-emotional education. Leaders might say, "This is what we do best," but holding on to outdated strengths prevents growth.

Schools need a culture of continuous learning. Teachers and leaders must prepare for new demands and building new skills ensures schools stay agile and ready to adapt.

Dominant Logic: A Barrier to Change

Dominant logic shapes how organizations think, decide and act. It creates stability and can help schools maintain their identity. But it also creates blind spots.

Complacency insists what worked before will always work. Cannibalization sees innovation as a threat rather than an opportunity. Competency convinces leaders their current expertise is enough.

Changing dominant logic means surfacing these beliefs and replacing them with a new narrative. Schools can't grow when their thinking remains anchored in the past.

A Path Out of the Traps

We must take bold steps to move beyond these traps. Change happens when we challenge assumptions and foster a culture that embraces growth.

- **Redefine Success**
  Focus on meeting future needs rather than preserving past accomplishments. Share stories of schools that took risks and found new ways to achieve excellence.

- **Encourage Experimentation**
  Allow freedom to test ideas on a small scale. Create space for innovation where failure is treated as a chance to learn.

- **Invest in People**
  Equip teachers and staff with tools to adapt. Professional development should focus on emerging challenges and opportunities.

- **Involve the Community**
  Build trust by involving parents, teachers and students in the conversation. Show how change aligns with the school's core mission.

- **Design for Adaptability**
  Make flexibility a priority in schedules, resources and systems. Build a foundation that can evolve with changing needs.

The world is moving fast. We need leaders who question assumptions and take risks. It means honoring the past by evolving it. Schools that embrace change prepare students not just to succeed in the world as it is but to lead in the world as it will be.

Innovation isn't a luxury. It's a responsibility.

Dominant logic shapes how organizations think, decide and act. It creates stability and can help schools maintain their identity. But it also creates blind spots.

Dominant Logic Exercise

This exercise for your group of innovators will help you identify and overcome organizational resistance traps.

Step 1. Warm-Up: Unmask the Traps (10 minutes)

Goal: Introduce the concept of organizational traps engagingly.

What You Do: Share three real-world examples (e.g., Blockbuster, Kodak, Nokia) and connect them to the traps (complacency, cannibalization, competency).

Ask Participants: Can you think of a time when a "success" blinded your school to change? What new ideas have been shelved because they felt too risky? What strengths might your school be relying on too heavily?

Outcome: Participants understand the traps and start thinking about them in their school's context.

Step 2. Main Task: The Innovation Escape Room (45 minutes)

Goal: Develop practical solutions to real challenges caused by resistance traps.

What You Do: Divide into three teams. Each team is "locked" in a virtual trap room.

1. Complacency Room: They must "escape" by identifying areas where success has masked the need for change. Example prompt: What long-standing practices could be failing today's students?

2. Cannibalization Room: They escape by reframing innovation as an opportunity, not a threat. Example prompt: What ideas are avoided because they seem risky or disruptive? How could they be tested?

3. Competency Room: Teams must escape by defining a way to build new strengths. Example prompt: What new skills or tools are missing in your school and how can you develop them?

Deliverable: Each team develops a 3-point "Escape Plan" to share with the group:

Identify the Trap: Describe the challenge (e.g., "We're stuck in tradition because...").

Propose One Bold Experiment: Define a simple, testable solution. Explain why it matters: How will this help students thrive in a changing world?

Step 3. The "Shark Tank" Pitch (30 minutes)

Goal: Push teams to refine and present their ideas.

What You Do: Each team gets 3 minutes to pitch their escape plan to a "panel" (the rest of the group or a few designated leaders).

Include:
- The trap they faced.
- The bold experiment they'll test.
- Why will this future-proof their school?

Panel members ask questions and vote on the most compelling escape plan. Outcome: Teams clarify their ideas under feedback and learn to advocate for innovation.

Step 4. Community Activation: Test and Build (15 minutes)

Goal: Ensure ideas are actionable and involve stakeholders.

What You Do: Teams quickly brainstorm two ways to involve the community. Who needs to be involved (parents, teachers, students)? How can they help shape or support the innovation?

Share ideas with the group.

Outcome: Each team leaves with a concrete next step to engage their school community.

Step 5. Wrap-Up: Commitment Wall (10 minutes)

Goal: Create accountability and excitement for action.

What You Do: Each participant writes a bold innovation commitment on a sticky note or card:

"I will lead by..."

"I will test..."

Stick these commitments on a visible "Commitment Wall" as a reminder of their pledge.

Supporting AI Prompt

Here is a prompt you can use with ChatGPT to help you dig deeper into your school's dominant logic:

"I am a school leader exploring how the dominant logic in my organization may be blocking innovation. Please guide me through these one step at a time:

- Identify dominant logic (beliefs, practices, assumptions).

- Understanding its impact on decision-making, risk-taking and change.

- Recognizing barriers it creates for innovation.

- Developing strategies to challenge and reshape it for a more innovative culture.

Conduct a conversation with me. During the conversation, use a mix of diagnostic questions, thought experiments and actionable suggestions to help me drive meaningful change."

Reasons People Resist Change

Many organizations struggle not because they lack creativity but because their people do not work in an environment conducive to innovation. These environments are caused by:

- Mistrust and miscommunication
- Comfort of the status quo
- Lack of capability building

Failing to address these traps means that resistance and stagnation are guaranteed. Success depends on understanding and overcoming these barriers. Let's explore these traps and discover ways to break the cycle.

1. Mistrust and Miscommunication

Trust is fragile but essential. When people mistrust leadership, resistance thrives. Negative experiences with past initiatives linger in the memory. They assume this time will be no different. They wonder if decisions are made with hidden agendas or whether their interests are considered. Resistance becomes a defensive response to protect what they value.

Miscommunication fuels mistrust. When we fail to explain the reasons for change clearly, your colleagues fill the void with their own narratives. Vague timelines and inconsistent messaging create confusion. Uncertainty about how changes affect individual roles leads to fear and fear turns into disengagement.

Many organizations struggle not because they lack creativity but because their people do not work in an environment conducive to innovation.

Breaking the Cycle

Leaders must prioritize understanding their people's concerns. Workshops and discussions create safe spaces for open dialogue. These forums allow people to voice their fears without judgment. Resistance often stems from anxieties, such as losing job security, personal impact, or increased workload. Listening builds trust.

Clarity is non-negotiable. Leaders must explain the "why" behind the change. They must highlight the consequences of inaction and emphasize how the change benefits them and the organization. Avoid generic platitudes. They must share data, decision-making processes and detailed plans. Transparency and authenticity help rebuild trust.

Visible leadership plays a critical role. Senior leaders must show unwavering commitment to the change. Your people must see that you believe in the vision and are actively working toward it. Involvement from respected influencers within the organization adds credibility. When they help shape the change, they feel ownership and trust grows.

2. The Comfort of the Status Quo

The familiar feels safe. People resist change when it threatens their sense of competence, stability or identity. Routines and processes represent expertise and control. Change disrupts that comfort. They worry they will lose relevance or struggle to adapt. The status quo becomes a shield against uncertainty.

Resistance often hides emotional responses. Fear, frustration and even grief are common reactions to perceived loss. Organizations with rigid cultures amplify these emotions. When "the way things have always been done" becomes sacred, innovation becomes a threat.

Moving Beyond Familiarity

We must address these emotions directly. Empathy is critical. Acknowledge the challenges. Use change management models, such as the Kübler-Ross Change Curve[4] or Bridges' Transition Model[5], to guide them through the process. Validate their feelings and provide support to help them adapt.

Reframe innovation as evolution, not rejection. Connect new initiatives to past successes. Show people how their expertise remains valuable, even as it

---

4. The Kübler-Ross Change Curve describes the emotional journey individuals experience when faced with significant change, moving through stages like denial, anger and acceptance.
5. Bridges' Transition Model focuses on the internal psychological transition people undergo during change, emphasizing the stages of letting go, navigating the uncertain neutral zone and embracing new beginnings.

evolves. Involve them in shaping the change. Participation builds confidence and reduces fear.

Momentum matters. Celebrate early wins to build enthusiasm. Small victories will help your colleagues see tangible benefits and create a sense of progress. Set realistic timelines that balance urgency with adaptability. They need space to adjust without feeling rushed or overwhelmed.

Collaboration fosters shared ownership. Inclusivity builds community and reduces the perception of change as imposed from the top.

People resist change when it threatens their sense of competence, stability or identity.

---

3. Lack of Capability Building

Innovation requires more than enthusiasm. It demands skills, tools and resources, and many organizations falter here. People resist when they feel unprepared. A lack of training, unclear expectations and limited support leave them vulnerable. Resistance becomes a way to avoid failure.

Unrealistic timelines exacerbate the problem. When people don't have enough time to adapt, they disengage. Organizations often underestimate the learning curve and overestimate how quickly their people can adjust.

Preparing for Success

Capability building starts with preparation. Leaders must assess skill gaps and provide targeted training. Generic workshops won't suffice. Training should focus on the specific tools and processes that will be used. Comprehensive programs build confidence and competence.

Inclusivity builds community and reduces the perception of change as imposed from the top.

Flexibility is key. Timelines must accommodate learning and adaptation. Rigid deadlines create unnecessary stress and resentment. Leaders who build time for adjustments promote a culture where people feel supported, not pressured.

Visible progress matters. Celebrate small successes along the way. Early wins validate the process and show that the organization is moving in the right direction.

Support must be ongoing. Change doesn't end with implementation. People need mentorship, feedback loops and access to resources that help them sustain their growth. When people feel equipped and supported, resistance diminishes.

Success in innovation requires more than creative ideas. It demands a culture that nurtures trust, embraces progress and prepares its people. When we confront resistance with empathy, clarity and support, we create an environment where innovation thrives.

Finding the Time

Teaching feels relentless. The pace and pressure often make it hard to imagine adding anything new to your plate. You don't need to overhaul your day or make grand gestures to spark meaningful change. Big things start small. That's where 15% Solutions comes in from Liberating Structure developed by Henri Lipmanowicz and Keith McCandless.[6]

When we confront resistance with empathy, clarity and support, we create an environment where innovation thrives.

The Power of Small Actions

This simple idea asks you to focus on what's already within your control. Your 15% is the portion of your work where you can act without asking for permission,

---

6. Lipmanowicz, K. M. H. (n.d.). Liberating Structures - 7. 15% Solutions. https://www.liberatingstructures.com/7-15-solutions/

extra resources or authority. It's about taking small, deliberate steps that create momentum and open new possibilities. This shift changes everything. It helps you move away from feeling stuck and instead focus on the opportunities hiding in plain sight.

How It Works

Start by identifying what you can influence. Maybe it's how you structure a lesson or approach a colleague with an idea. Even small efforts can lead to surprising results. These changes don't require massive time investments. They require awareness and intention.

Use this framework to make progress:

- **Start With Reflection**
  Take a few minutes to think about your current challenges. Ask yourself, "What's one thing I can do now with the freedom I already have?"

- **Share and Build**
  Talk with others in the accelerator group. Share your ideas. Listen to theirs. This process isn't about judgment. It's about exploring and strengthening possibilities together.

- **Take One Step**
  Pick one action and commit to it. Do it today or this week. Success comes from movement, not perfection.

You don't need to overhaul your day or make grand gestures to spark meaningful change.

Why It Matters

Small actions ripple outward. When one person starts making small changes, others notice. This approach creates energy and builds confidence. It also encourages a culture where innovation feels natural. Groups become more focused on what they can do instead of getting stuck in what feels impossible.

Consider a teacher who decided to send a weekly email sharing one practical teaching tip with their department. This effort took only minutes each week but quickly became a source of inspiration and conversation for colleagues. Another teacher makes a small shift in how they run department meetings. They introduced a quick brainstorming segment for actionable ideas. This tiny adjustment changed the team's collaboration and brought fresh ideas into daily practice.

Make It Part of Your Routine

This isn't a one-time exercise. Build it into your regular habits. Start meetings by asking, "What's one thing you've done with your 15%?" Celebrate progress, no matter how small it seems. Use 15% Solutions to break through roadblocks when challenges arise. These small shifts create momentum and help teams discover their power to make change together.

Think about your own 15%. Where do you have the freedom to act? What's one thing you could do today that might spark something bigger? Begin with that one step. Great journeys don't start with massive leaps. They begin with a simple, intentional move in the right direction.

Supporting AI Prompt

"I am an educator looking to identify small amounts of time in my week to maximize my efforts of influencing my school to (explain your initiative)."

---

5 Questions for Infinite Minds

1. How can you move beyond transactional persuasion to cultivate relational influence that aligns deeply with your school's shared values and long-term vision?

2. In what ways are you challenging the dominant logic of your school to prepare students for a world that demands adaptability and how can you model the courage to embrace uncertainty and growth?

3. How are you actively fostering an environment where trust and dialogue enable your team to progress from skepticism to shared ownership of transformative change?

4. How are you empowering your team to navigate the tension between tradition and transformation? What bold, polarizing stance might you take to ignite meaningful dialogue and progress?

5. Reflecting on the power of small, deliberate actions, how are you modeling a mindset of agency and creativity within your leadership? How can you cultivate this same mindset in your staff?

Download the interactive Infinite Education Playbook to complete this task in the playbook and access more accompanying activities for you and your accelerator group.

TL;DR

- Leadership that relies on influence rather than authority fosters genuine collaboration, trust and a shared vision that can withstand challenges and inspire long-term change.

- Influence is built through relational depth, guiding others from resistance to alignment by addressing fears, fostering dialogue and creating shared goals.

- The ability to inspire trust comes from consistency, authenticity and transparency, allowing leaders to transform skepticism into commitment without forcing compliance.

- People are drawn to purpose when they see their contributions as meaningful, their growth as prioritized and their concerns as heard, making trust and shared motivation the foundation of effective leadership.

- Lasting innovation requires leaders to confront and dismantle entrenched assumptions, reframing resistance not as opposition but as an opportunity for deeper understanding and progress.

Chapter 16

STEP 4–ALIGN

"Building a visionary company requires 1% vision and 99% alignment."
—James C. Collins

Innovative leadership isn't about short-term sparks. It's about building something that lasts. Many leaders rely on influence to bring people together. Influence can inspire and energize, creating excitement for a moment. But influence alone is not enough. Without alignment, inspiration fades and momentum dies.

Alignment takes influence and makes it real. It ensures that every action serves the same purpose. It creates clarity and unity. People understand their role. They see how their efforts fit into a bigger picture. When alignment happens, everything flows and energy turns into progress.

Influence may light the fire, but alignment keeps it burning. It guides us toward shared goals, builds systems that work, and ensures every classroom, lesson and decision moves in the same direction. Without alignment, even the best ideas fall apart.

Without alignment, inspiration fades and momentum dies.

Leaders who focus on alignment build trust. They make it easier for others to succeed. Teachers feel supported. The staff knows their work matters. Students benefit from a system built for them. Alignment brings consistency and fairness. It ensures no one gets left behind.

Moving from influence to alignment is the difference between hope and results. Leaders who embrace this shift unlock the full potential of their schools. The strategies and activities in this chapter will help you move from influence to aligning your school with your strategy.

Moving from influence to alignment is the difference between hope and results.

The Importance of Communication

Shifting a team toward a new strategy is one of the hardest tasks for any leader. Change disrupts routines, stirs uncertainty and makes people question their place in the future. Without clear and intentional communication, even the most innovative strategy will fail. The team will feel lost, disconnected and unmotivated. Communication is the tool that bridges this gap. It transforms doubt into belief and resistance into alignment.

Teams can thrive when they understand the bigger picture. They want to know their role and how their work contributes to success. Communication makes this possible. It drives clarity, engagement and action. Without it, alignment becomes impossible.

Clarity Drives Action

Your people can't follow a strategy they don't understand. Without clarity, confusion spreads and momentum stalls. People need to know three things:

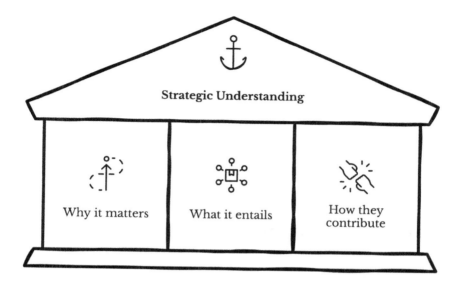

Crafting the message is essential. Focus on the most important points. Keep them simple and memorable. Aim for three to five key ideas that can be repeated without losing impact. These messages should address the reasons behind the strategy, its goals and how it solves problems or creates new opportunities. Even when you are tired of repeating these points, keep going because there will still be people who don't know them yet.

Plain language wins every time. Jargon alienates people and overly complex sentences confuse the message. Speak in ways that everyone can easily understand. Simple words have the power to move people when paired with clear intent.

For example: "Our school integrates comprehensive frameworks for ethical AI education, addressing algorithmic transparency, bias mitigation and compliance with emerging governance standards to empower responsible innovation."

The key ideas are:

- Ethical education through structured frameworks.
- Addressing challenges like transparency and bias.
- Aligning with regulations for responsible innovation.

The problem with this jargon-heavy message is that it can overwhelm people with technical terms and abstract concepts. It also focuses too much on methods, not on the real-world benefits or outcomes.

Instead of this, you could write something like: "We teach students to use AI responsibly so they can use these tools in a way that is fair, helpful and improves lives."

This works because it explains the strategy's purpose without using jargon. It also emphasizes the real-world benefits of aligning with this strategy.

Plain language wins every time. Jargon alienates people and overly complex sentences confuse the message.

Tailor Messages for Impact

Every team comprises different groups, each with its own concerns, priorities and ways of thinking. Your school will have diverse teams, from new teachers to office staff. A single message won't resonate with everyone. We need to tailor communication to meet the specific needs of each audience.

Executives focus on big-picture results. They want to know how the strategy aligns with organizational goals and delivers measurable outcomes. Managers need tools and information to lead their teams effectively. Frontline employees want to understand how their daily work will change and what support they'll receive. Parents, students or external stakeholders each require communication tailored to their priorities.

Understand your audience. Identify key groups within your organization. Speak their language. Address their concerns directly. Use examples that matter to them. When communication aligns with the audience, trust and engagement will follow.

When communicating to an executive team, alignment is crucial to the alignment of the rest of your colleagues and for ultimate success. In this circumstance, the message should be tailored to the individual. You need to know how to appeal to their priorities. For example, the person on your leadership team responsible for quality teaching and learning must be reassured that the innovation won't disrupt this. If one of them is responsible for managing building projects, they will need to know if your strategy will require physical changes to the school. In a tight budget situation, you may need to demonstrate to them how current spaces with minimal adjustments will support the strategy. Appealing to individuals is just as important to big overarching messages to the whole organization.

Understand your audience. Identify key groups within your organization. Speak their language. Address their concerns directly. Use examples that matter to them.

Actions Speak Louder Than Words

Teams don't just listen to what leaders say. They watch what they do. Words lose meaning when actions don't match. Leaders must embody the strategy through their behavior. This builds credibility and sets the tone for the rest of the team.

Face-to-face interactions make a difference. Walking the floor, hosting meetings or joining discussions shows commitment. These moments create trust and connection. Leaders who actively participate in the rollout of a strategy demonstrate its importance to the organization.

Updates should include more than just facts. Highlight progress and share stories of success. A teacher implementing a new tool or a team reaching a milestone reinforces the value of the strategy. These examples show the strategy in action and inspire others to follow suit.

Communication is Ongoing

One announcement won't align a team—repetition matters. People need time to absorb new ideas and they benefit from hearing them in different ways. Deliver messages consistently. Reinforce the strategy with updates, examples and reminders.

Use multiple channels to reach the whole team:

- Emails provide detailed information.
- Videos bring ideas to life.
- Intranets or internal apps ensure accessibility.
- Face-to-face meetings allow for dialogue and connection.

No single channel reaches everyone, so a mix is essential.

Time your communication thoughtfully. Align updates with key milestones or achievements. Celebrate wins. Acknowledging progress builds momentum and keeps people engaged. Consistent communication creates a rhythm that drives alignment forward.

Listening Builds Trust

Effective communication isn't a one-way street. Teams need to feel heard. Questions, concerns and feedback all play a role in aligning people. Leaders who ignore these voices risk losing their team's trust and commitment.

Create opportunities for feedback. Surveys, open forums and one-on-one discussions give people space to share their thoughts. Listen actively. Pay attention to both verbal and nonverbal cues. Summarize what you've heard to show understanding. Act on feedback to prove you value it.

More localized leaders will play a vital role here. Managers and team leads can facilitate conversations that uncover insights missed at higher levels. Equip them with tools to guide discussions and empower them to address concerns. When people feel heard, they are more likely to engage with the strategy.

Measure and Adjust

Communication isn't static. Strategies evolve and so do the team's needs. Measuring the effectiveness of your communication helps ensure it stays relevant and impactful. Success isn't about how much you communicate but the results it drives.

> **When people feel heard, they are more likely to engage with the strategy.**

Set clear metrics. Engagement rates, understanding of the strategy and behavioral alignment all provide valuable insights. Surveys and pulse reports can gauge how well messages resonate. Participation in training or feedback sessions shows how engaged people are.

Track progress. If engagement drops, refine your approach. If confusion lingers, clarify your message. Adjust communication to fit the needs of your team. Iteration ensures the strategy remains alive and aligned with organizational goals.

An Exercise for Your Accelerator Group

Here's a 1.5–2-hour activity you can do with the accelerator group to begin honing in on key messages.

Step 1: Experience
Activity: Rapid Brainstorm

Prompt: "Imagine a big change initiative where communication was a success. What did the leader say or do to make it work?"

Share insights in pairs, then have a group discussion.

Step 2: Understand Your Audience
Activity: Empathy Mapping

The group is split into small groups, each focusing on a specific audience (e.g., teachers, parents, or administrators). What excites them? What worries them? What do they want to hear?

Afterwards share and spot patterns as a big group.

Step 3: Craft Your Message
Activity: Message Sprint

Template: "We're introducing (change) to help (audience's need). This means (specific action) so we can achieve (benefit)."

Add an emotional hook or story for extra impact.

Do this in small groups.

Step 4: Test Your Message
Activity: Pitch and Feedback

Deliver your message to the larger group acting as your audience.

Structured feedback:
- What worked?
- What's unclear?
- How did it resonate?

Step 5: Wrap-Up: Commit to Action
Activity: Action Plan

Write down:
- Your audience.
- Your refined message.
- How and when you deliver it.
- How you'll gather feedback.

This can be a high-energy session with rapid feedback and interaction. It is action-oriented, so your accelerator group will leave with clear next steps.

Supporting AI Prompts

"We are honing strategic messages for a big change initiative. Act as a guide that will help us better understand our audience. We've identified different groups: (name the groups). We need to empathize with their needs. Help us by answering these questions to prompt deeper thinking:

- What might excite this group about the change?
- What might worry them?

- What do they need to hear to feel engaged and supported?

Once we share our ideas, help us spot patterns or gaps in our understanding and suggest how to address them in our messaging. Keep your guidance open-ended and empowering."

"We're crafting key messages for a change initiative using this template: 'We're introducing (change) to help (audience's need). This means (specific action) to achieve (benefit).' Help us refine our messaging by asking insightful questions like:

- Is the message clear and simple enough for the audience to immediately understand?
- Does it address the audience's biggest needs or concerns?
- Does it convey an emotional hook or story to make it memorable?

After sharing a draft, provide constructive feedback on clarity, resonance and impact. Suggest ways to improve the tone, specificity, or emotional connection without overhauling our work. Keep us in the driver's seat!"

Every school is a living system, full of cycles that mirror nature's rhythms.

Creative Destruction

The seeds of innovation have already been planted. Using Govindarjan's Three Boxes from chapter 11, you have pointed towards Box 3. Some skeptics have softened because of your influence and the influence of your accelerator group. The enthusiastic few have grown, shifting the culture toward the possibility of a shift towards Box 3 from Box 1. The question now isn't whether the strategy is worth pursuing; it's how to align the school's resources, energy and practices to make it a reality. How to create an aligned movement towards Box 3. This is where the Ecocycle Method, adapted from Lipmanowicz and McCandless's Liberating Structures, reveals its power.[1]

Schools as Living Systems

Every school is a living system, full of cycles that mirror nature's rhythms. Forests thrive not because they cling to their past but because they renew themselves. Old growth gives way to new life, dead wood returns nutrients to the soil and the ecosystem evolves. All organizations should follow this cycle. Complications happen when they don't.

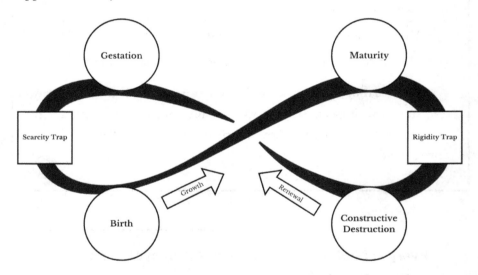

The Ecocycle frames this process in four distinct phases:

1. Creative Destruction

Activities that have lost their relevance or vitality reside here. They drain energy and resources that could be better spent elsewhere.

2. Gestation

This is the space of untapped potential. Ideas waiting for exploration and investment linger here, ready to transform into something meaningful.

1. Lipmanowicz, K. M. H. (n.d.-b). Liberating Structures - 31. Ecocycle Planning. https://www.liberating-structures.com/31-ecocycle-planning/

3. Birth

New initiatives emerge here. They are fragile and require nurturing. These represent the future.

4. Maturity

Practices in this phase are stable and reliable. They provide consistent value and are a school's foundation.

By mapping current activities, you and your accelerator group can identify where energy is well spent, wasted and still needs to be applied. The Ecocycle invites not just analysis but action.

The Seduction of Maturity

Maturity feels like the promised land. Established practices offer a sense of security. Routines work. Results are predictable. Yet, without vigilance, maturity can turn into stagnation. Practices that once inspired growth become barriers to it. Innovation struggles to take root when energy is locked in maintaining the status quo. This is the rigidity trap and it's where many of the education systems worldwide currently are.

At this stage, you face a pivotal challenge: deciding what to keep and what to let go. It is a deceptively simple decision but one that requires wisdom and collective will. The act of letting go is the creative destruction stage of the Ecocycle. It isn't about abandoning the past. It is about honoring what was useful and recognizing when it has run its course.

The Emotional Weight of Letting Go

Letting go is never just a practical matter. People are attached to practices that represent years of effort and identity. A teacher may see a long-standing program as a cornerstone of their work. A principal may feel pride in a strategy they once championed. Asking whether these practices still serve the school's vision can feel like questioning someone's value.

Schools risk clinging to practices that no longer align with their purpose without these conversations. For example, if part of your purpose is for your students to achieve their potential, then letting go of grade-level segregation might be essential. Leaders must create an environment where honesty is possible, not through critique but through curiosity. Why does this practice matter? What was its original purpose? Does it still serve that purpose? These questions honor the past while opening the door to the future.

Harnessing Collective Insight

The Ecocycle is not a solitary exercise. Its power lies in its ability to bring people together, each voice contributing to a shared understanding of where the school stands. Begin by inviting reflection. Ask teachers, administrators and other stakeholders to map their work. What consumes their time and energy? What feels essential? What feels burdensome?

Once individual reflections are gathered, bring people together to discuss their insights. Patterns will emerge. Some practices will shine as examples of stability and value. Others will reveal themselves as relics, well-intentioned but no longer effective. Still, others will spark excitement, representing possibilities waiting to be explored.

Use a visual map to represent these findings. Post-it notes on a large wall or digital tools for remote teams work equally well. Place each activity in one of the four Ecocycle phases, building a picture of the school's ecosystem. This process is not just about analysis. It is a catalyst for alignment. People see where their efforts connect, where duplication exists and where gaps are holding the school back.

The purpose is to ensure all your people and their tasks are identified on the Ecocycle. This will allow you to help them through the cycle, which is dynamic and continually flowing and will lead your people in alignment with your strategy.

Escaping Common Traps

We often find ourselves stuck in one of two traps. The first is the rigidity trap, where too much energy is spent preserving practices. The second is the poverty trap, where too many new initiatives spread resources too thin. The Ecocycle helps avoid these pitfalls by balancing efforts across all phases. This is a balanced view of alignment that slowly moves people to innovation.

> *Letting go is never just a practical matter. People are attached to practices that represent years of effort and identity.*

Leadership for Every Phase

The success of the Ecocycle depends on leaders who adapt their style to the needs of each phase. Every part of the cycle requires a different kind of courage from leaders:

1. The Heretic for Creative Destruction

Leaders in this phase must question the status quo, even when uncomfortable. They must create space for others to challenge outdated practices and offer alternatives. This type of leadership is essential now! This is a book for heretics.

2. The Networker for Gestation

Gestation relies on connectors. Leaders must bring people together, sparking collaboration and exploration. They must build networks and seek fresh ideas, laying the groundwork for future initiatives.

3. The Entrepreneur for Birth

Birth demands visionary leadership. Leaders must champion new ideas, take risks and encourage experimentation. They must also protect fragile initiatives and give them the time and resources they need to grow.

4. The Manager for Maturity

Maturity thrives on steady stewardship. Leaders must refine and optimize established practices, ensuring they deliver value without becoming rigid. Incremental improvement is key here.

A single leader can rarely act in all four of these roles. This is why school leadership must be diverse. Move away from a team of managers; otherwise, it will be impossible to get past the rigidity trap. The accelerator group is a perfect environment to raise up leaders who can be heretics and entrepreneurs. By embracing these roles, leaders ensure that every phase of the Ecocycle is productive and aligned with the school's vision.

Renewal Through Action

Renewal doesn't happen by chance. Schools must actively create space for new ideas to flourish. Pilot programs are an excellent way to test possibilities without overcommitting. Provide teachers and teams with the freedom to experiment. This begins with your accelerator group and must continually flow out from the group to the rest of the school. Support them with resources, encouragement and a willingness to learn from failure.

At the same time, be deliberate about letting go. Acknowledge the emotions involved but remain clear about the school's goals. Celebrate what has worked, then move forward with purpose. Each act of letting go creates the energy needed for something new to thrive.

A Culture That Thrives on Alignment

The Ecocycle is an essential planning tool for alignment, but it must also become our mindset. It teaches us to see alignment as a continuous journey rather than a one-time event. When we embrace this process, we become places where innovation is not a buzzword but a way of life.

By revisiting the Ecocycle regularly, schools ensure that their work remains focused and adaptive. Schedule periodic mapping sessions to reflect on progress. Use these moments to celebrate successes, learn from challenges and adjust strategies. Treat each cycle as an opportunity to grow stronger.

The power of the Ecocycle lies in its simplicity and depth. It provides a clear process for aligning strategy and action but also transforms how schools think about change. By embracing the natural rhythms of growth, destruction and renewal, schools become more than organizations. They become living systems capable of thriving in any environment.

Bring your team together. Reflect on where you are and where you want to go. Use the Ecocycle to guide your journey. Let it help you honor the past, navigate the present and create a future full of possibility. Together, you can transform your school into a place where alignment fuels innovation and every student and educator thrives.

An Exercise for Your Accelerator Group

This activity sets the stage for aligning the school's energy and resources to support your strategy. It helps you identify what to let go of, nurture and grow to create a unified push toward the future.

Step 1: Set the Vision

Begin with a brief overview of the strategy and its significance.

Frame the activity as a first step in aligning the school's current efforts with its vision for transformative change.

Step 2: Reflection

On sticky notes or a shared digital tool, ask participants to write down:

- What practices feel outdated or burdensome?

- What current initiatives excite them and align with the innovative strategy?

- What ideas remain unexplored but have potential?

Step 3: Create the Renewal Map

Draw the Ecocycle on a large poster or digital board with four sections:

- Creative Destruction: What should we let go of?

- Gestation: What untapped ideas align with our strategy?

- Birth: What new initiatives need nurturing to grow?

- Maturity: What established practices support the innovative vision?

Place each sticky note in the appropriate section as a group.

Step 4: Discuss Key Areas

Focus on:

- What to Stop: Practices that drain resources without aligning with the vision.

- What to Nurture: New ideas that need support to advance the strategy.

- What to Refine: Mature practices that still contribute value.

This can be done on sticky notes where participants complete the statement "Can we…". They then vote on the most compelling statement using sticky dots.

Step 5: Choose One Action
Using the results from the vote. Agree on one small "We will…" statement for each:

- Let go of one outdated practice.

- Invest in a promising idea.

- Support a fragile new initiative.

Outcome
This activity begins by developing a shared understanding of how current practices align with the innovative strategy. It is a practical first step toward creating momentum toward transformative change. This activity connects the school's present efforts to its bold future vision, ensuring every action contributes to the strategic shift.

Supporting AI Prompts

Prompt 1:

"I am preparing for an Ecocycle mapping activity. We want to evaluate practices across the phases of Creative Destruction, Gestation, Birth and Maturity to align with our innovative strategy. Can you help me design reflective questions, discussion prompts and a facilitation plan that encourages honest, constructive participation?"

Prompt 2:

"Our school needs leaders to embody the roles of the Heretic, Networker, Entrepreneur and Manager, as described in the Ecocycle method. Can you help me develop:

- Clear role descriptions for each phase.

- Practical strategies to identify and empower staff who can naturally step into these roles.

- Ways to provide training or mentoring to build capacity in these leadership roles while fostering diversity within our leadership team?"

Prompt 3:

"We aim to use the Ecocycle method to balance our resources across all phases and avoid the rigidity and poverty traps. Can you assist in:

- Creating an actionable checklist for ongoing review of our Ecocycle map to maintain alignment and balance.

- Developing strategies to shift resources from outdated practices to emerging initiatives without creating resistance.

- Crafting language for communication with staff that celebrates past successes while emphasizing the need for transformation and renewal."

We can align people across every school level: educators, departments, leadership teams and even the community. This ensures that innovation becomes a shared journey instead of a fragmented effort.

Three Dimensional Alignment

We have explored how the Ecocycle helps you and your team map your current activities. It is a powerful tool for creating alignment within a group or department. But here is the challenge. Schools are not single systems. They are layers of systems, with each one influencing and being influenced by the others. A single Ecocycle can only take us so far.

We need to see the bigger picture to align an entire school on its innovative strategy. We need to go three-dimensional. This is what Liberating Structures calls Panarchy.[2] It is about understanding how the many ecosystems within a school connect, overlap and impact one another. Using Panarchy, we can align people across every school level: educators, departments, leadership teams and even the community. This ensures that innovation becomes a shared journey instead of a fragmented effort.

Schools as Nested Systems

Think of your school as a forest. On the ground, you see individual plants growing. Some are thriving, others are struggling and some are brand-new shoots just beginning to emerge. Now lift your gaze to the trees. These are your departments and teams. They give the forest structure and shape. Finally, look higher at the canopy. This is the whole ecosystem. Larger forces like national policies, district policies and community expectations shape the school.

2. Lipmanowicz, K. M. H. (n.d.-c). Liberating Structures - 32. Panarchy. https://www.liberatingstructures.com/32-panarchy/

Everything is connected. The plants on the ground influence the health of the trees above them, just as the trees provide shade and nutrients for the plants below. The forest thrives or falters based on how well its layers work together.

Your school works the same way. Think about it:

A teacher tries a new artificial intelligence platform with their students. It might spark interest across their grade level or department if it works.

A department launches a new interdisciplinary project. It could inspire the whole school to reimagine its curriculum if it gains traction.

A district shifts funding priorities and suddenly, the resources that made classroom innovation possible are gone.

Panarchy helps us see these interactions clearly. It is a tool for understanding how alignment at one level can ripple across the others.

Taking the 3D View

So, how do we use Panarchy in a school? We start by mapping the nested systems. This is not complicated, but it does require you to pause and take stock of what is happening at every level.

You can think of this as zooming in and out:

You look at individual classrooms, teachers and students at the micro-level. Your influence efforts will have supported people in the beginning to innovate. What is happening that supports your strategy? What practices are working? What feels stuck?

At the meso level, you are looking at teams and departments. What programs or initiatives are emerging? Where is collaboration thriving and where is it hitting roadblocks?

You are looking at the whole school and beyond at the macro level. What are the big priorities? How are policies, funding and community expectations shaping what is possible?

As you map these layers, patterns will start to emerge. You might notice that a promising idea at the classroom level is being slowed down by outdated policies at the school level. Or you might find that a successful program at the department level is not getting the recognition or resources it needs to grow.

Aligning Through the Ecocycle

Once you have mapped your systems, the next step is to apply the Ecocycle to each one. This is where Panarchy becomes actionable.

Take a moment to revisit the Ecocycle framework:

- Creative Destruction: What needs to be let go?

- Gestation: What ideas are waiting for exploration or investment?

- Birth: What new initiatives need nurturing?

- Maturity: What practices are thriving but might risk stagnation?

You and your colleagues can ask these questions at each school level. Use sticky notes, whiteboards, or digital tools to map the answers. Place each activity in its appropriate phase.

Now is the fun part. Look across the levels. Ask yourself:

- How are the Ecocycles at different levels interacting?

- Where are opportunities for a small change at the micro-level to spark something bigger above?

- Where could stability and resources from the macro-level support growth below?

This is where Panarchy shines. It lets you see how the energy of the whole school flows and where alignment is needed.

Revolt and Remember

Panarchy is driven by two powerful dynamics: Revolt and Remember.

Revolt happens when small-scale innovations disrupt larger systems. Think about a teacher piloting a project-based learning approach. When it works, it spreads to their department and the whole school eventually adopts it. That is the power of Revolt.

Remember, it is the opposite. It is the stabilizing force that larger systems provide to smaller ones. When a school invests in professional development to support a new teaching method, it is Remember in action. Without it, innovations fizzle out.[3]

You need both. Revolt without Remember creates chaos. Remember without Revolt creates stagnation. Panarchy helps you balance these forces so that your school can naturally align with your strategy from the bottom up and from the top down.

Revolt happens when small-scale innovations disrupt larger systems.

Let's bring this to life with an example.

A middle school decides to focus on using artificial intelligence to personalize learning.

---

3. Resilience Alliance - Panarchy. (n.d.). https://www.resalliance.org/panarchy

At the micro-level, individual teachers are experimenting with AI-powered learning platforms that allow them to train a simple student-facing chatbot on their curriculum. Some are seeing great results, while others are unsure how to make it work.

At the meso level, department teams are sharing strategies for how to prompt these chatbots for optimal performance. They are creating templates for teachers and investigating new platforms that further their efforts in personalized learning.

At the macro level, the leadership team sees the value in this and partners with an AI company to make a bespoke school chatbot for students that can handle student data in a safe way. They allocate funds for training and make it a key part of their vision for the school.

By using Panarchy, the school aligns these efforts. Teachers feel supported because they know their work fits into a larger strategy. Teams share what is working, accelerating progress for everyone. The leadership team sees tangible results, which strengthens their commitment.

It looks like this when a school's energy aligns and flows in the same direction.

What About You?

As you read this, you might already be picturing the layers of your school. Start small. Map one layer of your school. Apply the Ecocycle and see where the energy is flowing. Then zoom out and ask how that layer connects to the ones above and below it.

This process is not about perfection. It is about seeing clearly and acting intentionally. Every time you revisit your Panarchy map, you will uncover new opportunities and insights.

Panarchy is more than a tool. It is a mindset. It teaches us to see schools as living systems full of potential and interconnection. It reminds us that change does not happen in isolation. It happens when we align our energy across all the levels of our work.

So, let's embrace the 3D view. Let's map our systems, align our efforts and create schools where innovation flows freely. Together, we can build ecosystems that are not just functional but thriving—where students, teachers and communities grow stronger daily.

An Exercise for Your Accelerator Group

This activity for your accelerator group aims to identify small innovations that can inspire broader change (Revolt) and pinpoint existing supports or structures that can stabilize and amplify these changes (Remember).

Step 1: Identify Small Innovations

Participants write down one or two small changes, experiments or new ideas they have seen or tried that could inspire broader change.

Write each on a sticky note.

Step 2: Identify Supports

On separate sticky notes, participants write one or two structures, policies or resources that help stabilize or spread innovation, for example: funding, training programs and leadership support.

Step 3: Connect and Discuss

Group the sticky notes into Revolt (innovations) and Remember (supports).

Discuss as a group:

- Which innovations could scale or succeed with more support?
- Which existing structures need to adapt to better support innovation?

Step 4: Choose Actions

As a group, pick one Revolt idea and one Remember opportunity to focus on.

Decide on one clear next step to either amplify the innovation or strengthen the support.

Participants will uncover how small innovations can drive larger change, identify specific supports that stabilize and scale innovations and leave with a clear next step to align and act on insights.

The Fuel That Empowers Alignment

The Panarchy framework sets pathways to align and direct your colleagues. These models clarify the stages of transformation but we need something else—the fuel to move us along these paths. The power to propel change lies in the interplay of ability, capability and competencies. Together, these forces will help your school to align with your strategy and transition through the Ecocycle with purpose.

Success in this framework hinges on cultivating the abilities, capabilities and competencies that effectively empower the school to function across all three boxes.

Movement through these cycles requires more than just talent or resources. It demands a schoolwide effort to manage the present, let go of the past and build the future simultaneously. The Three-Box Solution captures this delicate balance. Success in this framework hinges on cultivating the abilities, capabilities and competencies that effectively empower the school to function across all three boxes.

The Foundation: Ability, Capability and Competencies

Ability fuels execution. It resides within individuals—their skills, expertise and capacity to perform their roles. Everyone across your organization will possess ability in their area. These abilities sustain Box 1, your day-to-day performance engine. This ensures the school can meet current demands.

But ability alone is not enough. Even the most skilled educators struggle to affect the broader organization without the systems to align and scale these talents. It is capability that turns individual effort into collective strength. Capability refers to your school's ability to organize and deploy resources to effectively achieve its goals. It's not just about having skilled individuals but about the processes, structures and culture that allow the school to utilize these skills to act as a cohesive, high-functioning whole. For example, if a school has a lot of teachers who can use artificial intelligence in their classrooms effectively, then the school will likely be capable of providing whole school development sessions on how to use artificial intelligence in the classroom. When a school has strong capabilities, it can navigate the complexities of the ecocycle, coordinating growth and renewal while maintaining stability in the present.

At the intersection of ability and capability lies competency. Competencies represent the school's enduring strengths. They are the unique attributes that set a school apart and anchor its identity. Competencies are not fleeting skills or isolated successes but deeply integrated strengths that sustain value and guide strategic decisions. For schools navigating the Three-Box Solution, competencies ensure that future-focused efforts (Box 3) build on the foundation of what the school does exceptionally well. For example, a high school where students learn through multi-disciplinary projects rather than isolated classes, or an elementary school that ensures students primarily learn through play.

Why Competencies Matter

Competencies provide schools with more than an edge–they create clarity and focus in a landscape of uncertainty. In the business world, Honda's expertise in small engines and Apple's mastery of user-centric design exemplify how organizations leverage competencies to create value.

Competencies matter in schools because they:

- **Create Value for Students and Stakeholders**
  Families might not see the processes behind effective pedagogy, but they experience its results in student success, engagement and well-being.

- **Offer Sustainable Advantage**
  Competencies that are difficult to replicate protect the school's relevance and leadership position over time. For example, a deeply ingrained culture of equity or innovation becomes a hallmark no other school can easily imitate.

- **Support Growth Across Innovations**
  Strong competencies can be applied to new opportunities. A school that excels at its relationships with the local community can utilize this competency for a new strategy by bringing the community with it and getting the support it needs.

- **Focus Innovation**
  Understanding competencies helps schools evaluate ideas. Initiatives that align with existing strengths are more likely to succeed, while misaligned projects risk wasting resources and momentum.

Competencies provide schools with more than an edge–they create clarity and focus in a landscape of uncertainty.

Building Ability, Capability and Competencies

Abilities grow through targeted development. Professional learning programs that align with the school's strategic goals are essential. Mentorship and peer collaboration accelerate knowledge transfer while cross-training equips staff to contribute in multiple areas.

Capabilities develop through investment in systems and processes. We must create structures that support alignment and execution. Time for professional collaboration, effective data systems and clear decision-making protocols enhance capability. Culture plays a critical role. A culture of trust and collaboration ensures that systems work as intended and that staff feel empowered to innovate.

Competencies require focus and intentionality. Schools should leverage existing strengths as the foundation for growth. Experimentation uncovers new competencies. Small-scale pilots in areas like technology integration or interdisciplinary teaching allow schools to test and refine practices before scaling them across the organization. Embedding competencies into the school's identity ensures they remain a guiding force for future decisions.

Competencies provide schools with more than an edge—they create clarity and focus in a landscape of uncertainty.

Driving Innovation Through Capability

The Three-Box Solution highlights the importance of balancing the present, past and future. Building capability is essential for managing this balance. We must allow our accelerator group to focus on Box 3 innovation without being constrained by Box 1 demands. These teams bring fresh perspectives and experiment with new ideas, creating a safe space for failure and growth.

Further to developing the ability of our colleagues, we can also develop our capability by:

1. Recruiting New Talent

This injects energy and expertise into the organization. Outsiders often challenge conventional thinking and bring skills that align with future-focused goals.

2. Making Strategic Partnerships

Expand capability by providing access to resources the school lacks. Collaboration with community organizations, universities or tech companies accelerates learning and growth. Planned opportunism is when we prepare for future possibilities by building flexible skills and systems. This will position your school to seize opportunities as they arise.

Measuring and Adjusting for Continuous Progress

Alignment will stay on track only if we measure our progress continuously. Tracking individual growth, organizational performance and competency impact provides the data needed to refine efforts.

Feedback loops are critical. Listening to your teachers, students and families ensures the school stays attuned to its community's needs. Regular assessments of systems and processes highlight where alignment is working and where adjustments are needed. Flexibility allows schools to adapt without losing sight of their goals.

Recognizing milestones reinforces progress. Celebrating achievements motivates staff and builds confidence in the strategy. Schools that measure and adjust regularly create the resilience to navigate uncertainty and maintain momentum.

Feedback loops are critical. Listening to your teachers, students and families ensures the school stays attuned to its community's needs.

Empowered Alignment in Action

Empowered alignment integrates ability, capability and competencies into every stage of the school's transformation. Ability provides the skill to execute. Capability creates the systems to sustain collective action. Competencies anchor the school's efforts, ensuring innovation aligns with its unique strengths.

We move through these cycles with clarity and purpose when we harness our full potential. Alignment becomes more than a strategy. It is the road on which we are driving the school toward its most ambitious goals.

An Exercise for Your Accelerator Group

This activity used the Design Sprint Lightning Decision Jam activity. Let's use it to problem-solve how a school might develop the capability of implementing AI-driven personalized assessments for students.

Step 1: Highlight Positives
Participants write down what is already working well in the school's assessment practices (e.g., "teachers understand individual student needs," "we already use digital tools in classrooms").

Share positives with the group to build momentum.

Step 2: Identify Challenges
Individually, participants note down challenges specific to using AI for assessments (e.g., "teachers lack AI training," "data privacy concerns," "limited AI tools integrated with curriculum").

Cluster similar challenges on a board.

Step 3: Vote on Challenges
Participants get 3–5 dot stickers to vote on the most critical challenges.

Step 4: Prioritize Challenges
Rank the top-voted challenges to focus on the most pressing one (e.g., "teachers lack AI training").

Step 5: Generate Solutions
For the top challenge, participants brainstorm potential solutions individually and write them on sticky notes (e.g., "conduct AI training workshops," "partner with ed-tech companies," "pilot AI tools in one grade").

Step 6: Vote on Solutions
Participants vote on the most promising solutions using dot stickers.

Step 7: Prioritize Solutions

Map the solutions on an Impact vs. Effort Matrix to identify high-impact, low-effort ideas to pursue first.

Step 8: Create Action Items

For the top solution(s), define specific action steps.

Example:

- Action: Schedule AI training sessions for teachers.
- Responsible: Professional Development Team.
- Timeline: First session by next month.

Assign roles and timelines for implementation.

You should leave the session with a prioritized, actionable plan for beginning to implement AI-driven personalized assessments.

Supporting AI Prompts

Prompt 1:

"What specific training or collaborative activities can I implement to ensure teachers gain the skills needed to support our innovative strategy and how can I make this development accessible and aligned with daily responsibilities? This is our strategy: (Copy and paste or summarize your strategy)"

Prompt 2:

"What practical systems or processes can I put in place to enhance collaboration between staff, ensuring their abilities combine to build the collective capability needed for our innovative strategy? This is our strategy: (Copy and paste or summarize your strategy)"

Culture Built on Strategy

Leaders eager to create change often cling to the belief of starting with culture. We can define organizational culture as the collective values, beliefs, norms, behaviors and practices that characterize a particular workplace or company.[4]

The appeal is understandable. Surely, if you get this right, the strategy you build on top will progress easily. The issue is that without a guiding framework, it risks becoming a collection of habits, rituals and sentiments disconnected from purpose. A culture untethered from strategy cannot drive meaningful progress. It might create a pleasant environment but cannot sustain change or push an organization forward. Leaders who start with culture can find themselves lost when initial enthusiasm fades, unsure why the results don't match the energy.

This misstep happens because culture and strategy are often misunderstood as competing forces. The truth is more nuanced. Culture does not exist apart from strategy. It grows from it, aligns with it and takes shape from a well-defined vision. Culture without strategy is like a river without a source. It may flow for a time, but eventually, it dries up.

A culture untethered from strategy cannot drive meaningful progress. It might create a pleasant environment but cannot sustain change or push an organization forward.

Strategy as the Foundation

Every meaningful transformation begins with strategy. It defines purpose, sets priorities and provides a long-term vision. Strategy is not about following rigid plans or micromanaging every detail. It is about answering the fundamental questions: Why do we exist? What do we aim to achieve? How do we remain relevant and impactful over time?

---

4. He, G. (2023, December 10). Organizational Culture: Definition, Examples, & Best Practices. team-building.com. https://teambuilding.com/blog/organizational-culture?

When Satya Nadella became CEO of Microsoft in 2014, the company declined and faced much criticism over its lack of innovation. Nadella introduced a strategic vision emphasizing cloud computing and cross-platform services. This strategy necessitated a cultural shift towards collaboration, learning and customer-centricity. By starting with strategy, Microsoft revitalized its culture and, therefore, its innovation capabilities, leading to significant growth and a resurgence in market relevance.

In a strategic move in early 2024, Walmart shut down its innovation lab called Store No. 8. The purpose was to align innovation efforts more closely with all its people and ensure everyone was part of its innovation effort. This move fosters a culture where innovation is a shared responsibility across the organization. By integrating innovation into its core strategy, Walmart encouraged a new culture towards continuous improvement and responsiveness to market changes. Culture emanated from strategy.

Strategy lays the groundwork for everything else. Schools, like any complex organization, face various challenges and opportunities. Without a clear strategy, these elements overwhelm the system. Decisions become reactive rather than proactive. Efforts scatter in multiple directions without cohesion. The result is an organization that works hard but achieves little.

Culture Built on Strategy

Culture gains its strength and resilience from strategy. When tied to a clear vision and supported by aligned systems, culture becomes more than a set of values or behaviors. It becomes a living expression of the organization's purpose. It inspires and sustains progress, creating an environment where people feel motivated and empowered.

Your accelerator group model demonstrates how culture emerges from strategic alignment. This group operates as a microcosm of the organization's future. It fosters innovation, challenges norms and drives change. Its culture is not an accident. It reflects the school's strategic goals, both as a catalyst and a proving ground for new ideas.

This relationship between strategy and culture is symbiotic. Strategy provides the vision. Alignment creates the conditions for movement. Culture grows naturally from these elements, reinforcing and amplifying their effects. The result is an organization where values and actions align, creating a powerful and cohesive force.

Schools seeking lasting change must start with strategy. This does not mean ignoring culture. It means recognizing that culture is a product, not a starting point. It grows from the foundation of a well-defined strategy and the alignment framework.

A school that begins with strategy creates a roadmap for success. It defines its vision, aligns its efforts and fosters a culture that supports its goals. Teachers understand how their work contributes to student outcomes. Staff see how their roles fit into the larger picture. Students benefit from systems designed with their needs in mind.

This approach is not easy. It requires discipline, clarity and a willingness to challenge assumptions. Yet the rewards are worth it. A culture rooted in strategy does more than inspire. It delivers results. It transforms the organization into a force capable of leading change, not just reacting to it.

Culture gains its strength and resilience from strategy.

---

5 Questions for Infinite Minds

1. Do your team's daily actions align with your school's vision? What steps will you take to ensure everyone knows their role in achieving shared goals?

2. Are your messages about new strategies clear and easy to understand? How will you inspire people to act on them with confidence?

3. What outdated practices hold your school back? How will you let go of these in a way that respects the past while moving forward?

4. Do you notice small innovations that could lead to bigger changes? How will you support these ideas and help them grow across the school?

5. Does your school's culture help you reach your goals? What changes will you make to ensure it drives progress and inspires success?

Download the interactive Infinite Education Playbook to complete this task in the playbook and access more accompanying activities for you and your accelerator group.

TL;DR

- Alignment sustains innovation by connecting systems, actions and people to a shared purpose. It builds trust, empowers teachers and creates environments where students thrive. Influence ignites enthusiasm, but alignment drives lasting progress.

- Communication clarifies strategy and connects stakeholders to it. Simple and targeted messaging resonates with diverse groups. Leaders who act on their words build trust and foster commitment, keeping alignment strong.

- Schools thrive when they balance growth with renewal. The Ecocycle framework reveals what to let go of, what to nurture and what to refine. Leaders who guide these transitions ensure meaningful progress while respecting past efforts.

- Systems in schools work together at every level. Panarchy maps how classrooms, departments and leadership influence one another. Small changes grow into broader transformations when innovation aligns with supportive structures.

- Strategy drives meaningful culture. Clear purpose shapes systems and guides values. Schools with aligned strategies evolve into resilient communities capable of bold and lasting change.

Chapter 17

WHAT NEXT? THE NINE-STEP CENTER OF EXCELLENCE

The challenge set out in this book is by no means easy. It may well be the most difficult thing you have ever done. I have been there. I have had many failures and some successes. You may be shouting at me as you look at this page, "Can it actually be done?" Can we change education for the better? I know we can because I have witnessed it and worked at it with schools leading the way.

Maybe the question should not be "Can it be done?" but "How can it not be done?" The system needs to change. It is long overdue. Government policy will play a big part in this, but more importantly, we need individual schools to show how it can be done despite the system. Those early movers will find it most difficult. Hopefully, your impact as an early mover will show more educators that it can be done and will give them the courage to follow.

Leading innovation in your school could potentially be the most rewarding thing you ever do. But to do this and not share it would be a crime. So, I want to dedicate this conclusion to exploring how you and your accelerator group can use your learning, failures and progress to be a beacon to others—a Center of Excellence.

Your Center of Excellence

Building a Center of Excellence while actively innovating within your school is a dynamic and challenging undertaking, but it can yield significant benefits for the broader educational landscape.

To achieve this balance effectively, you need a deliberate strategy that integrates learning from your innovation journey with efforts to document, refine and share practices. Here's how your school can simultaneously innovate and prepare to support others through a Center of Excellence:

1. Build the Center of Excellence in parallel with your innovation.
2. Treat the innovation journey as a living lab.
3. Build a knowledge repository.
4. Establish collaborative partnerships.
5. Develop a communication and outreach strategy.
6. Focus on leadership development.
7. Plan for sustainability.
8. Align innovation efforts with the needs of other schools.
9. Evaluate progress and adjust as needed.

Let's dive in.

1. Build the Center of Excellence in Parallel with Your Innovation

Your Center of Excellence should evolve alongside your school's innovation journey. This parallel approach allows you to create a structure for capturing and refining your experiences in real time. Here are some strategies that will help:

- **Taskforce**
  While your accelerator group focuses on implementing and refining innovations, carefully assign two or three of them to observe, document and synthesize these efforts. This task force will be the foundation of your future Center of Excellence.

- **Feedback Loop**

  As you innovate, you and your task force can regularly create processes to capture insights, successes and failures. Use reflective journals, data analysis and staff debriefings to identify key takeaways that can inform your Center of Excellence.

- **Scalability**

  Test innovative ideas within your school while considering how they could be adapted for other schools. Document the conditions, resources and support required for success.

2. Treat the Innovation Journey as a Living Lab

Your school's innovation process is the foundation of the Center of Excellence. Frame your school as a living lab where new ideas are tested, refined and proven before being shared. This involves continuous experimentation and learning. It will help foster a culture of innovation. Here are some strategies that will help:

- **Mistakes and Challenges**

  Schools often hesitate to share failures, but your insights into what doesn't work are just as valuable as your successes. These lessons can help other schools avoid similar pitfalls.

- **Iterative Models**

  Implement a "try, learn, refine" approach to every innovation. This cyclical process will yield well-tested and adaptable strategies and models.

- **Engage Students and Staff**

  Involve stakeholders in reflecting on the innovation journey. Their perspectives provide critical insights that might be overlooked.

Frame your school as a living lab where new ideas are tested, refined and proven before being shared.

---

3. Build a Knowledge Repository

While innovating, invest in creating a knowledge repository that will become the backbone of your Center of Excellence. The repository can include course descriptions, lesson plans, videos of classroom practices, etc. This ensures that your learnings are systematically captured and organized. You can try:

- **Recording**
  Develop an online platform to store resources, case studies, podcasts, videos and guides based on your school's experiences. This repository will be invaluable for other schools looking to adopt similar practices.

- **Toolkits and Frameworks**
  As innovations are refined, toolkits, templates and frameworks can be created to implement these practices.

- **Outcomes and Evidence**
  Collect data on the impact of your innovations and organize it into easy-to-understand formats (e.g., reports and infographics). Evidence of effectiveness will be a cornerstone of your credibility.

4. Establish Collaborative Partnerships

Collaboration can amplify your school's innovation capacity while laying the groundwork for the Center of Excellence. Here are some ways you can do this:

- **Schools Partnerships**
  Identify partner schools that can serve as "beta testers" for your practices. Collaborating with other schools during innovation allows you to refine practices in diverse contexts.

- **Government and Educational Bodies**
  Share interim results with policymakers and education departments to align your Center of Excellence's goals with broader systemic needs. Early engagement ensures you are seen as a valuable resource for shaping educational policies.

- **Universities and Experts**
  Partner with research institutions and experts to validate your approaches and add academic rigor to your learnings.

5. Communication and Outreach Strategy

Building credibility and visibility for your Center of Excellence starts during the innovation phase. Share your school's journey widely to establish your expertise and attract interest. You can do this by:

- **Sharing Stories in Real Time**
  Use blogs, videos and social media to share your school's innovation journey as it happens. Highlight challenges, breakthroughs and lessons learned.

- **Host Events and Webinars**
  Invite other schools and stakeholders to learn about your innovations. Early engagement can create a network of interested collaborators who will later become users of the Center of Excellence.

- **Publish Progress Reports**
  Regularly publish updates and findings from your innovation efforts. This transparency builds trust and positions your school as a thought leader.

6. Focus on Leadership Development

Empowering your school's leaders to guide innovation and Center of Excellence development is crucial. A strong leadership team can ensure both initiatives are well-integrated and forward-looking. Here's what you can do for them:

- **Provide Professional Development**
  Equip leaders with skills in change management, innovation and knowledge sharing to drive the school's transformation and the creation of the Center of Excellence.

- **Foster Distributed Leadership**
  Encourage teachers and staff to take ownership of specific innovation

projects. Their experiences will enrich your resources and expand the Center of Excellence's credibility. Empowering teachers and staff to lead specific projects can enhance engagement and diversify leadership within the school.

7. Plan for Sustainability

While the school is innovating, it's essential to ensure the Center of Excellence is built for long-term impact. This involves embedding sustainability into both efforts. These strategies will help:

- **Create Succession Plans**
  Identify individuals who can take over Center of Excellence leadership roles as your school's priorities evolve.

- **Secure Funding and Resources**
  Seek external funding to support the Center of Excellence's growth. Partnerships with businesses, foundations and government entities can provide financial sustainability.

- **Embed the Center of Excellence Into the School's Mission**
  If it is a core part of your school's identity, this will increase the chances that it remains a priority even as leadership or strategies change.

8. Align Innovation Efforts With the Needs of Other Schools

To maximize the Center of Excellence's value, focus your innovation efforts on areas that resonate with challenges faced by other schools. You can do this by:

- **Conducting Needs Assessments**
  Engage with other schools to understand their pain points and areas of interest. Tailor your innovations to address these needs, too.

- **Piloting Scalable Solutions**
  Design innovations that are feasible for schools with varying resources.

This ensures your offerings are widely applicable.

- **Offering Customization Guidance**
  Provide resources that help schools adapt their innovations to their unique contexts.

Design innovations that are feasible for schools with varying resources. This ensures your offerings are widely applicable.

---

9. Evaluate Progress and Adjust as Needed

Building your Center of Excellence while innovating is a dynamic process. Regular evaluations ensure that both efforts remain aligned and impactful.

- **Set Clear Metrics**
  Define success indicators for both innovation projects and Cente of Excellence development.

- **Conduct Regular Reviews**
  Hold periodic meetings to assess progress, identify challenges and adjust strategies.

- **Celebrate Milestones**
  Recognize and celebrate successes to sustain momentum within your school and demonstrate value to external stakeholders.

By treating your innovation journey as a living lab, documenting and sharing learnings in real-time and fostering partnerships, your school can create a Center of Excellence that has a transformative impact on other schools and the broader education system. Balancing these efforts requires strong leadership, a commitment to collaboration and a focus on sustainability. The results will elevate your school and help shape the future of education for all.

5 Questions for Infinite Minds

1. How can you build a Center of Excellence in parallel with your innovation efforts to ensure real-time documentation, reflection, and scalability of your successes and failures?

2. What systems will you create to position your school as a living lab, where experimentation, mistakes, and lessons learned are embraced and shared to benefit others?

3. How will you establish collaborative partnerships with other schools, experts, and policymakers to validate, refine, and amplify your innovations?

4. What strategies will you implement to build a sustainable knowledge repository that captures toolkits, frameworks, and evidence-based practices for long-term use by other schools?

5. How will you evaluate and adjust both your innovation initiatives and the Center of Excellence to ensure continuous progress, relevance, and measurable impact?

Download the interactive Infinite Education Playbook to complete this task in the playbook and access more accompanying activities for you and your accelerator group.

TL;DR

- A Center of Excellence must grow alongside your school's innovation journey, with a dedicated task force to document real-time insights, successes, and failures that can be refined and shared for broader impact.

- Treat your school as a living lab where continuous experimentation, reflection, and learning—embracing both challenges and break-throughs—create adaptable, proven models for other schools to adopt.

- A sustainable knowledge repository, containing toolkits, frameworks, case studies, and evidence-based resources, ensures your innovations are accessible, practical, and scalable for diverse contexts.

- Collaborative partnerships with schools, universities, and policymakers amplify innovation, add credibility, and align efforts with the evolving needs of the wider education system.

- By embedding sustainability, clear evaluation metrics, and regular reflection into your Center of Excellence, you ensure continuous prog-ress, long-term impact, and the ability to shape the future of education for others.

Chapter 18: Bonus Chapter

THE RISE OF THE HERETIC

"Heretics are the only remedy against the entropy of human thought."
—Yevgeny Zamyatin

Every organization reaches a moment. A turning point. A time when the very structures that once propelled success begin to restrict progress. It's inevitable. Like all living systems, schools grow, mature and stagnate. At first, this stagnation is subtle. Policies remain unchanged. Practices, untouched. Beneath this stability lies the quiet truth that the status quo is no longer enough. This is when heretics rise.

Heretics are seen as disruptors, but they are so much more. They are visionaries who refuse to let institutions crumble under the weight of their history. They see what others cannot: that breaking is not destruction but transformation. Heretics are brave. Calculated. Compassionate. They question not to rebel but to renew. They disrupt not to dismantle but to rebuild.

To access the rest of the bonus chapter visit infiniteeducation.ai.

REFERENCES

Introduction

Ia. "The Intelligence Age." 23 Sept. 2024, ia.samaltman.com. Accessed 23 Sept. 2024.

Intelligent. "Nearly 4 in 10 employers avoid hiring recent college grads in favor of older workers." 2 Jan. 2024, www.intelligent.com/nearly-4-in-10-employers-avoid-hiring-recent-college-grads-in-favor-of-older-workers. Accessed 20 July 2024.

Langreo, Lauraine. "Teachers Desperately Need AI Training. How Many Are Getting It?" *Education Week*, 27 Mar. 2024, www.edweek.org/leadership/teachers-desperately-need-ai-training-how-many-are-getting-it/2024/03. Accessed 4 Apr. 2024.

Harari, Y. N. Homo Deus: *An Intoxicating Brew of Science, Philosophy and Futurism.* Random House, 2016.

Chapter 1

Technavio. "Professional Development Market Analysis North America, Europe, APAC, South America, Middle East and Africa - US, Canada, Germany, UK, China - Size and Forecast 2024-2028." Aug. 2024, www.technavio.com/report/professional-development-market-analysis. Accessed 1 Sept. 2024.

Carse, J. *Finite and Infinite Games.* Simon and Schuster, 2011.

How We XP. "How a Group of Schools in Northern England Reinvented School by Grouping Subjects." www.howwexp.org. Accessed 15 May 2024.

Chapter 2

Kingston University. (n.d.). "Kingston University renews calls for urgent action to prepare students for workplace increasingly dominated by AI as it unveils latest

Future Skills report. Kingston University London." Retrieved from https://
www.kingston.ac.uk/news/article/2904/06-dec-2023-kingston-university-re-
news-calls-for-urgent-action-to-prepare-students-for-workplace-increasingly-domi-
nated-by/

Lloyd, Will. "Yuval Noah Harari: 'Alien intelligence' will destroy us." *The Sunday Times*,
6 Sept. 2024, www.thetimes.com/culture/books/article/yuval-noah-harari-inter-
view-nexus-brief-history-information-networks-stone-age-ai-0qfrnb9hs. Accessed
12 Oct. 2024.

TED. "What Is an AI Anyway? | Mustafa Suleyman | TED." YouTube, 22 Apr. 2024,
www.youtube.com/watch?v=KKNCiRWd_j0. Accessed 30 May 2024.

Howarth, J. "57 NEW Artificial Intelligence Statistics (Oct 2024)." *Exploding Topics*.
Published 26 Sept. 2024, https://explodingtopics.com/blog/ai-statistics. Accessed
18 Oct. 2024.

Bick, Alexander, et al. *The Rapid Adoption of Generative AI*. 18 Sept. 2024, static1.
squarespace.com/static/60832ecef615231cedd30911/t/66f0c3fbabd-
c0a173e1e697e/1727054844024/BBD_GenAI_NBER_Sept2024.pdf. Accessed 30
Sept. 2024.

Walton Family Foundation. "The Value of AI in Today's Classrooms." 11 June 2024,
www.waltonfamilyfoundation.org/learning/the-value-of-ai-in-todays-classrooms.
Accessed 5 July 2024.

Takagi, Yu, and Shinji Nishimoto. "High-resolution image reconstruction with latent
diffusion models from human brain activity." *Biorxiv*, 11 Mar. 2023, www.biorxiv.
org/content/10.1101/2022.11.18.517004v3. Accessed 30 Mar. 2023.

Chapter 3

Carpenter, Nicole. "Why teens are suddenly obsessed with chess." *Polygon*, 12 Apr.
2023, www.polygon.com/tabletop-games/23679440/teens-love-chess-memes-
boom-2023. Accessed 8 Jan. 2024.

Godman, Heidi. "Even a little socializing is linked to longevity." *Harvard Health*, 1 July
2023, www.health.harvard.edu/mind-and-mood/even-a-little-socializing-is-linked-
to-longevity. Accessed 15 Jan. 2024.

Flowkyo. "C.G. Jung: *The Archetypes and the Collective Unconscious* (2nd Edition)." www.
academia.edu. Published Oct. 2022, www.academia.edu/88679511/C_G_Jung_
The_Archetypes_and_the_Collective_Unconscious_2nd_Edition. Accessed 20
June 2024.

Chapter 4

Wikipedia. "God of the gaps." 9 Sept. 2024, en.wikipedia.org/wiki/God_of_the_gaps. Accessed 15 Oct. 2024.

Tarud, Jonathan. "7 Recent AI Developments: Artificial Intelligence News." *Koombea*, 30 Sept. 2024, www.koombea.com/blog/7-recent-ai-developments. Accessed 3 Nov. 2024.

Chapter 5

Gawdat, Mo. "Mo Gawdat on AI: The Future of AI and How It Will Shape Our World." *YouTube*, 17 Sept. 2024, www.youtube.com/watch?v=HhcNrnNJY54. Accessed 10 Oct. 2024.

Suleyman, Mustafa, and Michael Bhaskar. *The Coming Wave: Technology, Power, and the Twenty-First Century's Greatest Dilemma.* First edition. Crown, 2023.

Chapter 6

Shapland, Dorothy. "Reflecting on 'What I do.'" askmsdorothy.blogspot.com/2011/09/reflecting-on-what-i-do.html. Accessed 22 July 2024.

Metcalf, Michael. "Ikigai meaning: 5 Steps to unlock your purpose and find joy." *Marlee.* www.getmarlee.com/blog/what-is-ikigai. Accessed 2 Mar. 2024.

Chapter 7

Gatto, J. T. *Dumbing Us Down: The Hidden Curriculum of Compulsory Schooling.* New Society Publishers, 2002.

Chapter 8

Fabrega, Ana Lorena. "The Origin of the Modern School System." *Ana Lorena Fabrega Blog,* 20 May 2022, afabrega.com/my-blog/the-origin-of-the-modern-school-system. Accessed 5 Apr. 2024.

Chapter 10

Govindarajan, V. *The Three Box Solution: A Strategy for Leading Innovation.* 2016.

Chapter 11

Govindarajan, V., and Chris Trimble. *The Other Side of Innovation: Solving the Execution

Challenge. 2013.

Govindarajan, V., and M. Tangri. *The Three-Box Solution Playbook: Tools and Tactics for Creating Your Company's Strategy*. Harvard Business Press, 2020.

Chapter 14

Dunne, A., & Raby, F. Speculative Everything: Design, Fiction, and Social Dreaming. MIT Press, 2013.

Lipmanowicz, K. M. H. "Liberating Structures - 9. What, So What, Now What? W3." Liberating Structures, n.d., https://www.liberatingstructures.com/9-what-so-what-now-what-w/. Accessed 12 Oct. 2024.

Lipmanowicz, K. M. H. "Liberating Structures - 3. Nine Whys." Liberating Structures, n.d., https://www.liberatingstructures.com/3-nine-whys/. Accessed 20 Oct. 2024.

Govindarajan, V., & Tangri, M. The Three-Box Solution Playbook: Tools and Tactics for Creating Your Company's Strategy. Harvard Business Press, 2020, pp. 39–44.

Tulloch, P. "How Libraries Can Drive Innovation Across a School." Tes Magazine, 16 Mar. 2023, https://www.tes.com/magazine/analysis/general/how-librar-ies-can-drive-innovation-across-school. Accessed 5 July 2024.

Wikipedia contributors. "OER4Schools." Wikipedia, 3 Aug. 2023, https://en.wikipedia.org/wiki/OER4Schools. Accessed 10 Oct. 2024.

Boyd, D., & Goldenberg, J. Inside the Box: A Proven System of Creativity for Breakthrough Results. Simon and Schuster, 2014.

The Sprint Book. n.d., https://www.thesprintbook.com/. Accessed 18 Oct. 2024.

Chapter 15

The Diary Of A CEO. "Former CIA Spy Reveals How They're Controlling You! - Andrew Bustamante [Video]." YouTube, 29 July 2024, https://www.youtube.com/watch?v=P_A8XElrAqA. Accessed 10 Oct. 2024.

Institute for Management Studies. "Strategies for Leading Innovation with Dr. Vijay Govindarajan & Charles Good | TGLP #52 [Video]." YouTube, 5 Dec. 2022, https://www.youtube.com/watch?v=QTStPtySRyM. Accessed 15 Oct. 2024.

Kübler-Ross, E., & Kessler, D. On Grief and Grieving: Finding the Meaning of Grief Through the Five Stages of Loss. Simon and Schuster, 2005.

Bridges, W., & Bridges, S. Transitions (40th Anniversary Edition): Making Sense of Life's Changes. Da Capo Lifelong Books, 2019.

Lipmanowicz, K. M. H. "Liberating Structures - 7. 15% Solutions." Liberating

Structures, n.d., https://www.liberatingstructures.com/7-15-solutions/. Accessed 12 Oct. 2024.

Chapter 16

Lipmanowicz, K. M. H. "Liberating Structures - 31. Ecocycle Planning." Liberating Structures, n.d., https://www.liberatingstructures.com/31-ecocycle-planning/. Accessed 20 Oct. 2024.

Lipmanowicz, K. M. H. "Liberating Structures - 32. Panarchy." Liberating Structures, n.d., https://www.liberatingstructures.com/32-panarchy/. Accessed 22 Oct. 2024.

Resilience Alliance. "Panarchy." Resilience Alliance, n.d., https://www.resalliance.org/panarchy. Accessed 6 Aug. 2024.

He, G. "Organizational Culture: Definition, Examples, & Best Practices." Teambuilding.com, 10 Dec. 2023, https://teambuilding.com/blog/organizational-culture. Accessed 1 Oct. 2024.

ACKNOWLEDGMENTS

Contributions

The leaders and innovators who provided insights into their work with their schools and colleges:

- Adrian Peer, Gateway Community Charters, California, USA
- Anna Haney-Withrow, Florida SouthWestern State College, Florida, USA
- Andrea Quantrill, Heart of Yorkshire College Group, England
- Bryony Evett Hackfort, Coleg Sir Gar Coleg Ceredigion, Wales
- Chris Loveday, Barton Peveril Sixth Form College, England
- Heather Gold, Ed.D, Gateway Community Charters, California, USA
- Henry Exham, Shrewsbury School, England
- Jennifer Verschoor, Northlands, Argentina
- Jess Baron, Ottawa Carleton District School Board, Canada
- Maryam Ferdosi, BBIS, Berlin Brandenburg International School, Germany
- Matthew Wemyss, Cambridge School of Bucharest, Romania
- Michael Armstrong, Breda Academy, Northern Ireland
- Rob Lea, Heart of Yorkshire College Group, England
- Tom Rogerson, Cottesmore School, England

Institutions

I have worked with many schools, colleges, universities, and businesses. Especially the following, for recently going deep with me on strategic development:

- Diocese of Albany Schools, New York
- Gateway Community Charters Schools, California
- Florida SouthWestern State College, Florida
- Leader at CEN, Connecticut
- BBIS Berlin Brandenburg International School, Germany
- Leaders at FETC, Florida
- Universidad Iberoamericana, Mexico
- Jersey College for Girls, Channel Islands
- Latin American Heads Conference
- Dukes Education, London

Artificial Intelligence Tools

How I used large language models to assist me in writing this book:

1. Research Assistance
- In some cases, Elicit.com and ChatGPT Search were used to research academic works and source materials.
- In some circumstances, Google's NotebookLM extracted supporting content from source materials.
- QuillBot was sometimes used to write citations.

2. Clarifying Ideas
- ChatGPT 4o, ChatGPT o1, Claude 3.5 Sonnet and Google Gemini were sometimes used to help me clarify ideas.

3. Crafting Prompts
- ChatGPT 4o and Claude 3.5 Sonnet were used to improve the prompts suggested in this book. These prompts originated from my ideas and were developed in workshops with leaders and educators.

4. Infographics
- Napkin.ai was used to create or inspire the infographics used in this book.

5. Spelling and Grammar
- Some Grammarly suggestions were accepted.

HOW DAN CAN HELP YOUR ORGANIZATION

As a global keynote speaker and consultant, Dan is at the forefront of helping organizations navigate the transformative intersection of artificial intelligence, innovation, and education. He works with schools, districts, colleges, and businesses to develop strategies that prepare them for the rapidly changing landscape of learning and leadership.

Dan believes that innovation is as much about empowering people as it is about adopting new technologies. While artificial intelligence opens up extraordinary possibilities, its real value lies in how it can drive meaningful change—enhancing learning, improving systems, and rethinking education's role in a changing world.

Dan partners with educators and leaders to explore how AI and strategic innovation can shape the future of learning. Through dynamic keynote speeches, engaging workshops, and hands-on consulting, he helps organizations adapt and thrive in an era of constant change.

Dan collaborates with a diverse range of organizations, from K-12 schools and higher education institutions to corporate teams. He partners with those who are asking bold questions about the future and are ready to take meaningful steps toward impactful solutions.

His work is tailored to each organization's unique challenges and goals, ensuring that the outcomes are both practical and transformative.

Dan's approach is grounded in a deep understanding of the stakes involved. The future of education isn't just about keeping pace with technological advances; it's about building systems and cultures that equip learners with the curiosity, resilience, and adaptability they need to succeed in an ever-changing world. Dan's work is fueled by this vision and a commitment to helping others bring it to life.

Dan has recently worked with:

- Bay-Arenac Intermediate School District, Michigan
- Bett UK
- British Council School, Madrid
- Commonwealth Scientific and Industrial Research Organisation (CSIRO), Australia
- Diocese of Albany, New York
- Festival of Education
- FETC
- Florida SouthWestern State College, Florida
- Forman School, Connecticut
- GEMS Education, Dubai
- Girls' Day School Trust
- Google for Education
- Latin American Heads Conference
- Miami-Dade County Public Schools
- National Catholic Educational Association
- New York State School Boards Association
- Norwalk Public Schools, Connecticut
- Northwest Council for Computer Education
- Oklahoma Society for Technology in Education
- Premier League
- Qatar Foundation
- Scottish School Leaders
- Universidad Iberoamericana, Mexico City

THE PREMIUM AI ACADEMY

This is the premier course for educators who refuse to be left behind in the revolution of artificial intelligence. This is a transformative journey into the heart of AI-powered education. Step confidently into the future, armed with the knowledge, strategies and tools to lead learning in ways that are as innovative as they are impactful.

Students, parents, and institutions are looking to educators for answers. With The AI Premium Academy, you'll gain the insight to not only meet this challenge but to thrive in it.

Here's how we'll empower you:

- **Command the AI Landscape:** Cut through the hype and master what AI truly means for education—practical, ethical and game-changing applications that will reshape your classroom.

- **Unlock Student Potential:** Use AI to create deeply personalized learning experiences that adapt to every student's unique needs, igniting curiosity and fostering lifelong growth.

- **Lead With Vision:** Transform fear of change into a driving force for innovation, positioning yourself as a trailblazer in the AI-powered future of education.

- **Bridge Humanity and Technology:** Learn how to blend AI's capabilities with the irreplaceable human connection that makes teaching a transformative act.

- **Turn Ideas Into Action:** Gain hands-on, actionable strategies to integrate AI into your practice, from intelligent tutoring systems to data-driven insights that enhance student outcomes.

This is your opportunity to become the educator every institution needs and every student deserves—an AI-savvy leader ready to redefine what learning can be.

Join The AI Premium Academy and take your place at the forefront of education's most exciting evolution at www.theaieducator.io/premiumacademy.

THE PREMIUM AI STRATEGY COURSE

Inspired by the groundbreaking ideas in this book *Infinite Education*, the Premium AI Academy program is your gateway to leading transformative change in a world reshaped by artificial intelligence.

In an era where innovation moves faster than ever, traditional education risks becoming obsolete. This course will challenge you to break free from outdated paradigms and embrace a future where learning is dynamic, personalized, and unbounded.

Here's what awaits you:

- **Visionary Leadership:** Discover the strategic frameworks that empower you to lead with clarity and purpose, creating a sustainable roadmap for innovation.

- **Human-Centered AI Integration:** Learn how to harness the power of AI as a collaborator to amplify creativity, problem-solving and emotional intelligence.

- **Infinite Learning Mindset:** Shift from finite, test-driven education models to fostering curiosity, adaptability and lifelong growth in students and educators alike.

- Actionable Innovation: Master tools and techniques to design learning environments that anticipate disruption, embrace change and inspire excellence.

Whether you're an educator, administrator or visionary leader, you'll leave equipped to transform classrooms, institutions and the very purpose of education. Together, let's ensure the next generation thrives.

The future of learning begins with you. Are you ready to lead it?

Join us at www.theaieducator.io/premiumstrategy.